RADICAL
SCHOOL
REFORM

EDITED BY
BEATRICE AND RONALD GROSS

SIMON AND SCHUSTER • NEW YORK

SBN 671–20412–2 Trade

Library of Congress Catalog Card Number: 72-92188
Designed by Edith Fowler
Manufactured in the United States of America
by American Book–Stratford Press, Inc., New York, N.Y.

ACKNOWLEDGMENTS

For guidance and stimulation during the process of editing this book, we are immensely grateful to George Dennison, Edgar Friedenberg, John Holt, and Richard Hooper. And for their generous cooperation and effort on behalf of the book we gladly thank Evans Clinchy, Boston Public Schools; Robert Davis, The Madison Project; Ellen Galinsky, Bank Street College of Education; Alan Howard, Toronto Waldorf School; George Leonard, *Look* Magazine; and Ole Sand, Center for the Study of Instruction.

We wish to express our thanks and appreciation to the authors, editors and publishers who permitted us to use the following material:

"The Way It Spozed to Be" from *The Way It Spozed to Be* by James Herndon, copyright © 1965, 1968 by James Herndon, reprinted by permission of Simon & Schuster, Inc.

Death at an Early Age. Copyright © 1967 by Jonathan Kozol. Reprinted by permission of the publisher, Houghton Mifflin Company.

"How Children Fail" from the book *How Children Fail* by John Holt. Copyright © 1964 by Pitman Publishing Corp. Reprinted by permission Pitman Publishing Corp.

"In Suburban Classrooms" condensed from *Culture Against Man* by Jules Henry. © copyright 1963 by Jules Henry and © copyright 1963 by Random House, Inc. Reprinted by permission of the publisher.

"Freedom and Learning: The Need for Choice" by Paul Goodman in May 18, 1968, *Saturday Review.* Copyright 1968 Saturday Review, Inc. Reprinted by permission of the author.

"The Future of Education" by Marshall McLuhan and George Leonard in *Look.* Copyright © 1967 by Cowles Communications, Inc. Reprinted by permission of Harold Ober Associates, Inc.

Kenneth B. Clark, "Alternative Public School Systems," *Harvard Educational Review,* 38, Winter 1968, 100–113. Copyright © 1968 by President and Fellows of Harvard College. Reprinted by permission of *Harvard Educational Review.*

"The Community-Centered School" by Preston R. Wilcox from *The Schoolhouse in the City,* edited by Alvin Toffler, published by Frederick A. Praeger, Inc., New York, 1968, in cooperation with Educational Facilities Laboratories.

"Autonomy and Learning" by Edgar Z. Friedenberg, by permission of the author.

"A Student Voice," Montgomery County Student Alliance, with permission of Norman Soloman, Montgomery County Student Alliance.

"What's Worth Knowing," reprinted from *Teaching as a Subversive Activity,* by Neil Postman and Charles Weingartner. Reprinted by permission of the publisher, Delacorte Press.

"Making Contact with the Disadvantaged" by Mario D. Fantini and Gerald Weinstein, adapted from *Toward a Contact Curriculum.* Reprinted with permission of the authors and the Anti-Defamation League of B'nai B'rith, 315 Lexington Avenue, New York, New York 10016.

6   Acknowledgments

"Organic Teaching" from *Teacher,* by Sylvia Ashton-Warner. Copyright ©
1963 by Sylvia Ashton-Warner. Reprinted by permission of Simon &
Schuster, Inc. and Martin Secker & Warburg Ltd.

"The British Infant Schools" by Joseph Featherstone. Reprinted by permission of *The New Republic,* © 1967, Harrison-Blaine of New Jersey, Inc.

"The Responsive Environments Laboratory" by Omar Khayyam Moore,
adapted from "Autotelic Responsive Environments for Learning." Reprinted by permission of the author.

"The First Street School" condensed from *First Street School,* by George
Dennison (*Liberation Magazine*) by permission of Random House, Inc.
Another version of this article appears in *The Lives of Children,* by George
Dennison. © copyright 1969 by George Dennison.

"Summerhill" from *Summerhill,* by A. S. Neill. Copyright © 1960 by Hart
Publishing Co. Reprinted by permission of the publisher.

"Fernwood" by Elizabeth Drews appeared in the *Journal of Humanistic
Psychology,* Fall, 1968. Reprinted by permission of the author.

"The New School—Vancouver" by Anne Long, by permission of the author.

"Good School in a Ghetto" by Evans Clinchy in November 16, 1968, *Saturday Review.* Copyright © 1968 Saturday Review, Inc. Reprinted by permission of author.

"The Pennsylvania Advancement School" by Farnum Gray. Parts of this
article were published in the February 1969 issue of *Colloquy* (Vol. 2,
No. 2, pp. 26–29). Reprinted by permission of the author.

"The CAM Academy" by permission of the CAM Academy.

"A Harlem Class Writes" by Herbert Kohl, reprinted in part with permission
from *The New York Review of Books.* Copyright © 1967 by Herbert
Kohl. Reprinted in part by permission of The World Publishing Company
from *36 Children* by Herbert Kohl. An NAL book. Copyright © 1967 by
Herbert Kohl.

For May,
who has devoted such intelligence and love
to our two children

Contents

Ghetto Education: New Directions

Student Participation

Making Contact: Toward a Relevant Curriculum

Part Three: SOMETHING ELSE: PRACTICE

Getting Out of Their Way: Environments for Learning

Following Their Lead: Exploring the Limits of Freedom

Teaching "Unteachables": The Acid Test

Introduction

We have bungled badly in education. Not merely in the ways noted by most school critics: too little money for education, outdated curricula, poorly trained teachers. But in more fundamental ways. It isn't just that our schools fail to achieve their stated purposes, that they are not the exalted places their proponents proclaim. Rather, many are not even decent places for our children to be. They damage, they thwart, they stifle children's natural capacity to learn and grow healthily. To use Jonathan Kozol's frightening but necessary metaphor: they destroy the minds and hearts of our children.

The school crisis has finally broken through to basics. The debates of the fifties about academic rigor and "life adjustment," the Sputnik-sparked worries that we were falling behind the Russians in producing scientists, Dr. Conant's concerns about marketable skills and Dr. Flesch's formulas to make Johnny read—all suddenly seem irrelevant.

In the big cities the Black communities are demanding full control of their schools, and in the suburbs the students are demanding control of theirs. In the cities the power structure is under attack, in the suburbs the value structure. Reforms are debated which would have been branded anti-American and "unconstructive" ten years ago: abandonment of public education in favor of a competitive system of private and public alternatives, Black schools in the ghetto as preferable to integrated schooling, political and economic reform as a prerequisite to better education, schools run by students themselves, or schools without subjects and teachers. To affirm such propositions would have put a writer beyond the pale of "responsible criticism" in the late fifties. But today we have many examples where the existing system of public education has failed and such alternatives have succeeded—street academies in the ghettos, freedom schools, experimental colleges, and free universities. Men who were considered wild-eyed romantics when they spoke have in a few short years begun to sound like the most realistic voices in education.

The sharpness of the crisis has made the most basic questions the most relevant and the most radical answers the most cogent. Radical means going to the root, posing the fundamental problems, and responding with theories and practices which are genuine alternatives to present theory and practice.

Radical has many meanings, in fact. In politics, radical means revolutionary: Black parents in the ghetto taking control of their schools. In social relations, radical means libertarian: an affirmation of the autonomy of the individual against the demands of the system. In a school situation, radical means unorthodox ways of promoting learning that fall outside the scope of conventional or even innovative school practice.

This book reflects the entire range of radical thought and practice, from the grand demand that compulsory public education be repealed and the formal educational system dismantled to reports of intensely practical teachers working constructively within the existing situation but nevertheless using truly unorthodox teaching techniques. But all these writers believe that we will not have significantly better schools until we have radically different schools.

It is important to distinguish these radical theories and practices from those "innovations"—like team teaching, teaching machines, the new math and other "new curricula," teaching via television, nongraded classes—which have appeared in many American schools in the past decade.

By the mid-fifties, Americans increasingly realized the importance of education in the economic sense. For the individual, it meant a chance for college and thereby an opportunity to find a job or occupation or profession in a world of work which was being transformed by automation and bureaucracies. A diploma was the passport to the affluent society.

For the nation, education was clearly the key to strength in a scientific and technological age. Sputnik, that superb visual aid, riveted home the practical relevance of Whitehead's dictum: "In the conditions of modern life the rule is absolute, the race which does not value trained intelligence is doomed." The ensuing sense of national urgency rallied an unprecedented corps of master plasterers to patch up the outmoded and intellectually disreputable façade of American education.

These "innovative" programs were undertaken in well-established schools with fairly conventional philosophies. They were not based on new ideas about the role of education, or the nature of the child, or the place of culture in a democratic society. They focused on practical methods of achieving the traditional end of schooling—the mastery of basic skills and subject matter—in schools strained by burgeoning enrollments and shortages of first-rate teachers. They were for the most part ingenious new techniques rather than radical reforms.

Such experimental approaches changed the climate of American public education in the late fifties and early sixties. So pervasive were they that the idea of "innovative education" was embodied in the most notable piece of federal legislation aiding schools: the Elementary and Secondary Education Act of 1965. One of the titles of that act specifically mandated money for innovative demonstration projects. What these innovations achieved has been important—but what they failed to achieve, unfortunately, has been even more important.

Even as these innovations relieved the rigid programs and teaching practices in many schools, a deeper malaise was developing, unnoticed, in American education. The seemingly enlightened educators who had pressed these changes toward flexibility and enrichment had focused their energies entirely on

making the process of learning in school more lively and reward-
ing. But they had not perceived that larger social forces were
calling into question the relevance of the entire enterprise of
formal education.

In the urban ghetto schools, starvation budgets, the impact of
the slum environment, teacher indifference, and sometimes unconscious racism had reduced the schools to mere disciplinary
institutions. And in the suburbs, the shadow of college preparation and social conformity had blighted the process of growing
up less brutally but with comparable efficiency. In all schools the
excitement of learning seemed to somehow shrivel from the time
the child entered till the time he left.

By the mid-sixties Black parents in the ghettos and white
students on the campuses and in the suburban high schools
began to revolt against the educational system. "Innovative"
approaches, enlightened and humane as they were, simply did
not seem to get at the deeper causes of the educational malaise.
The riots in the big-city slums and the demonstrations on the
campuses of the multiversities made it shockingly clear that the
educational system had reached a point where it could no longer
continue without basic, radical changes in its structure, control,
and operation. Radical reform is a vigorous recoil and response to
realities too long suppressed.

The call for radical reform takes many forms. Social critics like
Paul Goodman, Kenneth Clark, Edgar Friedenberg, and Marshall McLuhan articulate its theory. Teachers like Herbert Kohl,
John Holt, Sylvia Ashton-Warner, and Jonathan Kozol describe a
whole new way of teaching. Others of lesser renown report
radically new programs spotted around the country, from the
ghettos of Harlem and Watts to rural schools of Oregon and
Kentucky. They draw insights and ideas from Rousseau, Dewey,
Pestalozzi, Montessori, and A. S. Neill, from schools in Canada
and England and Africa. They cannot be subsumed—theorists or
practitioners—in any neat set of underlying principles.

For example, Black leaders in the ghettos want radical *political*
reform of education—changes in who says what goes. They feel
they must have this control because the schools under white
control have failed to teach their children those basic skills of

reading and writing which spell survival in the American economy today. For them, radical *educational* attacks on the existence of schools *per se* or extensive questioning of pedagogical assumptions are often not the most compelling priority. Their children can't read, and until they have power over their children's education no more basic criticisms can be meaningful to the ghetto parents they represent.

On the other hand, the most radical theorists—Goodman, Friedenberg, Henry, McLuhan—are not critics of the educational system in the usual sense, because they are not interested first and foremost in schooling. They are interested less in teaching and learning than in growth, dignity, autonomy, freedom, and the development of the full range of human potentialities.

But despite these divergences, there is a spirit that informs this thought and action as a whole, and that spirit has some distinguishable components. The radical critics all start with some kind of radical criticism of America as a sick society. They come at it from many angles: its competitive ethos, its cultural vulgarity, its neglect or suppression of minority groups, its inherent racism and imperialism, its failures in compassion, let alone enterprise, in regard to the wretched within its own boundaries and throughout the rest of the world. Their critique of the schools derives from this questioning of society, for they see the schools as mere agents of the society.

The radical critics then look at the schools. What they find in the classroom is suppression, irrelevance, inhumanity, manipulation, and the systematic stultification of most of what is promising in children and youth. The concept of "miseducation" covers much of this, and additionally distinguishes the tone of their writings. Whereas some of them score the schools' failures to accomplish what they set out to do or what the needs of society require them to do, the most radical attack them for being entirely too successful in doing the wrong things. From Marshall McLuhan to John Holt, these writers agree that more of the same is worse than nothing. They would give not a cent to bolster education as it now proceeds, but would first require dismantlement of the entire enterprise and its reconstitution along basically different lines.

Part One

SOME
REALITIES

It took new kinds of observers to see what was wrong with American schools, and to write about it so that the rest of us could see it with a shock of recognition. In these selections four such observers take you into the classroom, to see and hear and feel.

James Herndon and Jonathan Kozol went into ghetto schools to teach. They found the children being oppressed by a system which resulted, in Kozol's words, in "the destruction of the hearts and minds of Negro children." Both Herndon and Kozol were fired up by what they saw—and fired out of the system.

John Holt and Jules Henry went into classrooms in "privileged" schools. There the tyranny was subtler; the children were not physically brutalized. But they were being indoctrinated into what Henry calls the "necessary nightmare" which sustains American society.

In both cases—slum and suburb—the schools' real effects on children shockingly reflect the prevailing attitudes and values of the surrounding society. In most ghetto schools the chaos of the environment is mirrored in the behavior of the children. In many suburban classrooms the competitiveness of the culture is reinforced. In both cases a vicious cycle is created by the ways children are regarded and treated in school: finding their own knowledge and feelings about the world treated with contempt, they come to consider school learning irrelevant.

While it is too facile to equate the treatment of the slum youngster with that accorded the suburban child, the educational consequences of the two nightmares are similar. In both cases, children are thwarted, demeaned, and manipulated by a system —social and educational—which makes them sabotage their own prospects for healthy development.

THE URBAN SCHOOL NIGHTMARE

1. THE WAY IT SPOZED TO BE
JAMES HERNDON

James Herndon is teaching in California. He has been a merchant seaman, a file clerk, a machinist, an oboe player, and—most important—the author of a book describing his first year of teaching in a ghetto junior high school.

At least it looks like a school, I was saying, old, dark, the same brown window shades all pulled exactly three-quarters of the way down. . . . I was rather pleased about that. A real school, not one of those new ones I saw going up all over that looked like motels or bowling alleys. I was about to say that the motel-schools fooled nobody; they were still schools, and the same old crap was going to go on in them. Here, at least, everyone was notified right away by the looks of things that it was the same old crap.

7H came charging and whooping up the stairs from where they had been studying mathematics with Mr. Brooks. Later I came to recognize their particular cries coming up my way. There's Roy, I'd think, there Harvey, there Vincent, Alexandra, picking their

sounds out of the general outcry of the student body with a
mixture of admiration and dread. 7H dashed in, flung themselves
into seats and as quickly flung themselves out again. If 9D was
willing to ignore me until doomsday, 7H didn't. They scattered
from seat to seat, each trying to get as much free territory around
him as possible, jumping up again as the area got overcrowded
and ranging out to look for breathing space like Daniel Boone.
From these seats, wherever they were, they confronted me with
urgent and shouted questions, each kid, from his claim of several
empty desks, demanding my complete attention to him: Are you
a strict teacher? You going to make us write? When do we get to
go home? Where our books? Our pencils? Paper? You going to
give us them spellers? They were all finally outshouted by Roy, a
boy about five feet six or seven inches tall with tremendous
shoulders and arms, who stood in front of my desk, obscuring the
view for all the rest, and just laughed as loud as he could for
perhaps two minutes. Then he stopped and told everyone to shut
up, because he knew this teacher wanted to take the roll. After
some more shouting I finally did call it, listed the names of those
absent on absence slips and clipped them to the wall over the
door where a monitor from the office was to pick them up. I went
back to my desk, wondered if I ought to pass out pencils (I'd
learned something), thought a bit about books, and decided to
give out some spellers.

At that moment there came a tremendous outcry from over by
the door. I looked over and three or four kids were standing
there, looking up at the door and yelling their heads off. Naturally the rest of the class soon began shouting insults at them,
without any idea of what the trouble was. Everyone was standing up; calls of "watermelon-head!" filled the room. The kids by
the door wheeled and rushed up to me, furious and indignant.
Vincent, who was one of them, was crying. What the hell? I
began to yell in turn for everyone to shut up, which they soon
did, not from the effect of my order but out of a desire to find out
what was the matter; they sat back to hear the story. The four
were Roy, Harvey, Vincent and Alexandra, and what they demanded to know was why had I put their names up there on

those absence slips? They weren't absent! Was I trying to get them into trouble? We here, Mr. Hern-don! They didn't want to get in no trouble! Alexandra began to threaten me with her mama. Roy, tempted beyond his own indignation, began to make remarks about the color and hair quality of Alexandra's mama. It shows how upset Alexandra was; it was fatal to ever mention your mother at GW, which Alexandra of all kids knew quite well.

For a moment I thought maybe I had put the wrong names up by mistake, but I checked them and saw that wasn't so. I displayed the slips, spread out on my desk. Their names weren't there. The names on those slips were not theirs, I told them. Right? They weren't satisfied. They demanded a closer look at them slips. I handed the slips around, whereupon it became a scene out of some old movie when Stepin Fetchit turns the letter upside down and sideways before giving it to Bob Hope to read, explaining he doesn't read Chinese. The fact was, Harvey, Roy, Vincent and Alexandra were having a little trouble reading their own names.

Finally Alexandra let out a screech and started for the back of the room, where a little tiny kid, black and scrawny, jumped smoothly out of her way, grinning at her, holding onto a desk in front of him ready to jump again. Alexandra was demanding something from him; she was joined by Roy *et al;* and I finally made out that they were calling on him to verify my statement about their names and the slips. He wasn't doing that, apparently, so they all rushed back to me. All four now shouted that Virgil had told them their names were up there on them slips and they were getting into trouble for cutting school. The first day! The class began to hoot all over again. I started for Virgil, who left his chair and sped over by the windows.

I sped after him. Whooo-eee! Everything was great! Right away I saw I wasn't about to catch Virgil—I'd had some idea about making him recant in public—and stopped. Virgil promptly dashed out the door.

Just about then the monitor came along for the slips and I collected them and handed them over. The four kids still stood there. Were they in trouble or weren't they? They didn't know for sure, but probably they did know what they were up against here all of a sudden, just as I suddenly knew what I was going to be up against. As the monitor was leaving, a water bomb made from a folded sheet of school paper came flying through the open transom and exploded on the floor in the front of the room.

After school I hurried out to the nearest bar to have a beer and think it over. Things weren't the same as they had been this morning, or even at noon. There was Roy, a broad-shouldered, thick-chested *man* of thirteen, largely out of control, probably stronger than I. Vincent, a little kid, worried, thin, wore a sports coat and a tie for the first day of school. Harvey looked like a country boy, wearing jeans, a light jacket, high work shoes; it wasn't just his clothes, though, it was the way he walked— steady, serious, trying to puzzle it out, willing to, but no go. Alexandra—dark, handsome, proud, mean, bitter, able to whip any boy in the class except Roy—in looks and temperament a gypsy.

Their situation was simply that they couldn't read their own names when I wrote them on the slips. So that when Virgil told them I'd turned them in, they didn't have any way at all to find out if it was true or not. They had to believe it, at first anyway. They knew, somehow, that Virgil could read, and that was all the certainty they had to go on. Next they could ask me. Could I be trusted? After all, Virgil just told them I was trying to get them into trouble (and Virgil could read) and so it was only logical that I would lie about it. If Virgil was right, I couldn't be believed. But what about Virgil? There they were again, back to the simple fact that they couldn't tell their own names from anyone else's, and this was to be their situation every day and every period of the year.

But what about Virgil? Here was a kid who was not only mean enough but smart enough to figure out this foolproof method of driving four other kids nuts on the very first day of school, and who was also prepared in advance—for he hadn't had time to construct it out there in the hall—with a water bomb to throw in through the transom when he ran out . . . when I chased him out, as he said the next day by way of excusing his illegal departure.

I couldn't help it. I went down the next day before class and looked up old Virgil's IQ. It happened to be, at last testing, 138. I was going to ask one of the counselors just what he was doing in group H, but while I waited for them to show up I read farther down the card. After a lot of written comments like "troublemaker" and "adjustment difficulty to classroom situation" and a couple of referral dates to Juvenile Hall, I found the letter H, followed by the words *Teacher Recommendation*.

Why would a kid, or a whole row of kids, become frantic because they weren't getting any pencils? Why was it no one could pass out paper for a routine assignment without all the kids in the back rows pushing up to the front, grabbing at the paper, crumpling it and spilling it out onto the floor out of fear they wouldn't get any? Certainly it was clear by now that they were going to get paper and pencils, wasn't it? They always did, every day, every period, all year long.

I ought to mention that we always felt it necessary to pass out one piece of paper at a time per kid. Certainly if he used it all up he might have more. But most students wanted to have two, three, several at once, in order to have a pad to write on. They didn't like to write on the bare wood of the desks and, indeed, what a pleasant, luxurious feeling it is to write on a block of paper where the pencil seems to press down on something that gives and lets the lead glide along instead of on the unyielding surface, full of cracks and carving, over which the pencil or pen makes a thin and bumpy line. But we were always aware of the remonstrances of the administration at our meetings; somehow the shortage of supplies was always crucial—running out of everything was imminent. What were we going to do in May and June, they'd be saying, if we let the kids waste materials now? Nothing is more terrifying to most teachers than the prospect of days in a classroom full of kids without supplies—no long written assignments to assure order and a period of peace and rest. We felt responsible, and on some days we could see a kid who got hold of four or five sheets of paper, wrote a little on one of them and scattered the rest on the floor as a pretty bad, heedless, irresponsible citizen, not to mention destructive and wasteful. Still, it's possible to wonder why, in all of the vast, producing, consuming, buying, advertising, fantastically wasteful country of America, it had to be precisely this one article of three-hole, blue-lined, red-margined school paper that was in short supply, which had to be carefully guarded against waste, which it was immoral to waste, which had to be parceled out one sheet at a time, equally and fairly of course, but still one at a time as if it was oranges in a region where oranges were scarce around Christmastime.

It wasn't as if they even used the paper very much. In some classes very few actually wrote the assignment on that paper or even used it to doodle or write notes on or make paper planes from, and often kids left it untouched on their desks when they left; I could use it over again, or just leave it there pretending I hadn't seen it, as another little bonus for some fortunate student. Man! An extra sheet of school paper! Voices from all over the room would inform on the kid, who in turn would yell out denials and lies to protect his precious gift. If I went ahead and passed him out a sheet with all the rest, the class was shocked and outraged. He already got a piece! He got one, Mr. Herndon!

Yet plenty of kids had whole binders full of paper and those who did were quite generous with it, handing out sheets regularly to anyone who asked for it. These students with paper were indistinguishable from the rest when school paper was passed out.

Other items of property could also cause a terrible panic. Among these shoes were supreme, especially tennis shoes, which were always referred to as "tennis." Most kids carried one set of shoes around with them while wearing another pair and they were continually changing shoes in class, usually with the excuse that they were coming from or going to P.E. Tennis weren't trusted to hall or gym lockers; as in most schools, everybody knew everyone else's combinations so that the lockers were useless except as places to store absolutely worthless stuff. During class kids were continually picking up others' shoes or trying to step on new white shoes; this was especially common among girls and caused a great deal of uproar, often considerable weeping. New jackets and coats were important too and favorite shirts—let a teacher grab any kid by the collar or sleeve and he found himself facing a completely hysterical person, screaming about his clothes, his coat, his shirt, concerned only with the immediate salvation of that clothing and willing to forget any other consequence until the clothes were safe. Kids often spent entire periods simply protecting an article of clothing or a pair of tennis.

Try to narrow it down. Poverty, I've said, wasn't it. They had pocket money, most of them, and stuff bought with it. All personal property wasn't precious; their paper could be given away, money loaned, records swiped, without great outcry. Some things, though, were holy and these were mainly things that showed and looked good like the new jackets and shirts, which, once torn, were completely useless. For torn, they didn't look good, and in America you were supposed to look good, all clean, cool, sharp and above all new. There was a certain need to produce on demand, like Skates, the teacher in the next room, one hundred percent of the time. Think how it would look going out there to P.E. in your brown or black street shoes, pointy-toed, high or slippery-heeled, sliding around over the floor or asphalt, the coach asking, Where's your shoes? He (she) ain't got none! they would all yell . . . later too, your street shoes appearing scuffed, the shine gone, beat-up.

That was one point. But a point too was their concern over things they didn't actually want, the paper and probably those oranges, a concern to get their fair share of whatever was being passed out, passed out officially, what you were spozed to get in school, at Juvi, as an American, from the government, city, county, from the school, from the teachers. What was being passed out today, what probably would be passed out tomorrow, but on the other hand just might not be. What was being passed out one at a time. For actually, of all the things that were being passed out to them, it was always one at a time; there never was a surplus.

There was never a surplus. In vast, producing, consuming, wasteful America, the very image of surplus, it just happened that all the items which were being passed out officially one by one were those which had to be strictly guarded against misuse, malicious destruction, and waste.

One thing you could say for the welfare, there was never a surplus of it. Now, you weren't going to get enough money passed out to you, all at once, to last you for a year, or five years, or even for six months. Can you hear them saying, Welcome to town, and here's money in this bowl on the table and you just get you some, enough to last awhile, pay that high rent, buy those potato chips, get you some new tennis, and when you get back on your feet, when your ship comes in, you can give us back what you don't use? But you could get money enough for one month passed out to you, according to the law, fairly, if you could prove you didn't just come here to get that particular money, if you could prove you had to have it, if you could prove you hadn't no daddy, if you could prove you were entitled to it. Then you could get it for that month. Then, next month you could get it again, provided you could prove all those things all over again.

A definitive characteristic of The Tribe [the teachers' name for the students, who were "98% Negro, 99% deprived"] was its desire for a surplus.

The blacker a kid was, the kinkier his hair, the wider and flatter his nose, the larger and more everted his lips, the uglier he was and the more crap he had to take. Robert he got hit with the ugly stick, Mr. Hern-don, some kid would yell, and that was that for Robert. When it dark outside nobody can't even see Fletcher! Watch out somebody don't steal your head for a watermelon!

At first I was extremely surprised and shocked. I couldn't imagine how, with a whole white world ready and willing to call them all these names and always making the distinction between African-looking (ugly) Negroes and Caucasian-looking (handsome) Negroes, they could add to the situation themselves.

For a time I began to think that it was all a subtle way of finding out about me—if they said, for instance, that somebody was big-lipped, fuzzy-headed, black and therefore ugly, was I

going to somehow agree that he was uglier than the rest? Then I
could be exposed as a racist, just another white mother, and
could be dismissed. But as it kept on, day after day, all year long,
even after they had in many cases ceased to pay any attention to
me at all for long periods of time, I could see it wasn't for my
benefit. It was for themselves.

It never stopped. It was a characteristic of The Tribe. They
agreed that qualities which they all shared to some degree from
birth were to add up to *bad*. It was crucial that they join the
people most hostile to them all in order to establish relative
degrees of ugliness, in order that some might be less ugly. I got
over my surprise, got over trying to figure if it was meant for me,
and it soon became only very boring, like slightly risqué jokes
schoolkids are always telling you which you've heard a hundred
times. You couldn't ever say anything about dark, black, brown,
gray, shadow, night, head, nose, mouth, feet, legs, no raccoons,
no dancing of jigs, no spades, no skin, without invoking hoots of
laughter and a number of personal remarks. No one could read
about any melons (your head look like one), no one could read
about apes or monkeys (you look like one) . . . and if you
somehow managed to avoid all that, the rhymes would get you.
Say crack, back, track, Mac, hack, and you'd soon hear, Teacher,
did you say black? or May, Mr. Herndon say you too black! Or
there would be the bitter variation, Robert, go on leave me alone!
You too white (quite, flight, bright, knight and right). Whooo-
eee!

If I had imagined that the students of GW would present a
united front on the question of their own (relative) blackness, it
was a mistake. If I had supposed they were concerned with
testing me, that was a mistake too. They weren't interested in
degrees of liberal white attitudes like they spozed to be.

It was Opal Jameson who introduced me to the third major
characteristic of The Tribe. Opal was a member of 7B and ordinarily no member of that class would have been caught dead
indulging himself, at least in the classroom, in any of the characteristics of The Tribe. Except for Opal. Opal was a big, tall, very
black, strong girl with bad-luck features; she was aggressive,

argumentative, headstrong, unable to endure criticism of the mildest sort, uncooperative and, at the same time, very intelligent indeed—which was why she was still hanging on in the B group. I didn't think she'd remain there throughout the next two years at GW, but as it turned out of course, I never found out.

Opal's desire was to be my second-in-command. If allowed to pass out the paper, collect the work, correct the spelling papers, call out the assignment, check the book numbers and do all the various small administrative jobs in the classroom, she was happy, did her own work and didn't cause no trouble. Unfortunately she didn't always get to do this. First of all, these were big status jobs and many other kids in class wanted to share the glory; and second, she became so officious and overbearing in her performance of these duties—she argued with the kids about the neatness or the heading or the correctness of the work they were turning in, she moralized constantly about the scarcity of school materials and the evils of waste, she marked spelling words wrong if kids forgot to dot their i's—that we couldn't bear it all the time. When refused her prerogatives, she would consistently embark on some sort of antisocial behavior upon which I would have to comment; at the comment she would begin to argue, getting louder and louder and angrier and angrier until I would have to tell her to shut up and sit down. She would refuse to do this in no uncertain terms, whereupon I'd have to make a threat or advance toward her, at which point she would resort to the Plop Reflex.

My introduction to the reflex came about the third week of school, about two weeks before the time now, that I'm writing about, when I was thinking about The Tribe. It was apparently the time in which kids' hopes had about run out for another year, leaving about forty more weeks to go. Up until this time Opal had been happily doing all these administrative tasks for me, and I was quite happy to have someone do them, but it was brought to my attention by other kids that lots of students wanted to do these jobs, that why should Opal always get to do them, especially since Opal didn't always behave very well in class, and that it wasn't fair. We discussed this in class and I can now imagine

Opal listening to this with no very good feeling—no doubt it
happened just like this every year. In the end, a little boy named
Lorenzo was chosen to pass out paper the next day, and people
got started making schedules and monitor lists and all that.

The next day I started talking about the Indians and the
Bering Strait and something about Kon-Tiki, I remember, for we
were reading about the Indians who used to live nearby, the oak
trees which were all over, the shell mounds the Indians left by
the bay, and by and by I announced an assignment in the book.
Opal got up to pass out the paper. Immediately Lorenzo let out a
yell that he was supposed to do it. I agreed that he was right.
Opal simply said Sh!, grabbed the paper, and started up the row
with it. I told her to stop and give it to Lorenzo, about half
Opal's size, who was standing up by his seat, waiting for justice.
Opal ignored me and started thumbing off sheets of paper and
slapping them on desks. I insisted. She slammed all the paper
down on the floor and advanced upon me. She had a peculiar
stance when arguing: her feet flat on the floor, chin thrust out,
her body following it, leaning over, her butt stuck way out in
back of her, arms hanging straight down at her sides, so that she
looked like a V standing on one of its legs. Well, Lorenzo already
asked, I said, and it was already decided yesterday. She knew it.
She said that Lorenzo didn't know how to do it, all the paper
would be wasted, that she was spozed to do it, that I was just
mad at her and wouldn't let her do it. Finally, argument not
availing, she marched over to the kid, who, during the arguing,
had been picking up all the paper and was just beginning to pass
it out, and tried to snatch it away from him. The class began to
protest. Anarchy threatened. I wasn't about to have my only
reasonable class going crazy. Shut up and sit down, Opal! I
yelled. You are not passing out the paper. That's that! Opal, all
hope lost, let out a yell, launched herself backward exactly as if
she were a diver beginning a back one-and-a-half, flew into the
air, bounced off a desk and came down right square on her head
on the floor and lay there.

And that was the Plop Reflex. Remember how in the old comic
strip, *Mutt and Jeff*, some situation would be set up, something

would happen and then, by a twist, turn out unexpectedly? The
one, usually Mutt, the smart one, would be so amazed, so
astounded, so flabbergasted by the utter illogic of events, the
insanity of the situation and the stupidity of Jeff that he would
simply keel over with astonishment; the implication was that
everything was so absurd that no other action was left open to
him. It always happened in the last frame of the cartoon and all
you saw were the feet and part of the legs of Mutt, off the
ground, disappearing out of the frame, and in the air above the
feet and legs was always written the word PLOP!

Of course it wasn't Opal who really introduced the Plop Reflex
to me but Ruth that first day. But at the time I hadn't thought of
it as a characteristic of The Tribe, but only as a little added
attraction of Ruth's. As a characteristic, in action, it was limited
to the girls; not only that, but to the blacker, more African-
looking girls—those of the ugly stick. It just wouldn't have done
for a brown-skinned, straight-haired, thin-nosed chick to be
hurtling through the air like that. Just the same, it was definitive;
everyone shared in it, although only certain individuals were
chosen to perform it.

Its significance? I'd say it was terror. When all hope was lost,
when no one was going to understand, when your demand wasn't
going to be satisfied (even if that demand was impossible of
satisfaction)—then you could resort to terror. At least that's what
I felt and what The Tribe felt when the girls landed on their
heads with a bang. Possibilities, justice—none of it counted just
then, and your momentary terror came as a reflex too, a reaction
to an event which had just rendered you powerless.

7H was in no shape to learn or do anything. The heart of their
problem as a class was the simple skill of reading. There were
four kids who couldn't read their own names, three or four who
couldn't read anything else, and the rest of the class who could
read a little but were always shaky about it. They were unsure if
they would be able to avoid derision at any given moment, and
so tried to assert their superiority over each other in the very area
of their common incompetence. Any time we tried to work on
beginning word recognition, letters, sounds, the majority

sounded off about "that baby stuff," and as a result the non-readers had to sound off about it too; they couldn't admit not knowing how to read and so they couldn't ever begin to learn, because in order to learn they'd have to begin, right there in class, with simplicities, easily identified by all as "learning to read," and open themselves up to scorn. Nothing doing.

On the other hand, everything we were supposed to be doing in class presupposed that everybody could read. If you couldn't read it, what could you do?

7H had quite a few answers to that. Confronted with the word, Roy, for instance, laughed. He jumped up, threw back his head and laughed. He advanced to my desk and laughed, he roared with laughter, he raced around the room laughing. Everything was so funny he couldn't stop laughing long enough to read. Vincent got nervous. His face broke out in red blotches, and his eyes watered so badly that he had to take out his handkerchief and wipe them, so that of course the only reason he couldn't read was that his eyes were watering so—otherwise, he implied, he could read the hell out of it. Harvey always looked at me indignantly and asked why did I always pick on him to read the hardest parts? Now them other easy parts, I could read them real good, he'd say, but you just trying to make me read all the hard parts and I ain't going to do it!

Alexandra alone faced the reading issue with defiance and aplomb—she read like hell. Whatever was given to her, she just read right along, stumbling occasionally, but always recovering and getting everything right. This drove me crazy until I discovered that she was listening to Judy sitting right behind her muttering the words and Alexandra, sharp and cool, reading aloud after her. So I moved Judy one day, and Alexandra still read right along although considerably slower and with some mistakes; she not only had to be looking over at Judy in order to read her lips, but she also had to look down at the page once in awhile to give a semblance of reality and it was pretty difficult. She read Judy's lips! It's not so astounding, I guess; they'd been together in classes for years so Alexandra had had lots of practice. On days when Judy was absent Alexandra just pulled potato chips or candy out of her purse before her turn and began to eat them ostentatiously. If this didn't prompt a remark from me the other kids would object loudly; Alexandra would then begin to argue about eating in class (her mama *told* her to eat them potato chips!) and pretty soon Alexandra would get mad and announce how she wasn't going to do no reading today because I was so mean!

On the first day I found out she was reading Judy's lips, I went slightly crazy; I lectured her for ten minutes on how difficult it was to read lips, how simple it was by comparison to read, how if she'd have spent one-tenth of the time learning to read that she'd spent avoiding it . . . finally she yelled out furiously that she could so read, and why was I trying to lie and say she couldn't read? Judy piped up and said she was Alexandra's best friend and she ought to know, and Alexandra could so read, and that she—Judy—just read along with Alexandra to keep her company because we friends, Mr. Herndon! The rest of the class was taking sides by that time and began advising me on what Alexandra had done in the second or fifth grades and what *that* teacher said and did; finally someone remembered that I'd mentioned the secret word *lips* and said no wonder Alexandra could read Judy's lips, they were so big and fat and ugly, and so we had to hear from all sides about big-lip and liver-lip and watermelon-head and so on down the line. During this time Alexandra gained the upper hand, having very thin lips, and Judy, for all her fat-lip, could read better than anyone else. So everything was fine, except we were right back where we began.

The other nonreaders, or almost nonreaders, applied similar tactics, to the effect that it was more honorable to appear bad than stupid. When it came their turns to read they simply did something outrageous, we had our uproar, got over it, and Virgil or Judy would finish reading the story.

At one point I decided to get Judy and Virgil to help teach the others. It was the obvious thing to do and was fine in one sense— that is, everyone knew that Virgil and Judy were smart, smarter than anyone else in the class by a long shot, and so it was no disgrace to be instructed by them. Everyone was happy to co-operate. I had Virgil and Judy sitting at desks turned around to face three or four other desks, all equipped with flash cards, simple sentences written on large sheets, syllable sounds, rhyming words—everything all set, just as the unit plans say. I stood by, ready to lend a hand and also to keep the rest of the class busy or at least fairly quiet. Everyone enjoyed it a lot, but it didn't work.

The trouble was Virgil and Judy. Judy was a short, stocky little girl, black, African-looking, intelligent, and she possessed a terrible impatience and a temper. For one thing, having had to take everybody's crap for so long about her looks, she was not going to hold back pointing out their lacks in the area of brains. She liked being teacher, and often worked at it quite seriously, but she almost always went too fast, got impatient, criticized, mocked and called everyone stupid, which no one could take without making a remark in turn about Judy's head.

Virgil hadn't changed any since the first day, which makes it obvious how his group went. He showed them a word and then told them it meant something else; he wrote long words or nonsense words and slipped them into the stack of flash cards, or else he would ask Wade or Harvey how to spell antidisestablishmentarianism—and of course the ability to spell that word, in no matter what school, always represents the acme of intelligence and culture.

While this was going on, he advised them not to consult me because I was still trying to figure out ways to get them in trouble; this kept them where he wanted them, in a place where there was no appeal, no chance to find out anything for certain. He didn't even want them to trust *him*—Virgil wanted above all a permanent state of uneasiness for everyone.

Two days after vacation I received a note from the secretary that Mrs. X (another name I don't remember) was coming down to talk to me. Mrs. X was the District Language and Social Studies consultant for GW.

Mrs. X didn't visit my classes. She met me in the teachers' room during my free period and opened the conversation by telling me that she came, as she did with all the new teachers, to offer any help or advice she could.

This Mrs. X was white, elderly, tall, stringy, wore a print dress—the very picture, I must say, of the old-lady schoolteacher. She asked me if I had any problems I cared to mention. Did I? I began to outline them—9D's apathy, 7H's conglomeration of inabilities. I raced enthusiastically into a point-by-point description of the problems of 7H for a starter; I considered myself something of an expert on the subject. I spoke as if we two were going to reform the entire system, then and there.

Before I'd gotten fairly started, she interrupted. Now, we all have our problems, she said, and sometimes we're tempted to consider our own problems as being unique. But with *these* children (leaving out The Word, as usual) I've found that a simpler, more direct approach works best. I feel already that you may be making it all too complicated for yourself. In my experience, the best advice I can give you beginning teachers is, hold out a carrot.

A carrot? I didn't get it.

You know, she said brightly, the carrot, or perhaps we should say a sugar cube. If you want the goat to pull the cart, but he doesn't want to, you hold a carrot out in front of him. He tries to reach the carrot because he does want it. In doing so he pulls the cart. *If*, she said with a kind of wink, *if* you've attached the carrot to the cart.

I must have seemed a little stupid to her. Seeing that I just sat there, she tried to explain. Teaching these children is like training animals. For each task you want them to do, you must offer them a carrot.

You mean, I finally said, you try to get the goat to pull the cart without his realizing it. That is, the goat actually does what you want him to do, but all the time he thinks he's just trying to get that carrot. He doesn't realize he's pulling the cart. Not only that, but pulling the cart isn't something that any goat, any normal goat, ever wants to do, but . . .

I think you're trying to make it complicated again, she said, frowning.

You mean, I tried again, to get the student to do the assignment because of some reward he's going to get, not because he realizes that the assignment is valuable or interesting to him. You mean, the assignment itself can't be the carrot . . .

She felt happier. That's it, she said. Of course the reward must vary. There are individual differences as we know. A carrot for one, a sugar cube for another.

Mercifully the bell rang. Mrs. X went back to her desk in the district office, downtown. I sneaked a quick smoke, my mind filled with carrots and outrage, and arrived upstairs a bit late to greet 9D.

The next day I was invited, during my free period, to Mr. Grisson's office for a talk. As it turned out, that was normal procedure after a visit from the consultant. I was still outraged about them carrots and also I was tired of taking up my free time—during which I planned to drink coffee and smoke cigarettes—with substitutes and consultants. I believe I had some idea that Grissum and I, both being involved in the "real" situation, would soon settle these damn people.

So when he asked me how things went with Mrs. X, I was ready. I stated that she was hardly a person to be advising beginning teachers, seeing as how she thought that teaching kids was about the same as training a dog to play dead. He didn't seem disturbed. Instead, as I paused for breath, he said, I believe your problem is one of projection. You are not projecting.

Again I didn't get it.

Your voice, he said; projection, like an actor, or a good officer. The tone of command. Men, or children, hearing the voice properly projected, stop, pay attention, and tend to do what the voice says. Your voice hasn't that effect. You find yourself, for instance, shouting to get their attention.

That was the first I knew that he had any idea what went on in my room. Well, I said, I more or less think that the reason I shout is because they're all talking at once and otherwise they wouldn't hear me.

He shook his head. That's not the point. The point is to have them firmly in control by your voice as soon as they enter. Before they ever get into that state. Now, I'm going to arrange for you to have voice lessons. You'll be able to take them here, at the school, during your free period. You'll find it to be of great value, wherever you go and whatever you do.

Fine, I said, not knowing what else to say. I was rather astounded. I didn't have the slightest idea what he was talking about; also, I'd momentarily forgotten about my free period.

It's an excellent experience, he said. You'll be notified when the program starts.

The interview was clearly over. Still, I didn't feel we understood each other. Voice lessons were OK, but I had something else to say.

Mr. Grisson, I said, I'm sure voice lessons will be of value (I wasn't sure), but the thing is, I don't feel the problem is that I can't get them under control. I've had quite a bit of advice on that subject and I'm sure it's not very difficult to do that. The thing is, *I* don't want to *get them* under control. I want them to see some reason for getting *themselves* under control.

He began to look at me intently. I rushed on. It seemed to me, I told him, that they'd been having this firm control for years now, and it hadn't worked. They still hadn't seen any advantage in self-control, so obviously it hadn't worked!

Your description is correct, he said, but your conclusions, as I interpret them, are wrong. For if they've not yet learned self-control, then they must be controlled until they do learn it. You are the person to do that. It does them no good to be out of control, and it is dangerous. It is dangerous to them, and to the orderly running of the unit, the school.

He was intent and serious; he had a few things to say himself, apparently.

History shows, he said, that democracy is only granted to those populations who can manage their own affairs, who can do what is necessary without being forced to. The moment they no longer can, a leader, a monarch, even a dictator, takes over and orders them to do what they cannot make themselves do. That may be unpleasant for them, but it is inevitable.

Springtime at GW was the time for riots. The Tribe had given up and was becoming violent. By April the story of the year was over—some details, some dramatics left to tell, but the score was already in. All the promises had lost their appeal and The Tribe was busting out. Fights. Fires. Broken windows. Food thrown all over. Neighborhood complaints about vandalism. Teachers who had kept things in check all year began to have their troubles. We began to hear about So-and-so who was threatened by a group of kids, someone else who was swung on by a student, another who hit some kid. Down the hall old Mrs. Z was knocked flat in the hall by a girl whom she'd ordered down to the office for chewing gum. She'd ordered that girl and all the rest of them down to the office all year long, but now she had ordered once too often. Riots began to take place in the rooms—books torn up and papers thrown around, desks overturned and pushed out into the halls, the helpless teacher calling for assistance. Oddly enough, the faculty took it in stride. It happens every year, they seemed to say. We try. We hold 'em for as long as we can. . . .

Skates was an exception to the general fatalistic mood. The paragraph to copy didn't do the trick these days, the kids weren't going along with jokes and bantering. One day during a hard spring rain his afternoon class began to raise hell. They did the usual—tore up books, scattered the contents of cabinets all over, threw paper out the window. Skates gave up and dashed out of the room to get help, and the kids locked him out. By the time he got back in with the aid of the custodian and Mr. Grisson, the contents of his desk had been thrown out the window too, the desk itself overturned, his grade book torn up, and so on. Jim, he told me, it was a real, honest-to-God riot.

Skates's feelings were really hurt. Why me? he asked me over and over again. Why me?

I'm on their side, he kept saying. He was really upset. One detail of the riot, which he took to be directed at him personally, bothered him more than the rest. The kids had thrown his hat out the window along with the rest of the stuff; it had sailed down into the gutter. When Skates got back in the room and looked out the window, there he saw his hat floating in that muddy water along with the papers and books, and somehow it was that sight which was too much for him. He was almost crying as he told me about it. They threw my hat out! he kept saying. Why did they want to throw out my hat?

He'd always felt that he and The Tribe were just passing the time together while waiting for history to catch up with them; the idea was to make the time pass pleasantly and offer mutual support in the meantime. If there were irritating or troublesome moments along the way, that was OK with him, for basically he liked the kids just as they were. . . . The majority of the teachers were different, of course, and they weren't affected personally at all. They had believed all along that there was a war going on; outnumbered, they used every trick and all the moral authority granted them by the school and the country of America to hold the fort as long as it might be held. Now, retreating, still punishing the enemy whenever possible, giving ground, they hadn't given up and they weren't depressed. They would regroup, they told themselves, and come back next year for those battles, which they expected would follow the same pattern of war.

Let me say clearly in advance that I don't know how Harvey learned to read. I don't know when he learned. I couldn't say this method worked or that one, whether phonics or word recognition, reading groups, flash cards, tape recorder, structural linguistics, or "Cowboy Small."

On one of those last days, a commotion came from his reading group. I went over. Harvey stood up and announced to me, Mr. Hern-don, I can so read! Everyone jeered, with some justification. It wasn't as if Harvey had ever admitted he couldn't read.

You go on and test me, Mr. Hern-don! cried Harvey. That was new, so I went over and got a copy of *Red Feather*. I turned to a page I was pretty sure he hadn't memorized and gave it to him. He held it standing up and, sure enough, began to read it. It was a section where Red Feather, the Indian boy, is learning to make arrows from the old arrow maker. I could remember reading it myself as a child. Harvey read about making the shaft straight by pulling it through a hole bored in a block of hardwood or a piece of sandstone, I can't remember which. He stumbled a little, stopped and puzzled, moving his lips, but he read it. Everyone knew he was reading, not just reciting something he knew by heart.

When he finished I said, We ought to give Harvey a hand. Everybody clapped and cheered; naturally there were a few calls of *watermelon-head* and *chump* mixed in. After the ovation Harvey couldn't shut up; he was in a daze. He kept talking like a reformed drunkard, telling about how bad things were when he couldn't read, how he knew all the letters, but put them together and they just didn't mean anything to him *before*, but *now* . . . and what he planned to read next . . . them comics . . .

Finally someone couldn't stand it any more and yelled out, Harvey, why don't you shut up! You ain't nothing but a little colored boy!

That tore it! I thought. But Harvey didn't care. He had a big, pink ringworm spot on his forehead, I remember, and he said reasonably, just as if it weren't completely unheard of at GW, I know I'm just a little colored boy. What about it?

In the old days—six years ago—the kids got along with the system. (Would they now, since we have legislated against safety valves?) The kids are different now. Upon reflection, they too come up with the word *deprived*. If more kids can't or won't go along with us, it is because we have more deprived kids. If virtually all the kids from "lower-income" and "minority" groups are in our own low-ability groups, we turn to the counselors, the social workers, the clinics. Them is deprived kids, goes the cry, and someone ought to do something about it.

Deprived of what? Of intelligence? Do we claim that lower-class kids are just naturally dumber than middle-class kids, and that why they all in that dumb class? Naturally not. We have a list. They are deprived of ego strength, of realistic goal-orientation, of family stability, of secure peer relationships; they lack the serene middle-class faith in the future. Because of all that, they also lack self-control, cannot risk failure, won't accept criticism, can't take two steps back to go one forward, have no study habits, no basic skills, don't respect school property, and didn't read "Cowboy Small."

You can add to this list, or you can find another. But what such a list adds up to is something simple: some kids can't take it as well as others.

If the kids went along with us in the old days, it was for two reasons: first, there were fewer of them and we were able to allow them enough leeway to live; and second, they were white, middle-class kids in America. Not that the system in general was right for them—only that they fit the ideal of America in 1960 without much worry about it, had a richer life-diet outside of school, and so were tough enough to take it.

All right. Some can take it, and some can't. Those who cannot expose the point—it's not any good for anyone. My wife's father was once bitten by a cottonmouth, and survived. Another man from the same community was bitten and died. No one argued that the experience was good for either one of them. Sitting in a classroom or at home pretending to "study" a badly written text full of false information, adding up twenty sums when they're all the same and one would do, being bottled up for seven hours a day in a place where you decide nothing, having your success or failure depend, a hundred times a day, on the plan, invention and whim of someone else, being put in a position where most of your real desires are not only ignored but actively penalized, undertaking nothing for its own sake but only for that illusory carrot of the future—maybe you can do it, and maybe you can't, but either way, it's probably done you some harm.

The only thing is, I now know they aren't unique—that GW is not unique. More colorful, no doubt, more vehement in showing us the error of our ways, less cooperative . . . but, as Sullivan said, rather more like the rest of us than less.

What to do? You can read suggestions for change in a lot of recent books by serious and intelligent men. I suppose I could add mine. But frankly, I have almost no hope that there will be any significant change in the way we educate our children—for that, after all, would involve liberty, the last thing we may soon expect—and so I have thought merely to describe one time for you, parents, kids, readers, the way it is.

2. DEATH AT AN EARLY AGE
JONATHAN KOZOL

Jonathan Kozol received a National Book Award in 1968 for Death at an Early Age. *Since then he has been Educational Director of the Storefront Learning Center in Boston and has continued to teach, write, and live in the Boston ghetto.*

The room in which I taught my Fourth Grade was not a room at all, but the corner of an auditorium. The first time I approached that corner, I noticed only a huge torn stage curtain, a couple of broken windows, a badly listing blackboard and about thirty-five bewildered-looking children, most of whom were Negro. White was overcome in black among them, but white and black together were overcome in chaos. They had desks and a teacher, but they did not really have a class. What they had was about one quarter of the auditorium. Three or four blackboards, two of them broken, made them seem a little bit set apart. Over at the other end of the auditorium there was another Fourth Grade class. Not much was happening at the other side at that minute so that for the moment the noise did not seem so bad. But it became a real nightmare of conflicting noises a little later on. Generally it was not until ten o'clock that the bad crossfire started. By ten-thirty it would have attained such a crescendo that the children in the back rows of my section often couldn't hear my questions and I could not hear their answers. There were no carpetings or sound-absorbers of any kind. The room, being large, and echoing, and wooden, added resonance to every sound. Sometimes the other teacher and I would stagger the lessons in which our classes would have to speak aloud, but this was a makeshift method and it also meant that our classes had to be induced to maintain an unnatural and otherwise unnecessary rule of silence during the rest of the time. We couldn't always do it anyway, and usually the only way out was to try to outshout each other so that both of us often left school hoarse or wheezing. While her class was reciting in unison you could not hear very much in mine. When she was talking alone I could be heard above her but the trouble then was that little bits of her talk got overheard by my class. Suddenly in the middle of our geography you could hear her saying:

"AFTER YOU COMPARE, YOU HAVE GOT TO BRING DOWN."

Or "PLEASE GIVE THAT PENCIL BACK TO HENRIETTA!"

Neither my class nor I could help but be distracted for a moment of sudden curiosity about exactly what was going on. Hours were lost in this way. Yet that was not the worst. More troublesome still was the fact that we did not ever *feel* apart. We were tucked in the corner and anybody who wanted could peek in or walk in or walk past. I never minded an intruder or observer, but to notice and to stare at any casual passer-by grew to be an irresistible temptation for the class. On repeated occasions I had to say to the children: "The class is still going. Let them have their discussion. Let them walk by if they have to. You should still be paying attention over here."

Soon after I came into that auditorium, I discovered that it was not only our two Fourth Grades that were going to have their classes here. We were to share the space also with the glee club, with play rehearsals, special reading, special arithmetic, and also at certain times a Third or Fourth Grade phonics class. I began to make head-counts of numbers of pupils and I started jotting them down:

Seventy children from the two regular Fourth Grades before the invasion.

Then ninety one day with the glee club and remedial arithmetic.

One hundred and seven with the play rehearsal.

One day the sewing class came in with their sewing machines

and then that seemed to become a regular practice in the hall. Once I counted one hundred and twenty people. All in the one room. All talking, singing, yelling, laughing, reciting—and all at the same time. Before the Christmas break it became apocalyptic. Not more than one half of the classroom lessons I had planned took place throughout that time.

"Mr. Kozol—I can't hear you."

"Mr. Kozol—what's going on out there?"

"Mr. Kozol—couldn't we sing with them?"

One day something happened to dramatize to me, even more powerfully than anything yet, just what a desperate situation we were really in. What happened was that a window whose frame had rotted was blown right out of its sashes by a strong gust of wind and began to fall into the auditorium, just above my children's heads. I had noticed that window several times before and I had seen that its frame was rotting, but there were so many other things equally rotted or broken in the school building that it didn't occur to me to say anything about it. The feeling I had was that the Principal and custodians and Reading Teacher and other people had been in that building for a long time before me and they must have seen the condition of the windows. If anything could be done, if there were any way to get it corrected, I assumed they would have done it by this time. Thus, by not complaining and by not pointing it out to anyone, in a sense I went along with the rest of them and accepted it as something inevitable. One of the most grim things about teaching in such a school and such a system is that you do not like to be an incessant barb and irritation to everybody else, so you come under a rather strong compulsion to keep quiet. But after you have been quiet for a while there is an equally strong temptation to begin to accept the conditions of your work or of the children's plight as natural. This, in a sense, is what had happened to me during that period and that, I suppose, is why I didn't say anything about the rotting window. Now one day it caved in.

First there was a cracking sound, then a burst of icy air. The next thing I knew, a child was saying: "Mr. Kozol—look at the window!" I turned and looked and saw that it was starting to fall

in. It was maybe four or five feet tall and it came straight inward
out of its sashes toward the heads of the children. I was standing,
by coincidence, only about four or five feet off and was able to
catch it with my hand. But the wind was so strong that it nearly
blew right out of my hands. A couple of seconds of good luck—
for it was a matter of chance that I was standing there—kept
glass from the desks of six or seven children and very possibly
preserved the original shape of half a dozen of their heads. The
ones who had been under the glass were terrified but the thing
that I noticed with most wonder was that they tried very hard
to hide their fear in order to help me get over my own sense of
embarrassment and guilt. I soon realized I was not going to be
able to hold the thing up by myself and I was obliged to ask one
of the stronger boys in the class to come over and give me a
hand. Meanwhile, as the children beneath us shivered with the
icy wind and as the two of us now shivered also since it was a
day when the mercury was hovering all morning close to freezing, I asked one of the children in the front row to run down and
fetch the janitor.

When he asked me what he should tell him, I said: "Tell him
the house is falling in." The children laughed. It was the first time
I had ever come out and said anything like that when the children could hear me. I am sure my reluctance to speak out like
that more often must seem odd to many readers, for at this
perspective it seems odd to me as well. Certainly there were
plenty of things wrong within that school building and there was
enough we could have joked about. The truth, however, is that I
did not often talk like that, nor did many of the other teachers,
and there was a practical reason for this. Unless you were ready
to buck the system utterly, it would become far too difficult to
teach in an atmosphere of that kind of honesty. It generally
seemed a great deal easier to pretend as well as you could that
everything was normal and okay. Some teachers carried out this
posture with so much eagerness, in fact, that their defense of the
school ended up as something like a hymn of praise and adora-
tion. "You children should thank God and feel blessed with good
luck for all you've got. There are so many little children in the

world who have been given so much less." The books are junk,
the paint peels, the cellar stinks, the teachers call you nigger, and
the windows fall in on your heads. "Thank God that you don't
live in Russia or Africa! Thank God for all the blessings that
you've got!" Once, finally, the day after the window blew in, I
said to a friend of mine in the evening after school: "I guess that
the building I teach in is not in very good condition." But to state
a condition of dilapidation and ugliness and physical danger in
words as mild and indirect as those is almost worse than not
saying anything at all. I had a hard time with that problem—the
problem of being honest and of confronting openly the extent to
which I was compromised by going along with things that were
abhorrent and by accepting as moderately reasonable or unavoidably troublesome things which, if they were inflicted on
children of my own, I would have condemned savagely.

After the window blew in on us that time, the janitor finally
came up and hammered it shut with nails so that it would not fall
in again but also so that it could not open. It was a month before
anything was done about the large gap left by a missing pane.
Children shivered a few feet away from it. The Principal walked
by frequently and saw us. So did supervisors from the School
Department. So of course did the various lady experts who
traveled all day from room to room within our school. No one can
say that dozens of people did not know that children were sitting
within the range of freezing air. At last one day the janitor came
up with a piece of cardboard or pasteboard and covered over
about a quarter of that lower window so that there was no more
wind coming in but just that much less sunshine too. I remember
wondering what a piece of glass could cost in Boston and I had
the idea of going out and buying some and trying to put it in
myself. That rectangle of cardboard over our nailed-shut window
was not removed for a quarter of the year. When it was removed,
it was only because a television station was going to come and
visit in the building and the School Department wanted to make
the room look more attractive. But it was winter when the

window broke, and the repairs did not take place until the middle of the spring.

In case a reader imagines that my school may have been unusual and that some of the other schools in Roxbury must have been in better shape, I think it's worthwhile to point out that the exact opposite seems to have been the case. The conditions in my school were said by many people to be considerably better than those in several of the other ghetto schools.

Perhaps a reader would like to know what it is like to go into a new classroom in the same way that I did and to see before you suddenly, and in terms you cannot avoid recognizing, the dreadful consequences of a year's wastage of real lives.

You walk into a narrow and old wood-smelling classroom and you see before you thirty-five curious, cautious and untrusting children, aged eight to thirteen, of whom about two-thirds are Negro. Three of the children are designated to you as special students. Thirty per cent of the class is reading at the Second Grade level in a year and in a month in which they should be reading at the height of Fourth Grade performance or at the beginning of the Fifth. Seven children out of the class are up to par. Ten substitutes or teacher changes. Or twelve changes. Or eight. Or eleven. Nobody seems to know how many teachers they have had. Seven of their lifetime records are missing: symptomatic and emblematic at once of the chaos that has been with them all year long. Many more lives than just seven have already been wasted but the seven missing records become an embittering symbol of the lives behind them which, equally, have been lost or mislaid. (You have to spend the first three nights staying up until dawn trying to reconstruct these records out of notes and scraps.) On the first math test you give, the class average comes out to 36. The children tell you with embarrassment that it has been like that since fall.

You check around the classroom. Of forty desks, five have tops with no hinges. You lift a desk-top to fetch a paper and you find that the top has fallen off. There are three windows. One cannot be opened. A sign on it written in the messy scribble of a hurried

teacher or some custodial person warns you: DO NOT UNLOCK THIS
WINDOW IT IS BROKEN. The general look of the room is as of a
bleak-light photograph of a mental hospital. Above the one poor
blackboard, gray rather than really black, and hard to write on,
hangs from one tack, lopsided, a motto attributed to Benjamin
Franklin: "*Well begun is half done.*" Everything, or almost everything like that, seems a mockery of itself.

Into this grim scenario, drawing on your own pleasures and
memories, you do what you can to bring some kind of life. You
bring in some cheerful and colorful paintings by Joan Miró and
Paul Klee. While the paintings by Miró do not arouse much
interest, the ones by Klee become an instantaneous success. One
picture in particular, a watercolor titled "Bird Garden," catches
the fascination of the entire class. You slip it out of the book and
tack it up on the wall beside the doorway and it creates a traffic
jam every time the children have to file in or file out. You discuss
with your students some of the reasons why Klee may have
painted the way he did and you talk about the things that can be
accomplished in a painting which could not be accomplished in a
photograph. None of this seems to be above the children's heads.
Despite this, you are advised flatly by the Art Teacher that your
naïveté has gotten the best of you and that the children cannot
possibly appreciate this. Klee is too difficult. Children will not
enjoy it. You are unable to escape the idea that the Art Teacher
means herself instead.

For poetry, in place of the recommended memory gems, going
back again into your own college days, you make up your mind
to introduce a poem of William Butler Yeats. It is about a lake
isle called Innisfree, about birds that have the funny name of
"linnets" and about a "bee-loud glade." The children do not all go
crazy about it but a number of them seem to like it as much as
you do and you tell them how once, three years before, you were
living in England and you helped a man in the country to make
his home from wattles and clay. The children become intrigued.
They pay good attention and many of them grow more curious
about the poem than they appeared at first. Here again, however,
you are advised by older teachers that you are making a mistake:

Yeats is too difficult for children. They can't enjoy it, won't appreciate it, wouldn't like it. You are aiming way above their heads . . . Another idea comes to mind and you decide to try out an easy and rather well-known and not very complicated poem of Robert Frost. The poem is called "Stopping By Woods on a Snowy Evening." This time, your supervisor happens to drop in from the School Department. He looks over the mimeograph, agrees with you that it's a nice poem, then points out to you—tolerantly, but strictly—that you have made another mistake. "Stopping By Woods" is scheduled for Sixth Grade. It is not "a Fourth Grade poem," and it is not to be read or looked at during the Fourth Grade. Bewildered as you are by what appears to be a kind of idiocy, you still feel reproved and criticized and muted and set back and you feel that you have been caught in the commission of a serious mistake.

On a series of other occasions, the situation is repeated. The children are offered something new and something lively. They respond to it energetically and they are attentive and their attention does not waver. For the first time in a long while perhaps there is actually some real excitement and some growing and some thinking going on within that one small room. In each case, however, you are advised sooner or later that you are making a mistake. Your mistake, in fact, is to have impinged upon the standardized condescension on which the entire administration of the school is based. To hand Paul Klee's pictures to the children of this classroom, and particularly in a twenty-dollar volume, constitutes a threat to this school system. It is not different from sending a little girl from the Negro ghetto into an art class near Harvard Yard. Transcending the field of familiarity of the administration, you are endangering its authority and casting a blow at its self-confidence. The way the threat is handled is by a continual and standardized underrating of the children: They can't do it, couldn't do it, wouldn't like it, don't deserve it . . . In such a manner, many children are tragically and unjustifiably held back from a great many of the good things that they might come to like or admire and are pinned down instead to books the teacher knows and to easy tastes that she can handle. This includes, above all, of course, the kind of material that is contained in the Course of Study.

Try to imagine, for a child, how great the gap between the outside world and the world conveyed within this kind of school must seem: A little girl, maybe Negro, comes in from a street that is lined with car-carcasses. Old purple Hudsons and one-wheel-missing Cadillacs represent her horizon and mark the edges of her dreams. In the kitchen of her house roaches creep and large rats crawl. On the way to school a wino totters. Some teenage white boys slow down their car to insult her, and speed on. At school, she stands frozen for fifteen minutes in a yard of cracked cement that overlooks a hillside on which trash has been unloaded and at the bottom of which the New York, New Haven and Hartford Railroad rumbles past. In the basement, she sits upon broken or splintery seats in filthy toilets and she is yelled at in the halls. Upstairs, when something has been stolen, she is told that she is the one who stole it and is called a liar and forced abjectly to apologize before a teacher who has not the slightest idea in the world of who the culprit truly was. The same teacher, behind the child's back, ponders audibly with imagined compassion: "What can you do with this kind of material? How can you begin to teach this kind of child?"

Gradually going crazy, the child is sent after two years of misery to a pupil adjustment counselor who arranges for her to have some tests and considers the entire situation and discusses it with the teacher and finally files a long report. She is, some months later, put onto a waiting-list some place for once-a-week therapy but another year passes before she has gotten anywhere near to the front of a long line. By now she is fourteen, has lost whatever innocence she still had in the back seat of the old Cadillac and, within two additional years, she will be ready and eager for dropping out of school.

Once at school, when she was eight or nine, she drew a picture of a rich-looking lady in an evening gown with a handsome man bowing before her but she was told by an insensate and wild-eyed teacher that what she had done was junk and garbage and the picture was torn up and thrown away before her eyes. The

rock and roll music that she hears on the Negro station is considered "primitive" by her teachers but she prefers its insistent
rhythms to the dreary monotony of school. Once, in Fourth
Grade, she got excited at school about some writing she had
never heard about before. A handsome green book, brand new,
was held up before her and then put into her hands. Out of this
book her teacher read a poem. The poem was about a Negro—a
woman who was a maid in the house of a white person—and she
liked it. It remained in her memory. Somehow without meaning
to, she found that she had done the impossible for her: she had
memorized that poem. Perhaps, horribly, in the heart of her
already she was aware that it was telling about her future: fifty
dollars a week to scrub floors and bathe little white babies in the
suburbs after an hour's street-car ride. The poem made her want
to cry. The white lady, the lady for whom the maid was working,
told the maid she loved her. But the maid in the poem wasn't
going to tell any lies in return. She knew she didn't feel any love
for the white lady and she told the lady so. The poem was
shocking to her, but it seemed bitter, strong and true. Another
poem in the same green book was about a little boy on a merry-
go-round. She laughed with the class at the question he asked
about a Jim Crow section on a merry-go-round, but she also was
old enough to know that it was not a funny poem really and it
made her, valuably, sad. She wanted to know how she could get
hold of that poem, and maybe that whole book. The poems were
moving to her . . .

This was a child in my class. Details are changed somewhat
but it is essentially one child. The girl was one of the three
unplaced special students in that Fourth Grade room. She was
not an easy girl to teach and it was hard even to keep her at her
seat on many mornings, but I do not remember that there was
any difficulty at all in gaining and holding onto her attention on
the day that I brought in that green book of Langston Hughes.

Of all of the poems of Langston Hughes that I read to my
Fourth Graders, the one that the children liked most was a poem
that has the title "Ballad of the Landlord." . . . This poem may
not satisfy the taste of every critic, and I am not making any

claims to immortality for a poem just because I happen to like it a great deal. But the reason this poem did have so much value and meaning for me and, I believe, for many of my students, is that it not only seems moving in an obvious and immediate human way but that it *finds* its emotion in something ordinary. It is a poem which really does allow both heroism and pathos to poor people, sees strength in awkwardness and attributes to a poor person standing on the stoop of his slum house every bit as much significance as William Wordsworth saw in daffodils, waterfalls and clouds. At the request of the children later on I mimeographed that poem and, although nobody in the classroom was asked to do this, several of the children took it home and memorized it on their own. I did not assign it for memory, because I do not think that memorizing a poem has any special value. Some of the children just came in and asked if they could recite it. Before long, almost every child in the room had asked to have a turn.

All of the poems that you read to Negro children obviously are not going to be by or about Negro people. Nor would anyone expect that all poems which are read to a class of poor children ought to be grim or gloomy or heart-breaking or sad. But when, among the works of many different authors, you do have the will to read children a poem by a man so highly renowned as Langston Hughes, then I think it is important not to try to pick a poem that is innocuous, being like any other poet's kind of poem, but I think you ought to choose a poem that is genuinely representative and then try to make it real to the children in front of you in the way that I tried. I also think it ought to be taken seriously by a teacher when a group of young children come in to him one morning and announce that they have liked something so much that they have memorized it voluntarily. It surprised me and impressed me when that happened. It was all I needed to know to confirm for me the value of reading that poem and the value of reading many other poems to children which will build upon, and not attempt to break down, the most important observations and very deepest foundations of their lives.

BOSTON PUBLIC SCHOOLS
SCHOOL COMMITTEE
15 BEACON STREET, BOSTON 8, MASSACHUSETTS

ATTORNEY
THOMAS S. EISENSTADT
MEMBER

A careful investigation of the facts pertaining to the discharge of Mr. Jonathan Kozol reveal that the administration of the Boston Public Schools were fully justified in terminating his service.

Contrary to publicized reports, I have found that the poem incident was not the sole reason for Mr. Kozol's discharge. Rather, this particular incident was merely the climax to a series of incidents involving this teacher. On numerous occasions during his six months of service . . . Mr. Kozol was advised and counseled by his Principal, Miss ——, and his Supervisor, Mr. ——, to restrict his reading and reference materials to the list of approved publications. These admonitions were brought about by Mr. Kozol's continual deviation from the 4th grade course of study.

It has been established as a fact that Mr. Kozol taught the poem, "Ballad of the Landlord" to his class and later distributed mimeographed copies of it to his pupils for home memorization. It is also true that a parent of one of the pupils registered a strong objection to the poem to the school principal. Miss ——, properly carrying out her responsibility to all of the pupils and to their parents, admonished the neophyte teacher for his persistent deviation from the course of study. She further suggested that the poem "Ballad of the Landlord" was unsuitable for 4th graders since it could be interpreted as advocating defiance of authority. At this point Mr. Kozol became rude and told Miss —— that he was a better judge of good literature than she.

The confirmation of the above facts is adequate justification for the discharge of a temporary teacher hired on a day-to-day trial basis. It has been stated quite adequately that the curriculum of this particular school, which is saturated with compensatory programs in an effort to specially assist disadvantaged pupils, does allow for innovation and creative teaching. However, this flexibility does not and should not allow for a teacher to implant in the minds of young children any and all ideas. Obviously, a measure of control over the course of study is essential to protect the 94,000 Boston school children from ideologies and concepts not acceptable to our way of life. Without any restrictions, what guarantees would parents have that their children were not being taught that Adolf Hitler and Nazism were right for Germany and beneficial to mankind?

It should be understood that the fact of the poem's author [sic] happened to be a Negro had no bearing on this matter whatsoever. As a matter of fact, Mr. Kozol was asked by the school principal why other works of Langston Hughes, non-controversial in nature, were not selected for study. In fact, a reference source suggested in the course of study recommends use of the book entitled, "Time for Poetry," published by Foresman which contains six of Langston Hughes' poems; and the Administrative Library contains the book, "More Silver Pennies," by MacMillian [sic] which includes more of Langston Hughes' poems, and also poems by the Negro poet Countee Cullen.

When Miss —— reported the incident to Deputy Superintendent Sullivan and requested Mr. Kozol's removal from the teaching staff of the —— School, it climaxed a series of complaints made to Miss Sullivan's office concerning this particular teacher. Superintendent Ohrenberger's decision after carefully weighing the facts of the case was to relieve Mr. Kozol from further service in the Boston Public Schools.

It should be understood that many temporary teachers are released from service every year by the administration of the Boston Public Schools. They are released for a variety of reasons. The overwhelming majority of such cases are discharged because in the opinion of the administrators and supervisors the certain temporary teachers are found unsuitable in training, personality, or character. Mr. Kozol, or anyone else who lacks the personal discipline to abide by rules and regulations, as we all must in our civilized society, is obviously unsuited for the highly responsible profession of teaching.

In conclusion, I must add that Mr. Kozol did bring to his pupils an enthusiastic spirit, a high degree of initiative, and other fine qualities found in the best teachers. It is my hope that Mr. Kozol will develop his latent talents and concomitantly develop an understanding and respect for the value of working within the acceptable codes of behavior.

THE
SUBURBAN SCHOOL
NIGHTMARE

3. HOW CHILDREN FAIL
John Holt

John Holt has been teaching and observing children for more than fifteen years. In addition to teaching and acting as a consultant for elementary and high schools, he is the author of How Children Fail, How Children Learn, *and numerous magazine articles.*

April 21

I watched Ruth during the period of the Math test. At least four-fifths of the time she was looking out the window; or else she played with her pencil, or chewed her fingernails, or looked at Nell to see what information she might pick up. She did not look in the least worried or confused. It looked as if she had decided that Math tests were to be done, not during the regular test period, when everyone else does them, but during conference period on Friday, with teacher close at hand, so that if she got into a jam she could get instant help.

She seems to find the situation of not knowing what to do so painful that she prefers to do nothing at all, waiting instead for a time when she can call for help the moment she gets stuck. Even in conference period today she did next to nothing. She was trying to sneak something out of her desk. She moves rather jerkily, so every time she raised the desk lid, I saw it out of the corner of my eye and looked at her. This was rather frustrating for her; however, she kept right on trying for most of the period, not a bit abashed by being caught at it all the time.

Remember when Emily, asked to spell "microscopic," wrote MINCOPERT? That must have been several weeks ago. Today I wrote MINCOPERT on the board. To my great surprise, she recognized it. Some of the kids, watching me write it, said in amazement, "What's that for?" I said, "What do you think?" Emily answered, "It's supposed to be 'microscopic.'" But she gave not the least sign of knowing that she was the person who had written MINCOPERT.

On the diagnostic spelling test, she spelled "tariff" as TEARERFIT. Today I thought I would try her again on it. This time she wrote TEARFIT. What does she do in such cases? Her reading aloud gives a clue. She closes her eyes and makes a dash for it, like someone running past a graveyard on a dark night. No looking back afterward, either.

Reminds me of a fragment of "The Ancient Mariner"—perhaps the world's best short ghost story:

> Like one, that on a lonesome road
> Doth walk in fear and dread,
> And having once turned round walks on,
> And turns no more his head;
> Because he knows, a frightful fiend
> Doth close behind him tread.

Is this the way some of these children make their way through life?

MAY 8

MEMO TO THE RESEARCH COMMITTEE:

I have mentioned Emily, who spelled "microscopic" MINCOPERT. She obviously made a wild grab at an answer, and having written it down, never looked at it, never checked to see if it looked right. I see a lot of this one-way, don't-look-back-it's-too-awful strategy among students. Emily in particular has shown instances of it so striking that I would like you to know about them.

Some time after the spelling test in question, I wrote MINCO-PERT on the blackboard. Emily, and one other student, a good speller, interestingly enough, said that it was supposed to be "microscopic." Everyone found this very amusing, including Emily. She is a child who shows in her voice, look, coloring, and gestures much of what she is thinking, and she has not shown the least indication that she knows she is the creator of MINCOPERT. In fact, her attitude suggests that she rejects scornfully the idea that *she* would ever be so foolish as to spell the word in such a way.

Today she handed me, for display, a piece of tag board on which she had pasted some jokes that a friend had cut out of a newspaper. I found when I got to the last one that she had put the paste on the joke side, so that all there was to read was the meaningless fragment of a news story. I was surprised that she would paste a joke on backwards, without even looking to see whether she had it on the right way. When it was posted, and the other kids were looking at it, I said to Emily, "You'll have to explain that last joke to us; we don't get it." I thought she might look at it, for the first time, see that it was meaningless, and realize that she had pasted it on backside up. To my amazement, she smiled and said with the utmost nonchalance, "As a matter of fact, I don't get it myself." She *had* looked at it. She was perfectly ready to accept the fact that she had posted a joke that was meaningless. The possibility that she had made a mistake, and that the real joke was on the other side, did not occur to her.

I am curious about the ability of children to turn things around in their minds. One day, in room period, I asked the children to write on paper certain words that I had showed them, and then write what these would look like if seen in a mirror. I told them to be sure to write the words exactly as I did, with the same use of capital or lower-case letters. First I wrote CAT. Emily wrote CAt. It didn't trouble her that two letters were capitals, and one lower case—if she noticed it at all. She assumed that seen in a mirror the order of letters would be reversed, so she wrote TaC. The lower-case *t* became capital; the *A* became lower case. The next word was BIRD. She completely forgot what she had just done about reversing the order of the letters. This time she assumed that the trick was to write each letter backwards, while keeping them in the original order. On her paper she had written BIrD. She reversed the *B* correctly, wrote the *I*, then looked at the lower-case *r*, which must have looked to her like an upside-down *L*, decided, "I must turn this right side up," and wrote *L*. Then she decided that the letters *B* and *D* should not be reversed, so her final answer was BILD. Answer to what question? She hadn't the faintest idea. Whatever task she had set out to do at the beginning had gone from her mind long before she got to the end of it; it had become changed into something else, something to do with writing letters upside down, or backwards, or something.

This child *must* be right. She cannot bear to be wrong, or even to imagine that she might be wrong. When she is wrong, as she often is, the only thing to do is to forget it as quickly as possible. Naturally she will not tell herself that she is wrong; it is bad enough when others tell her. When she is told to do something, she does it quickly and fearfully, hands it to some higher authority, and awaits the magic words, "right," or "wrong." If the word is "right," she does not have to think about that problem any more; if the word is "wrong," she does not want to, cannot bring herself to think about it.

This fear leads her to other strategies, which other children use as well. She knows that in a recitation period the teacher's attention is divided among twenty students. She also knows the teacher's strategy of asking questions of students who seem confused, or not paying attention. She therefore feels safe waving her hand in the air, as if she were bursting to tell the answer, whether she really knows it or not. This is her safe way of telling me that she, at least, knows all about whatever is going on in class. When someone else answers correctly she nods her head in emphatic agreement. Sometimes she even adds a comment, though her expression and tone of voice show that she feels this is risky. It is also interesting to note that she does not raise her hand unless there are at least half a dozen other hands up.

Sometimes she gets called on. The question arose the other day, "What is half of forty-eight?" Her hand was up; in the tiniest whisper she said, "Twenty-four." I asked her to repeat it. She said, loudly, "I said," then whispered "twenty-four." I asked her to repeat it again, because many couldn't hear her. Her face showing tension, she said, very loudly, "I said that one-half of forty-eight is . . ." and then, very softly, "twenty-four." Still, not many of the students heard. She said, indignantly, "OK, I'll shout." I said that that would be fine. She shouted, in a self-righteous tone, "The question is, what is half of forty-eight. Right?" I agreed. And once again, in a voice scarcely above a whisper, she said, "Twenty-four." I could not convince her that she had shouted the question but not the answer.

Of course, this is a strategy that often pays off. A teacher who asks a question is tuned to the right answer, ready to hear it, eager to hear it, since it will tell him that his teaching is good and that he can go on to the next topic. He will assume that anything that sounds close to the right answer is meant to be the right answer. So, for a student who is not sure of the answer, a mumble may be his best bet. If he's not sure whether something is spelled with an *a* or an *o*, he writes a letter that could be either one of them.

The mumble strategy is particularly effective in language classes. In my French classes, the students used to work it on me, without my knowing what was going on. It is particularly effective with a teacher who is finicky about accents and proud of his own. To get such a teacher to answer his own questions is a cinch. Just make some mumbled, garbled, hideously un-French answer, and the teacher, with a shudder, will give the correct answer in elegant French. The student will have to repeat it after him, but by that time he is out of the worst danger.

Game theorists have a name for the strategy which maximizes your chances of winning and minimizes your losses if you should lose. They call it "minimax." Kids are expert at finding such strategies. They can always find ways to hedge, to cover their bets. Not long ago, in room period, we were working with a balance beam. A wooden arm or beam is marked off at regular intervals and balanced on a pivot at its midpoint. The beam can be locked in a balanced position with a peg. We put a weight at a chosen point on one side of the beam, then give the student another weight, perhaps the same, perhaps heavier, perhaps lighter, which he is to place on the other side of the beam so that, when the beam is unlocked, it will stay in the balanced position. When a student has placed the weight, the other members of his group say, in turn, whether they think the beam will balance or not.

One day it was Emily's turn to place the weight. After much thought, she placed it wrongly. One by one, the members of the group said that they thought it would not balance. As each one spoke, she had less and less confidence in her choice. Finally, when they had all spoken and she had to unlock the beam, she looked around and said brightly, "I don't think it's going to balance either, personally." Written words can not convey the tone of her voice: she had completely dissociated herself from that foolish person (whoever it was) who had placed the weight on such a ridiculous spot. When she pulled the peg and the beam swung wildly, she almost seemed to feel vindicated. Most of the children hedge their bets, but few do it so unashamedly, and some even seem to feel that there is something dishonorable in having so little courage of your own convictions.

July 25

OBSERVING IN BILL HULL'S CLASS:

Of all I saw and learned this past half-year, one thing stands out. What goes on in class is not what teachers think—certainly not what I had always thought. For years now I have worked with a picture in mind of what my class was like. This reality, which I felt I knew, was partly physical, partly mental or spiritual. In other words, I thought I knew, in general, what the students were doing, and also what they were thinking and feeling. I see now that my picture of reality was almost wholly false. Why didn't I see this before?

Sitting at the side of the room, watching these kids, not so much to check up on them as to find out what they were like and how they differed from the teen-agers I have worked with and know, I slowly became aware of something. You can't find out what a child does in class by looking at him only when he is called on. You have to watch him for long stretches of time without his knowing it.

During many of the recitation classes, when the class supposedly is working as a unit, most of the children paid very little attention to what was going on. Those who most needed to pay attention, usually paid the least. The kids who knew the answer to whatever question you were asking wanted to make sure that you knew they knew, so their hands were always waving. Also, knowing the right answer, they were in a position to enjoy to the full the ridiculous answers that might be given by their less fortunate colleagues. But, as in all classes, these able students are a minority. What of the unsuccessful majority? Their attention depended on what was going on in class. Any raising of the emotional temperature made them prick up their ears. If an argument was going on, or someone was in trouble, or someone was being laughed at for a foolish answer, they took notice. Or, if you were explaining to a slow student something so simple that all the rest knew it, they would wave their arms and give agonized, half-suppressed cries of "O-o-o-o-oh! O-o-o-o-oh!" But most of the time, when explaining, questioning, or discussing was going on, the majority of children paid little attention or none at all. Some daydreamed, and no amount of calling them back to earth with a crash, much as it amused everyone else, could break them of the habit. Others wrote and passed notes, or whispered, or held conversations in sign language, or made doodles or pictures on their papers or desks, or fiddled with objects.

There doesn't seem to be much a teacher can do about this, if he is really teaching and not just keeping everyone quiet and busy. A teacher in class is like a man in the woods at night with a powerful flashlight in his hand. Wherever he turns his light, the creatures on whom it shines are aware of it, and do not behave as they do in the dark. Thus the mere fact of his watching their behavior changes it into something very different. Shine where he will, he can never know very much of the night life of the woods.

So, in class, the teacher can turn the spotlight of his attention, now on this child, now on that, now on them all; but the children know when his attention is on them, and do not act at all as they do when it is elsewhere. A teacher who is really thinking about what a particular child is doing or asking, or about what he, himself, is trying to explain, will not be able to know what all the rest of the class is doing. And if he does notice that other children are doing what they should not, and tells them to stop, they know they have only to wait until he gets back, as he must, to his real job.

For children, the central business of school is not learning, whatever this vague word means; it is getting these daily tasks done, or at least out of the way, with a minimum of effort and unpleasantness. Each task is an end in itself. The children don't care how they dispose of it. If they can get it out of the way by doing it, they will do it; if experience has taught them that this does not work very well, they will turn to other means, illegitimate means, that wholly defeat whatever purpose the task-giver may have had in mind.

They are very good at this, at getting other people to do their tasks for them. I remember the day not long ago when Ruth opened my eyes. We had been doing math, and I was pleased with myself because, instead of telling her answers and showing her how to do problems, I was "making her think" by asking her questions. It was slow work. Question after question met only silence. She said nothing, did nothing, just sat and looked at me through those glasses, and waited. Each time, I had to think of a question easier and more pointed than the last, until I finally found one so easy that she would feel safe in answering it. So we inched our way along until suddenly, looking at her as I waited for an answer to a question, I saw with a start that she was not at all puzzled by what I had asked her. In fact, she was not even thinking about it. She was coolly appraising me, weighing my patience, waiting for the next, sure-to-be-easier question. I thought, "I've been had!" The girl had learned how to make me do her work for her, just as she had learned to make all her previous teachers do the same thing. If I wouldn't tell her the answers, very well, she would just let me question her right up to them.

Schools and teachers seem generally to be as blind to children's strategies as I was. Otherwise, they would teach their courses and assign their tasks so that students who really thought about the meaning of the subject would have the best chance of succeeding, while those who tried to do the tasks by illegitimate means, without thinking or understanding, would be foiled. But the reverse seems to be the case. Schools give every encouragement to *producers*, the kids whose idea is to get "right answers" by any and all means. In a system that runs on "right answers," they can hardly help it. And these schools are often very discouraging places for *thinkers*.

APRIL 28

The other day the fourth graders were playing Twenty Questions.

Many of them are very anxious when their turn comes to ask a question. We ask them to play Twenty Questions in the hope that, wanting to find the hidden thought, they will learn to ask more informative and useful questions.

They see the game quite differently: "When my turn comes, I have to ask a question." They are not the least interested in the object of the game, or whether their question gains useful information. The problem is simply to think of a question, any old question. The first danger is that you will just be sitting there, unable to think of a question. The next danger is that when you ask a question, other kids will think it is silly, laugh at it, say, "That's no good."

So the problem becomes not just thinking up a question, but thinking up a question that will sound good. The best way to do this is to listen to kids that you know are pretty sharp, and ask questions that sound like theirs. Thus, a child who found in one game that "Is it water?" was a useful question, went on asking it in game after game, even when other questions had established that the information sought for had nothing to do with water.

Many of our kids play the same way. Pat, Rachel, and some others never have any idea what the object of the game is, or what information has been gained by questions already asked. All they want, when their turn comes, is to have a question that won't be laughed at. Jessie plays it even safer than that. She just refuses to ask a question, says, "I pass," and looks very pleased with herself after she says it, too.

Another popular strategy is the disguised blind guess. When kids first play this game, every question is a guess. Then some of them see that it is silly to guess right at the beginning, and that the sensible thing to do is narrow down the possibilities. They criticize very severely teammates who start guessing too soon. So the trick becomes to ask a guessing question that doesn't sound like a guess, like Nat's classic, "Was he killed by Brutus?" This has become something of a joke in his group. Still, every question he asks conceals a guess.

One day we were using the atlas, and the field of the game was geographical locations. Sam wanted to ask if it was Italy, but that was a guess, so he said, "Does it look like a boot?" Every time it is his turn, he says, "Can I make a guess?" The strategy of narrowing down possibilities has not occurred to him, or if it has, he does not know how to make use of it.

Betty makes multiple guesses. Thinking of either Corsica or Sardinia, she asked, "Does it begin with C or S?" Another time she said, "Does it begin with B, D, C, P, or T?" This is not bad strategy. On another occasion she said to a cautious teammate, "Don't say 'Could it be?'; say 'Is it?' " She's a positive little critter.

Sometimes we try to track down a number with Twenty Questions. One day I said I was thinking of a number between 1 and 10,000. Children who use a good narrowing-down strategy to find a number between 1 and 100, or 1 and 500, go all to pieces when the number is between 1 and 10,000. Many start guessing from the very beginning. Even when I say that the number is very large, they will try things like 65, 113, 92. Other kids will narrow down until they find that the number is in the 8,000's; then they start guessing, as if there were now so few numbers to choose from that guessing became worthwhile. Their confidence in these shots in the dark is astonishing. They say, "We've got it this time!" They are always incredulous when they find they have not got it.

They still cling stubbornly to the idea that the only good answer is a *yes* answer. This, of course, is the result of their miseducation, in which "right answers" are the only ones that pay off. They have not learned how to learn from a mistake, or even that learning from mistakes is possible. If they say, "Is the number between 5,000 and 10,000?" and I say *yes*, they cheer; if I say *no*, they groan, even though they get exactly the same amount of information in either case. The more anxious ones will, over and over again, ask questions that have already been answered, just for the satisfaction of hearing a *yes*. Their more sophisticated teammates point out in vain that it is silly to ask a question when you already know the answer.

FEBRUARY 26

The unbelievable incompetence of some of the kids sometimes drives me wild. They can't find anything. They have no paper or pencil when it's time for work. Their desks are a mess. They lose library books. If they do homework at home, they leave it there; if they take home material to do homework, they leave the assignment at school. They can't keep their papers in a notebook. Yet they are not stupid or incapable children; they do many things well.

Ted is a very intelligent, alert, curious, humorous, and attractive boy, with a record of unbroken failure and frustration in school. He is an excellent athlete, strong, quick, and well coordinated. But his school papers are as torn, smudged, rumpled, and illegible as any I have ever seen. The other day the class was cleaning out desks, and I was "helping" him. We got about a ream of loose papers out of the desk, and I asked him to put them in the notebook. As always, when he is under tension, his face began to get red. He squirmed and fidgeted, and began to mutter, "They won't fit, the notebook's the wrong size,"—which wasn't true. Finally he assembled a thick stack of papers and began to try to jam them onto one of the rings in his notebook, not noticing that the holes in the papers were at least a half-inch from the ring. As he pushed and fumbled and muttered, I felt my blood pressure rising until, exasperated almost to rage, I said loudly, "For Heaven's sake, leave it alone, do it later, I can't stand to watch any more of it!"

Thinking over this scene, and many others like it, I was suddenly reminded of a movie, *A Walk in the Sun,* based on the novel by Harry Brown. It showed the adventures of a leaderless platoon of infantrymen during the first day of the invasion of Italy. At one point, while the platoon is moving through some woods, they are surprised by an enemy light tank, which, amid a good deal of confusion, they manage to ambush. When this action is over the soldiers find that their sergeant, who has been growing rapidly more anxious, and is clearly the victim of battle fatigue, has given way completely. They find him hugging the ground, shaking all over, babbling incoherently. They leave him behind, as they move inland toward their vaguely conceived objective. One of the soldiers remarks as they go that the sergeant has finally dug himself a foxhole that they can't get him out of.

It seems to me that children dig themselves similar foxholes in school, that their fumbling incompetence is in many ways comparable to the psychoneurotic reactions of men who have been under too great a stress for too long. Many will reject this comparison as being wildly exaggerated and inappropriate. They are mistaken. There are very few children who do not feel, during most of the time they are in school, an amount of fear, anxiety, and tension that most adults would find intolerable. It is no coincidence at all that in many of their worst nightmares adults find themselves back in school. I was a successful student, yet now and then I have such nightmares myself. In mine I am always going to a class from which, without the slightest excuse, I have been absent for months. I know that I am hopelessly behind in the work, and that my long absence is going to get me in serious trouble, of what sort I am not sure. Yet I feel I cannot stay away any longer, I have to go.

It is bad enough to be a teacher and feel that the children in your charge are using the conscious and controlled parts of their minds in ways which, in the long run and even in the short, are unprofitable, limiting, and self-defeating; to see them dutifully doing the assigned work and to be sure that they are not getting a scrap of intellectual nourishment out of it; to know that what they seem to have learned today they will have forgotten by next month, or next week, or even tomorrow.

But it is a good deal worse to feel that many children are reacting to school in ways that are not under their control at all. To feel that you are helping make children less intelligent is bad enough, without having to wonder whether you may be helping to make them neurotic as well.

MARCH 20

Today Jane did one of those things that, for all her rebellious and annoying behavior in class, make her one of the best and most appealing people, young or old, that I have ever known. I was at the board, trying to explain to her a point on long division, when she said, in self-defense, "But Miss W. [her fourth-grade teacher] told us that we should take the first number . . ." Here she saw the smallest shadow of doubt on my face. She knew instantly that I did not approve of this rule, and without so much as a pause she continued, ". . . it wasn't Miss W., it was someone else . . ." and then went on talking about long division.

I was touched and very moved. How many adults would have seen what she saw, that what she was saying about Miss W.'s teaching was, in some slight degree, lowering my estimate of Miss W.? Even more to the point, how many adults, given this opportunity to shift the blame for their difficulties onto the absent Miss W., would instead have instantly changed their story to protect her from blame? For all our yammering about loyalty, not one adult in a thousand would have shown the loyalty that this little girl gave to her friend and former teacher. And she scarcely had to think to do it; for her, to defend one's friends from harm, blame, or even criticism was an instinct as natural as breathing.

Teachers and schools tend to mistake good behavior for good character. What they prize above all else is docility, suggestibility; the child who will do what he is told; or even better, the child who will do what is wanted without even having to be told. They value most in children what children least value in themselves. Small wonder that their effort to build character is such a failure; they don't know it when they see it. Jane is a good example. She has been a trial to everyone who has taught her. Even this fairly lenient school finds her barely tolerable; most schools long since would have kicked her out in disgrace. Of the many adults who have known her, probably very few have recognized her extraordinary qualities or appreciated their worth. Asked for an estimate of her character, most of them would probably say that it was bad. Yet, troublesome as she is, I wish that there were more children like her.

June 3

I've corrected and scored the final math tests. The results are not quite as dismal as last week; most people did a little better. But one exception suggests that drill is not always as helpful as most people think. Caroline took the first test after being out two weeks, during which she missed much review work. She surprised me by getting 15 out of 25. Today, after taking the other test a week ago, and after a week of further review, she got only 7 right. It looks as if she learns more when she is out of school than when she is in it.

Looking at the low grades, I feel angry and disgusted with myself for having given these tests. The good students didn't need them; the poor students, during this month or more of preparation and review, had most of whatever confidence and common sense they had picked up during the year knocked right out of them. Looking at Monica today, on the edge of tears, unable to bring herself even to try most of the problems, I felt that I had literally done her an injury.

There was a lot of room for improvement in the rather loose classes I was running last fall, but the children were doing some real thinking and learning, and were gaining confidence in their own powers. From a blind *producer* Ben was on his way to being a very solid and imaginative *thinker;* now he has fallen back into recipe-following production strategy of the worst kind. What is this test nonsense, anyway? Do people go through life taking math tests, with other people telling them to hurry? Are we trying to turn out intelligent people, or test-takers?

There must be a way to educate young children so that the great human qualities that we know are in them may be developed. But we'll never do it as long as we are obsessed with tests. At faculty meetings we talk about how to reward the *thinkers* in our classes. Who is kidding whom? No amount of rewards and satisfactions obtained in the small group thinking sessions will make up to Monica for what she felt today, faced by a final test that she knew she couldn't do and was going to fail. Pleasant experiences don't make up for painful ones. No child, once painfully burned, would agree to be burned again, however enticing the reward. For all our talk and good intentions, there is much more stick than carrot in school, and while this remains so, children are going to adopt a strategy aimed above all else at staying out of trouble. How can we foster a joyous, alert, wholehearted participation in life, if we build all our schooling around the holiness of getting "right answers"?

DECEMBER 4

Some time ago, in an article on race stereotypes, I read something that stuck in my mind, but that only recently has seemed to have anything to do with children.

The author spent some time in a German concentration camp during the war. He and his fellow prisoners, trying to save both their lives and something of their human dignity, and to resist, despite their impotence, the demands of their jailers, evolved a kind of camp personality as a way of dealing with them. They adopted an air of amiable dull-wittedness, of smiling foolishness, of cooperative and willing incompetence—like the good soldier Schweik. Told to do something, they listened attentively, nodded their heads eagerly, and asked questions that showed they had not understood a word of what had been said. When they could not safely do this any longer, they did as far as possible the opposite of what they had been told to do, or did it, but as badly as they dared. They realized that this did not much impede the German war effort, or even the administration of the camp; but it gave them a way of preserving a small part of their integrity in a hopeless situation.

After the war, the author did a good deal of work, in many parts of the world, with subject peoples; but not for some time did he recognize, in the personality of the "good black boy" of many African colonies, or the "good nigger" of the American South, the camp personality adopted during the war by himself and his fellow prisoners. When he first saw the resemblance, he was startled. Did these people, as he had done, put on this personality deliberately? He became convinced that this was true. Subject peoples both appease their rulers and satisfy some part of their desire for human dignity by putting on a mask, by acting much more stupid and incompetent than they really are, by denying their rulers the full use of their intelligence and ability, by declaring their minds and spirits free of their enslaved bodies.

Does not something very close to this happen often in school? Children are subject peoples. School for them is a kind of jail. Do they not, to some extent, escape and frustrate the relentless, insatiable pressure of their elders by withdrawing the most intelligent and creative parts of their minds from the scene? Is this not at least a partial explanation of the extraordinary stupidity that otherwise bright children so often show in school? The stubborn and dogged "I don't get it" with which they meet the instructions and explanations of their teachers—may it not be a statement of resistance as well as one of panic and flight?

I think this is almost certainly so. Whether children do this consciously and deliberately depends on the age and character of the child. Under pressure that they want to resist but don't dare to resist openly, some children may quite deliberately *go stupid;* I have seen it and felt it. Most of them, however, are probably not this aware of what they are doing. They deny their intelligence to their jailers, the teachers, not so much to frustrate them but because they have other and more important uses for it. Freedom to live and to think about life for its own sake is important and even essential to a child. He will only give so much time and thought to what others want him to do; the rest he demands and takes for his own interests, plans, worries, dreams. The result is that he is not all there during most of his hours in school. Whether he is afraid to be there, or just does not want to be there, the result is the same. Fear, boredom, resistance—they all go to make what we call stupid children.

To a very great degree, school is a place where children learn to be stupid. A dismal thought, but hard to escape. Infants are not stupid. Children of one, two, or even three throw the whole of themselves into everything they do. They embrace life, and devour it; it is why they learn so fast, and are such good company. Listlessness, boredom, apathy—these all come later. Children come to school *curious;* within a few years most of that curiosity is dead, or at least silent. Open a first or third grade to questions, and you will be deluged; fifth graders say nothing. They either have no questions or will not ask them. They think, "What's this leading up to? What's the catch?" Last year, thinking that self-consciousness and embarrassment might be silencing the children, I put a question box in the classroom, and said that I would answer any questions they put into it. In four months I got one question—"How long does a bear live?" While I was talking about the life span of bears and other creatures, one child said impatiently, "Come on, get to the point." The expressions on the children's faces seemed to say, "You've got us here in school; now make us do whatever it is that you want us to do." Curiosity, questions, speculation—these are for outside school, not inside.

Boredom and resistance may cause as much stupidity in school as fear. Give a child the kind of task he gets in school, and whether he is afraid of it, or resists it, or is willing to do it but bored by it, he will do the task with only a small part of his attention, energy, and intelligence. In a word, he will do it stupidly—even if correctly. This soon becomes a habit. He gets used to working at low power, he develops strategies to enable him to get by this way. In time he even starts to think of himself as being stupid, which is what most fifth graders think of themselves, and to think that his low-power way of coping with school is the only possible way.

It does no good to tell such students to pay attention and think about what they are doing. I can see myself now, in one of my ninth-grade algebra classes in Colorado, looking at one of my flunking students, a boy who had become frozen in his school stupidity, and saying to him in a loud voice, "Think! Think! Think!" Wasted breath; he had forgotten how. The stupid way—timid, unimaginative, defensive, evasive—in which he met and dealt with the problems of algebra were, by that time, the only way he knew of dealing with them. His strategies and expectations were fixed; he couldn't even imagine any others. He really was doing his dreadful best.

We ask children to do for most of a day what few adults are able to do even for an hour. How many of us, attending, say, a lecture that doesn't interest us, can keep our minds from wandering? Hardly any. Not I, certainly. Yet children have far less awareness of and control of their attention than we do. No use to shout at them to pay attention. If we want to get tough enough about it, as many schools do, we can terrorize a class of children into sitting still with their hands folded and their eyes glued on us, or somebody; but their minds will be far away. The attention of children must be lured, caught, and held, like a shy wild animal that must be coaxed with bait to come close. If the situations, the materials, the problems before a child do not interest him, his attention will slip off to what does interest him, and no amount of exhortation or threats will bring it back.

A child is most intelligent when the reality before him arouses in him a high degree of attention, interest, concentration, involvement—in short, when he cares most about what he is doing. This

is why we should make schoolrooms and schoolwork as interesting and exciting as possible, not just so that school will be a
pleasant place, but so that children in school will act intelligently
and get into *the habit* of acting intelligently. The case against
boredom in school is the same as the case against fear; it makes
children behave stupidly, some on purpose, most because they
cannot help it. If this goes on long enough, as it does in school,
they forget what it is like to grasp at something, as they once
grasped at everything, with all their minds and senses; they
forget how to deal positively and aggressively with life and experience, to think and say, "I see it! I get it! I can do it!"

4. IN SUBURBAN CLASSROOMS

Jules Henry

*Jules Henry has taught at the University of Chicago
and at Columbia University and is presently a professor of anthropology at Washington University in
St. Louis. In addition to* Culture Against Man, *he is
the author of* Jungle People.

The function of education has never been to free the mind and
the spirit of man, but to bind them; and to the end that the mind
and spirit of his children should never escape *Homo sapiens* has
employed praise, ridicule, admonition, accusation, mutilation,
and even torture to chain them to the culture pattern. Throughout most of his historic course *Homo sapiens* has wanted from his
children acquiescence, not originality. It is natural that this
should be so, for where every man is unique there is no society,
and where there is no society there can be no man. Contempo-

rary American educators think they want creative children, yet it is an open question as to what they expect these children to create. And certainly the classrooms—from kindergarten to graduate school—in which they expect it to happen are not crucibles of creative activity and thought. It stands to reason that were young people truly creative the culture would fall apart, for originality, by definition, is different from what is given, and what is given is the culture itself. From the endless, pathetic "creative hours" of kindergarten to the most abstruse problems in sociology and anthropology, the function of education is to prevent the truly creative intellect from getting out of hand. Only in the exact and the biological sciences do we permit unlimited freedom, for we have (but only since the Renaissance, since Galileo and Bruno underwent the Inquisition) found a way—or *thought* we had found a way—to bind the explosive powers of science in the containing vessel of the social system.

American classrooms, like educational institutions anywhere, express the values, preoccupations, and fears found in the culture as a whole. School has no choice; it must train the children to fit the culture as it is. School can give training in skills; it cannot teach creativity. All the American school can conceivably do is nurture creativity when it appears. And who has the eyes to see it? Since the creativity that is conserved and encouraged will always be that which seems to do the most for the culture, which seems at the moment to do the most for the obsessions and the brutal preoccupations and anxieties from which we all suffer, schools nowadays encourage the child with gifts in mathematics and the exact sciences. But the child who has the intellectual strength to see through social shams is of no consequence to the educational system.

Creative intellect is mysterious, devious, and irritating. An intellectually creative child may fail, for example, in social studies, simply because he cannot understand the stupidities he is taught to believe as "fact." He may even end up agreeing with his teachers that he is "stupid" in social studies. Learning social studies is, to no small extent, whether in elementary school or the university, learning to be stupid. Most of us accomplish this task before we enter high school. But the child with a socially creative imagination will not be encouraged to play among new social systems, values, and relationships; nor is there much likelihood of it, if for no other reason than that the social studies teachers will perceive such a child as a poor student. Furthermore, such a child will simply be unable to fathom the absurdities that seem transparent *truth* to the teacher. What idiot believes in the "law of supply and demand," for example? But the children who do tend to *become* idiots, and learning to be an idiot is part of growing up! Or, as Camus put it, learning to be *absurd*. Thus the child who finds it impossible to learn to think the absurd the truth, who finds it difficult to accept absurdity as a way of life, the intellectually creative child whose mind makes him flounder like a poor fish in the net of absurdities flung around him in school, usually comes to think himself stupid.

The schools have therefore never been places for the stimulation of young minds. If all through school the young were provoked to question the Ten Commandments, the sanctity of revealed religion, the foundations of patriotism, the profit motive, the two-party system, monogamy, the laws of incest, and so on, we would have more creativity than we could handle. In teaching our children to accept fundamentals of social relationships and religious beliefs without question we follow the ancient highways of the human race, which extend backward into the dawn of the species, and indefinitely into the future. There must therefore be more of the caveman than of the spaceman about our teachers.

Much of what I have to say in the following pages pivots on the inordinate capacity of a human being to learn more than one thing at a time. Although it is true that all the higher orders of animals can learn several things at a time, this capacity for polyphasic learning reaches unparalleled development in man. A child writing the word "August" on the board, for example, is not only learning the word "August" but also how to hold the chalk without making it squeak, how to write clearly, how to keep going even though the class is tittering at his slowness, how to appraise the glances of the children in order to know whether he is doing it right or wrong, et cetera. If the spelling, arithmetic, or

music lesson were only what it appeared to be, the education of
the American child would be much simpler; but it is all the
things the child learns *along with* his subject matter that really
constitute the drag on the educational process as it applies to the
curriculum.

A classroom can be compared to a communications system, for
certainly there is a flow of messages between teacher (trans-
mitter) and pupils (receivers) and among the pupils; contacts
are made and broken, messages can be sent at a certain rate of
speed only, and so on. But there is also another interesting characteristic of communications systems that is applicable to classrooms, and that is their inherent tendency to generate *noise*.
Noise, in communications theory, applies to all those random
fluctuations of the system that cannot be controlled. They are the
sounds that are not part of the message: the peculiar quality
communicated to the voice by the composition of the telephone
circuit, the static on the radio, and so forth. In a classroom lesson
on arithmetic, for example, such *noise* would range all the way
from the competitiveness of the students, the quality of the
teacher's voice ("I remember exactly how she sounded when she
told me to sit down"), to the shuffling of the children's feet. The
striking thing about the child is that along with his arithmetic—
his "messages about arithmetic"—he learns all the noise in the
system also. It is this inability to avoid *learning the noise with the
subject matter* that constitutes one of the greatest hazards for an
organism so prone to polyphasic learning as man. It is this that
brings it about that an objective observer cannot tell which is
being learned in any lesson, the *noise* or the formal subject
matter. But—and mark this well—it is *not* primarily the message
(let us say, the arithmetic or the spelling) that constitutes the
most important subject matter to be learned, but the noise! The
most significant cultural learnings—primarily the cultural drives
—are communicated as *noise*.

Let us take up these points by studying selected incidents in
some of the suburban classrooms my students and I studied over
a period of six years.

The first lesson a child has to learn when he comes to school is that lessons are not what they seem. He must then forget this and act as if they were. This is the first step toward "school mental health"; it is also the first step in becoming absurd. In the first and second grades teachers constantly scold children because they do not raise their hands enough—the prime symbol of having learned what school is all about. After that, it is no longer necessary; the kids have "tumbled" to the idea.

The second lesson is to put the teachers' and students' criteria in place of his own. He must learn that the proper way to sing is tunelessly and not the way *he* hears the music; that the proper way to paint is the way the teacher says, not the way he sees it; that the proper attitude is not pleasure but competitive horror at the success of his classmates, and so on. And these lessons must be so internalized that he will fight his parents if they object. The early schooling process is not successful unless it has accomplished in the child an acquiescence in its criteria, unless the child *wants* to think the way school has taught him to think. He must have accepted alienation as a rule of life. What we see in the kindergarten and the early years of school is the pathetic surrender of babies. How could it be otherwise?

The observer is just entering her fifth-grade classroom for the observation period. The teacher says, "Which one of you nice, polite boys would like to take [the observer's] coat and hang it up?" From the waving hands, it would seem that all would like to claim the title. The teacher chooses one child, who takes the observer's coat. The teacher says, "Now, children, who will tell [the observer] what we have been doing?"

The usual forest of hands appears, and a girl is chosen to tell. . . . The teacher conducted the arithmetic lessons mostly by asking, "Who would like to tell the answer to the next problem?" This question was usually followed by the appearance of a large and agitated forest of hands, with apparently much competition to answer.

What strikes us here are the precision with which the teacher was able to mobilize the potentialities in the boys for proper social behavior, and the speed with which they responded. One is impressed also with the fact that although the teacher could have said, "Johnny, will you please hang up [the observer's] coat?" she chose rather to activate all the boys, and thus give *them* an opportunity to activate their Selves, in accordance with the alienated Selfhood objectives of the culture. The children were thus given an opportunity to exhibit a frantic willingness to perform an act of uninvolved solicitude for the visitor; in this way each was given also a chance to communicate to the teacher his eagerness to please her "in front of company."

The mere appearance of the observer in the doorway sets afoot a kind of classroom destiny of self-validation and actualization of pupil-teacher communion, and of activation of the cultural drives. In the observer's simple act of entrance the teacher perceives instantly the possibility of exhibiting her children and herself, and of proving to the visitor, and once again to herself, that the pupils are docile creatures, eager to hurl their "company" Selves into this suburban American tragicomedy of welcome. From behind this scenery of mechanical values, meanwhile, the most self-centered boy might emerge a *papier mâché* Galahad, for what he does is not for the benefit of the visitor but for the gratification of the teacher and of his own culturally molded Self. The large number of waving hands proves that most of the boys have already become absurd; but they have no choice. Suppose they sat there frozen?

From this question we move to the inference that the skilled teacher sets up many situations in such a way that *a negative attitude can be construed only as treason.* The function of questions like, "Which one of you nice polite boys would like to take [the observer's] coat and hang it up?" is to bind the children into absurdity—to compel them to acknowledge that absurdity is existence, to acknowledge that it is better to exist absurd than not to exist at all.

It is only natural, then, that when the teacher next asks, "Now who will tell what we have been doing?" and "Who would like to tell the answer to the next problem?" there should appear "a large and agitated forest of hands," for failure to raise the hand could be interpreted only as an act of aggression. The "arithmetic" lesson, transformed by the teacher, had become an affirmation of her matriarchal charisma as symbol of the system.

The reader will have observed that the question is not put, "Who *has* the answer to the next problem?" but "Who *would like to tell*" it? Thus, what at one time in our culture was phrased as a challenge to skill in arithmetic, becomes here an invitation to group participation. What is sought is a sense of "groupiness" rather than a distinguishing of individuals. Thus, as in the singing lesson an attempt was made to deny that it was a group activity, in the arithmetic lesson the teacher attempts to deny that it is an individual one. The essential issue is that *nothing is but what it is made to be by the alchemy of the system.*

In a society where competition for the basic cultural goods is a pivot of action, people cannot be taught to love one another, for those who do cannot compete with one another, except in play. It thus becomes necessary for the school, without appearing to do so, to teach children how to hate, without appearing to do so, for our culture cannot tolerate the idea that babes should hate each other. How does the school accomplish this ambiguity? Obviously through competition itself, for what has greater potential for creating hostility than competition? One might say that this is one of the most "creative" features of school. Let us consider an incident from a fifth-grade arithmetic lesson.

Boris had trouble reducing "12/16" to the lowest terms, and could only get as far as "6/8." The teacher asked him quietly if that was as far as he could reduce it. She suggested he "think." Much heaving up and down and waving of hands by the other children, all frantic to correct him. Boris pretty unhappy, probably mentally paralyzed. The teacher, quiet, patient, ignores the others and concentrates with look and voice on Boris. She says, "Is there a bigger number than two you can divide into the two parts of the fraction?" After a minute or two, she becomes more urgent, but there is no response from Boris. She then turns to the class and says, "Well, who can tell Boris what the number is?" A forest of hands appears, and the teacher calls Peggy. Peggy says that four may be divided into the numerator and the denominator.

Thus Boris' failure has made it possible for Peggy to succeed; his depression is the price of her exhilaration; his misery the occasion for her rejoicing. This is the standard condition of the American elementary school, and is why so many of us feel a contraction of the heart even if someone we never knew succeeds merely at garnering plankton in the Thames: because so often somebody's success has been bought at the cost of our failure. To a Zuñi, Hopi, or Dakota Indian, Peggy's performance would seem cruel beyond belief, for competition, the wringing of success from somebody's failure, is a form of torture foreign to those non-competitive redskins. Yet Peggy's action seems natural to us; and so it is. How else would you run our world? And since all but the brightest children have the constant experience that others succeed at their expense they cannot but develop an inherent tendency to hate—to hate the success of others, to hate others who are successful, and to be determined to prevent it. Along with this, naturally, goes the hope that others will fail. This hatred masquerades under the euphemistic name of "envy."

Looked at from Boris' point of view, the nightmare at the blackboard was, perhaps, a lesson in controlling himself so that he would not fly shrieking from the room under the enormous public pressure. Such experiences imprint on the mind of every man in our culture the *Dream of Failure*, so that over and over again, night in, night out, even at the pinnacle of success, a man will dream not of success, but of failure. *The external nightmare is internalized for life.* It is this dream that, above all other things, provides the fierce human energy required by techno-logical drivenness. It was not so much that Boris was learning arithmetic, but that he was learning the *essential nightmare. To be successful in our culture one must learn to dream of failure.*

From the point of view of the other children, of course, they were learning to yap at the heels of a failure. And why not? Have they not dreamed the dream of flight themselves? If the culture does not teach us to fly from failure or to rush in, hungry for success where others have failed, who will try again where others have gone broke? Nowadays, as misguided teachers try to soften the blow of classroom failure, they inadvertently sap the energies of success. The result will be a nation of chickens unwilling to take a chance.

When we say that "culture teaches drives and values" we do not state the case quite precisely. One should say, rather, that culture (and especially the school) provides the occasions in which drives and values are *experienced in events* that strike us with *overwhelming and constant force*. To say that culture "teaches" puts the matter too mildly. Actually culture invades and infests the mind as an obsession. If it does not, culture will not "work," for only an obsession has the power to withstand the impact of critical differences; to fly in the face of contradiction; to engulf the mind so that it will see the world only as the culture decrees that it shall be seen; to compel a person to be absurd. The central emotion in obsession is fear, and the central obsession in education is fear of failure. In order not to fail most students are willing to believe anything and to care not whether what they are told is true or false. Thus one becomes absurd through being afraid; but paradoxically, *only by remaining absurd can one feel free from fear*. Hence the immovableness of the absurd.

In examining education as a process of teaching the culture pattern, I have discussed . . . an arithmetic lesson, and the hanging up of a coat. Now let us consider a spelling lesson in a fourth-grade class.

"SPELLING BASEBALL"

The children form a line along the back of the room. They are to play "spelling baseball," and they have lined up to be chosen for the two teams. There is much noise, but the teacher quiets it. She has selected a boy and a girl and sent them to the front of the room as team captains to choose their teams. As the boy and girl pick the children to form their teams, each child chosen takes a seat in orderly succession around the room. Apparently they know the game well. Now Tom, who has not yet been chosen, tries to call attention to himself in order to be chosen. Dick shifts his position

to be more in the direct line of vision of the choosers, so that
he may not be overlooked. He seems quite anxious. Jane,
Tom, Dick, and one girl whose name the observer does not
know, are the last to be chosen. The teacher even has to
remind the choosers that Dick and Jane have not been
chosen. . . .

The teacher now gives out words for the children to spell,
and they write them on the board. Each word is a pitched
ball, and each correctly spelled word is a base hit. The children move around the room from base to base as their teammates spell the words correctly. With some of the words the
teacher gives a little phrase: "Tongue, watch your tongue,
don't let it say things that aren't kind; butcher, the butcher is
a good friend to have; dozen, twelve of many things; knee,
get down on your knee; pocket, keep your hand out of your
pocket, and anybody else's. No talking! Three out!" The
children say, "Oh, oh!"

The outs seem to increase in frequency as each side gets
near the children chosen last. The children have great difficulty spelling "August." As they make mistakes, those in the
seats say, "No!" The teacher says, "Man on third." As a child
at the board stops and thinks, the teacher says, "There's a
time limit; you can't take too long, honey." At last, after
many children fail on "August" one child gets it right and
returns, grinning with pleasure, to her seat. . . . The motivation level in this game seems terrific. All the children seem
to watch the board, to know what's right and wrong, and
seem quite keyed up. There is no lagging in moving from
base to base. The child who is now writing "Thursday" stops
to think after the first letter, and the children snicker. He
stops after another letter. More snickers. He gets the word
wrong. There are frequent signs of joy from the children
when their side is right.

Since English is not pronounced as it is spelled, "language
skills" are a disaster for educators as well as for students. We
start the problem of "spelling baseball" with the fact that the

spelling of English is so mixed up and contradictory and makes such enormous demands on the capacity for being absurd that nowadays most people cannot spell. "Spelling baseball" is an effort to take the "weariness, the fever, and the fret" out of spelling by absurdly transforming it into a competitive game. Over and over again it has seemed to our psychologist designers of curriculum scenery that the best way to relieve boredom is to transmute it into competition. Since children are usually good competitors, though they may never become good spellers, and although they may never learn to *spell* "success" (which really should be written *sukses*), they know what it *is*, how to go after it, and how it feels not to have it. A competitive game is indicated when children are failing, because the drive to succeed in the *game* may carry them to victory over the *subject matter*. At any rate it makes spelling less boring for the teacher and the students, for it provides the former with a drama of excited children, and the latter with a motivation that transports them out of the secular dreariness of classroom routine. "Spelling baseball" is thus a major effort in the direction of making things seem not as they are. But once a spelling lesson is cast in the form of a game of baseball a great variety of *noise* enters the system, because the sounds of *baseball* (the baseball "messages") cannot but be *noise* in a system intended to communicate *spelling*. Let us therefore analyze some of the baseball noise that has entered this spelling system from the sandlots and the bleachers.

We see first that a teacher has set up a choosing-rejecting system directly adopted from kid baseball. I played ball just that way in New York. The two best players took turns picking out teammates from the bunch, coldly selecting the best hitters and fielders first; as we went down the line it didn't make much difference who got the chronic muffers (the kids who couldn't catch a ball) and fanners (the kids who couldn't hit a ball). I recall that the kids who were not good players danced around and called out to the captains, "How about me, Slim? How about me?" Or they called attention to themselves with gestures and intense grimaces, as they pointed to their chests. It was pretty noisy. Of course, it didn't make any difference because the captains knew whom they were going to try to get, and there was not much of an issue after the best players had been sorted out to one or the other team. It was an honest jungle and there was nothing in it that didn't belong to the high tension of kid baseball. But nobody was ever left out; and even the worst were never permitted to sit on the sidelines.

"Spelling baseball" is thus sandlot baseball dragged into the schoolroom and bent to the uses of spelling. If we reflect that one could not settle a baseball game by converting it into a spelling lesson, we see that baseball is bizarrely *irrelevant* to spelling. If we reflect further that a kid who is a poor speller might yet be a magnificent ballplayer, we are even further impressed that learning spelling through baseball is learning by absurd association. In "spelling baseball" words become detached from their real significance and become assimilated to baseballs. Thus a spelling game that promotes absurd associations provides an indispensable bridge between the larger culture, where doubletalk is supreme, and the primordial meaningfulness of language. It provides also an introduction to those associations of mutually irrelevant ideas so well known to us from advertising—girls and vodka gimlets, people and billiard balls, lipstick and tree-houses, et cetera.

In making spelling into a baseball game one drags into the classroom whatever associations a child may have to the impersonal sorting process of kid baseball, and in this way some of the *noise* from the baseball system enters spelling. But there are differences between the baseball world and the "spelling baseball" world also. Having participated in competitive athletics all through my youth, I seem to remember that we sorted ourselves by skills, and we recognized that some of us were worse than others. In baseball I also seem to remember that if we struck out or muffed a ball we hated ourselves and turned flips of rage, while our teammates sympathized with our suffering. In "spelling baseball" one experiences the sickening sensation of being left out as others are picked—to such a degree that the teachers even have to remind team captains that some are unchosen. One's failure is paraded before the class minute upon minute, until, when the worst spellers are the. only ones left, the conspicuousness of the failures has been enormously increased. Thus the *noise* from baseball is amplified by a *noise* factor specific to the classroom.

It should not be imagined that I "object" to all of this, for in the first place I am aware of the indispensable social functions of the spelling game, and in the second place, I can see that the rendering of failure conspicuous, the forcing of it on the mind of the unchosen child by a process of creeping extrusion from the group, cannot but intensify the quality of the essential nightmare, and thus render an important service to the culture. Without nightmares human culture has never been possible. Without hatred competition cannot take place.

One can see from the description of the game that drive is heightened in a complex competitive interlock: each child competes with every other to get the words right; each child competes with all for status and approval among his peers; each child competes with the other children for the approval of the teacher; and, finally, each competes as a member of a team. Here failure will be felt doubly because although in an ordinary spelling lesson one fails alone, in "spelling baseball" one lets down the children on one's team. Thus though in the game the motivation toward spelling is heightened so that success becomes triumph, so does failure become disaster. The greater the excitement the more intense the feeling of success and failure, and the importance of spelling or failing to spell "August" becomes exaggerated. But it is in the nature of an obsession to exaggerate the significance of events.

We come now to the *noise* introduced by the teacher. In order to make the words clear she puts each one in a sentence: "Tongue: watch your tongue; don't let it say things that aren't kind." "Butcher: the butcher is a good friend to have." "Dozen: twelve of many things." "Knee: get down on your knee." "Pocket: keep your hand out of your pocket, and anybody else's." More relevant associations to the words would be, "The leg bends at the knee." "A butcher cuts up meat." "I carry something in my pocket," etc. What the teacher's sentences do is introduce a number of her idiosyncratic cultural preoccupations, without clarifying anything; for there is no *necessary* relation between butcher and friend, between floor and knee, between pocket and improperly intrusive hands, and so on. In her way, therefore, the teacher establishes the same irrelevance between words and associations as the game does between spelling and baseball. She amplifies the *noise* by introducing ruminations from her own inner communication system.

CARPING CRITICISM

The unremitting effort by the system to bring the cultural drives to a fierce pitch must ultimately turn the children against one another; and though they cannot punch one another in the nose or pull each other's hair in class, they can vent some of their hostility in carping criticism of one another's work. Carping criticism is so destructive of the early tillerings of those creative impulses we cherish, that it will be good to give the matter further review.

Let us now consider two examples . . . from a fifth-grade class as the children report on their projects and read original stories.

Bill has given a report on tarantulas. As usual the teacher waits for volunteers to comment on the child's report.

MIKE: The talk was well illustrated and well prepared.

BOB: Bill had a *piece of paper* [for his notes] and teacher said he should have them on *cards*. . . .

Bill says he could not get any cards, and the teacher says he should tear the paper the next time he has no cards.

BOB: He held the paper behind him. If he had had to look at it, it wouldn't have been very nice.

The children are taking turns reading to the class stories they have made up. Charlie's is called *The Unknown Guest.*

"One dark, dreary night, on a hill a house stood. This house was forbidden territory for Bill and Joe, but they were going in anyway. The door creaked, squealed, slammed. A voice warned them to go home. They went upstairs. A stair cracked. They entered a room. A voice said they might as well stay and find out now; and their father came out. He laughed and they laughed, but they never forgot their adventure together."

TEACHER: Are there any words that give you the mood of the story?

LUCY: He could have made the sentences a little better. . . .

TEACHER: Let's come back to Lucy's comment. What about his sentences?

GERT: They were too short.

Charlie and Jeanne have a discussion about the position of the word "stood" in the first sentence.

TEACHER: Wait a minute; some people are forgetting their manners. . . .

JEFF: About the room: the boys went up the stairs and one "cracked," then they were in the room. Did they fall through the stairs, or what?

The teacher suggests Charlie make that a little clearer. . . .

TEACHER: We still haven't decided about the short sentences. Perhaps they make the story more spooky and mysterious.

GWYNNE: I wish he had read with more expression instead of all at one time.

RACHEL: Not enough expression.

TEACHER: Charlie, they want a little more expression from you. I guess we've given you enough suggestions for one time. [Charlie does not raise his head, which is bent over his desk as if studying a paper.] Charlie! I guess we've given you enough suggestions for one time, Charlie, haven't we? [Charlie half raises his head, seems to assent grudgingly.]

It stands to reason that a competitive system must do this; and adults, since they are always tearing each other to pieces, should understand that children will be no different. School is indeed a training for later life not because it teaches the 3 Rs (more or less), but because it instills the essential cultural nightmare fear of failure, envy of success, and absurdity.

Part Two

SOMETHING ELSE: THEORY

Radical reform of schooling—as distinguished from mere "innovation" in the organization or content of instruction—demands that basic postulates be re-examined, challenged, and where necessary replaced. Is formal education necessary or desirable? Should there be schools? Should education be compulsory? Should teachers and school administrators run the schools? Should there be a curriculum? Should there be goals of education which are considered applicable to all normal children?

Paul Goodman begins with a vision of how the whole system of American education could be freed from the bureaucratic constraints which stifle real learning and growth. He argues that we should dismantle it completely, from preschool to professional training, and restructure it entirely on the basis of free choice.

Looking at the entire educational system from a quite different radical perspective, Marshall McLuhan and George Leonard envisage what the school of the future might look like if we completely harnessed the new communications technologies to the task of cultivating the widest possible range of human potentialities. They believe that the school experience must be linked up with the most potent sources of energy and information in our society.

While considering these visions of a freed-up, turned-on school experience, however, we must face the immediate prob-

lem of what to do about the untenable failure of ghetto education. Alternative public school systems with divergent goals and
methods, or decentralized public school systems which serve
their communities in new and different ways, may be the answer if the existing big-city bureaucracies prove incapable of
renewal. Kenneth Clark and Preston Wilcox probe the possibilities.

The theory of radical school reform does not stop with the
institutional framework of schooling. It attempts to define the
quality of life within the classroom. Two qualities are valued
most: freedom and relevance.

Freedom is central because it is the necessary condition of
finding the way to viable teaching and learning. Breaking out
of the constraints and compulsions of the surrounding culture
and society, of the hierarchical and authoritarian structure of
educational institutions, of obsolete attitudes toward children—
these are necessary preconditions to basic change.

The public schools' control of young people's lives is supported by the law, which makes attendance compulsory, and
also by the collective opinion of adult society, which insists that
schooling is good for kids and that if the kids don't like it there's
something wrong with *them*. Edgar Friedenberg discusses how
sufficient student participation can be injected into such an
authoritarian system to permit some real learning to take place.

Friedenberg's principles are applied to a specific school situation in the statement of the Montgomery County (Maryland)
Student Alliance, the most cogent and eloquent manifesto yet
issued by precollege students.

But breaking out is not enough—freedom is not an end in
itself. The purpose of breaking out of sick and dead patterns
is to build or invent healthy, lively ones. The use of freedom in
education is to make contact between teacher and student, and
between both of them and things worth knowing. Postman
and Weingartner, Fantini and Weinstein, and Sylvia Ashton-
Warner ask how the school experience can be made truly relevant for children. They explore basic ways by which teachers

can assure that what is taught touches the child's true concerns, both intellectual and emotional. Whether the children are suburban WASPs, Blacks in the American ghetto, or Maoris in Australia, they need to find in school answers to questions which they themselves feel are interesting and important. If they do not, the consequences may be portentous. "Inescapably war and peace wait in an infant room," writes Sylvia Ashton-Warner, "wait and vie."

VISIONS:
THE SCHOOL
IN SOCIETY

⌐5.⌐ NO PROCESSING WHATEVER
PAUL GOODMAN

*Paul Goodman holds a Ph.D. in Humanities from
the University of Chicago. His books include* Com-
munitas (*with Percival Goodman*), Growing Up Absurd, The Community of Scholars, *and* Compulsory
Mis-Education. *Through his magazine articles and
widespread lecturing he has become widely admired
by students and a respected adviser on educational
problems.*

The belief that a highly industrialized society requires twelve to
twenty years of prior processing of the young is an illusion or a
hoax. The evidence is strong that there is no correlation between
school performance and life achievement in any of the professions, whether medicine, law, engineering, journalism, or business. Moreover, recent research shows that for more modest
clerical, technological, or semiskilled factory jobs there is no
advantage in years of schooling or the possession of diplomas.
We were not exactly savages in 1900 when only 6 per cent of
adolescents graduated from high school.

Whatever the deliberate intention, schooling today serves mainly for policing and for taking up the slack in youth unemployment. It is not surprising that the young are finally rebelling against it, especially since they cannot identify with the goals of so much social engineering—for instance, that 86 per cent of the federal budget for research and development is for military purposes.

We can, I believe, educate the young entirely in terms of their free choice, with no processing whatever. Nothing can be efficiently learned, or, indeed, learned at all—other than through parroting or brute training, when acquired knowledge is promptly forgotten after the examination—unless it meets need, desire, curiosity, or fantasy. Unless there is a reaching from within, the learning cannot become "second nature," as Aristotle called true learning. It seems stupid to decide a priori what the young ought to know and then to try to motivate them, instead of letting the initiative come from them and putting information and relevant equipment at their service. It is false to assert that this kind of freedom will not serve society's needs—at least those needs that should humanly be served; freedom is the only way toward authentic citizenship and real, rather than verbal, philosophy. Free choice is not random but responsive to real situations; both youth and adults live in a nature of things, a polity, an ongoing society, and it is these, in fact, that attract interest and channel need. If the young, as they mature, can follow their bent and choose their topics, times, and teachers, and if teachers teach what they themselves consider important—which is all they can skillfully teach anyway—the needs of society will be adequately met; there will be more lively, independent, and inventive people; and in the fairly short run there will be a more sensible and efficient society.

It is not necessary to argue for free choice as a metaphysical proposition; it is what is indicated by present conditions. Increasingly, the best young people resolutely resist authority, and we will let them have a say or lose them. And more important, since the conditions of modern social and technological organization are so pervasively and rigidly conforming, it is necessary, in order to maintain human initiative, to put our emphasis on protecting the young from top-down direction. The monkish and academic methods which were civilizing for wild shepherds create robots in a period of high technology. The public schools which did a good job of socializing immigrants in an open society now regiment individuals and rigidify class stratification.

Up to age twelve, there is no point to formal subjects or a prearranged curriculum. With guidance, whatever a child experiences is educational. Dewey's idea is a good one: It makes no difference *what* is learned at this age, so long as the child goes on wanting to learn something further. Teachers for this age are those who like children, pay attention to them, answer their questions, enjoy taking them around the city and helping them explore, imitate, try out, and who sing songs with them and teach them games. Any benevolent grownup—literate or illiterate—has plenty to teach an eight-year-old; the only profitable training for teachers is a group therapy and, perhaps, a course in child development.

We see that infants learn to speak in their own way in an environment where there is speaking and where they are addressed and take part. If we tried to teach children to speak according to our own theories and methods and schedules, as we try to teach reading, there would be as many stammerers as there are bad readers. Besides, it has been shown that whatever is useful in the present eight-year elementary curriculum can be learned in four months by a normal child of twelve. If let alone, in fact, he will have learned most of it by himself.

Since we have communities where people do not attend to the children as a matter of course, and since children must be rescued from their homes, for most of these children there should be some kind of school. In a proposal for mini-schools in New York City, I suggested an elementary group of twenty-eight children with four grownups: a licensed teacher, a housewife who can cook, a college senior, and a teen-age school dropout. Such a group can meet in any store front, church basement, settlement house, or housing project; more important, it can often go about the city, as is possible when the student-teacher ratio is 7 to 1.

Experience at the First Street School in New York has shown that the cost for such a little school is less than for the public school with a student-teacher ratio of 30 to 1. (In the public system, most of the money goes for administration and for specialists to remedy the lack of contact in the classroom.) As A. S. Neill has shown, attendance need not be compulsory. The school should be located near home so the children can escape from it to home, and from home to it. The school should be supported by public money but administered entirely by its own children, teachers, and parents.

In the adolescent and college years, the present mania is to keep students at their lessons for another four to ten years as the only way of their growing up in the world. The correct policy would be to open as many diverse paths as possible, with plenty of opportunity to backtrack and change. It is said by James Conant that about 15 per cent learn well by books and study in an academic setting, and these can opt for high school. Most, including most of the bright students, do better either on their own or as apprentices in activities that are for keeps, rather than through lessons. If their previous eight years had been spent in exploring their own bents and interests, rather than being continually interrupted to do others' assignments on others' schedules, most adolescents would have a clearer notion of what they are after, and many would have found their vocations.

For the 15 per cent of adolescents who learn well in schools and are interested in subjects that are essentially academic, the present catch-all high schools are wasteful. We would do better to return to the small preparatory academy, with perhaps sixty students and three teachers—one in physical sciences, one in social sciences, one in humanities—to prepare for college board examinations. An academy could be located in, and administered by, a university and staffed by graduate students who like to teach and in this way might earn stipends while they write their theses. In such a setting, without dilution by nonacademic subjects and a mass of uninterested fellow students, an academic adolescent can, by spending three hours a day in the classroom, easily be prepared in three or four years for college.

Forcing the nonacademic to attend school breaks the spirit of most and foments alienation in the best. Kept in tutelage, young people, who are necessarily economically dependent, cannot pursue the sexual, adventurous, and political activities congenial to them. Since lively youngsters insist on these anyway, the effect of what we do is to create a gap between them and the oppressive adult world, with a youth subculture and an arrested development.

School methods are simply not competent to teach all the arts, sciences, professions, and skills the school establishment pretends to teach. For some professions—e.g., social work, architecture, pedagogy—trying to earn academic credits is probably harmful because it is an irrelevant and discouraging obstacle course. Most technological know-how has to be learned in actual practice in offices and factories, and this often involves unlearning what has been laboriously crammed for exams. The technical competence required by skilled and semiskilled workmen and average technicians can be acquired in three weeks to a year on the job, with no previous schooling. The importance of even "functional literacy" is much exaggerated; it is the attitude, and not the reading ability, that counts. Those who are creative in the arts and sciences almost invariably go their own course and are usually hampered by schools. Modern languages are best learned by travel. It is pointless to teach social sciences, literary criticism, and philosophy to youngsters who have had no responsible experience in life and society.

Most of the money now spent for high schools and colleges should be devoted to the support of apprenticeships; travel; subsidized browsing in libraries and self-directed study and research; programs such as VISTA, the Peace Corps, Students for a Democratic Society, or the Student Nonviolent Coordinating Committee; rural reconstruction; and work camps for projects in conservation and urban renewal. It is a vast sum of money—but it costs almost $1,500 a year to keep a youth in a blackboard jungle in New York; the schools have become one of our major industries. Consider one kind of opportunity. Since it is important for the very existence of the republic to countervail the now overwhelming national corporate style of information, entertainment, and research, we need scores of thousands of small independent television stations, community radio stations, local newspapers that are more than gossip notes and ads, community theaters, high-brow or dissenting magazines, small design offices for neighborhood renewal that is not bureaucratized, small laboratories for science and invention that are not centrally directed. Such enterprises could present admirable opportunities for bright but unacademic young people to serve as apprentices.

Ideally, the polis itself is the educational environment; a good community consists of worthwhile, attractive, and fulfilling callings and things to do, to grow up into. The policy I am proposing tends in this direction rather than away from it. By multiplying options, it should be possible to find an interesting course for each individual youth, as we now do for only some of the emotionally disturbed and the troublemakers. Voluntary adolescent choices are often random and foolish and usually transitory; but they are the likeliest ways of growing up reasonably. What is most essential is for the youth to see that he is taken seriously as a person, rather than fitted into an institutional system. I don't know if this tailor-made approach would be harder or easier to administer than standardization that in fact fits nobody and results in an increasing number of recalcitrants. On the other hand, as the Civilian Conservation Corps showed in the Thirties, the products of willing youth later can be valuable even economically, whereas accumulating Regents blue-books is worth nothing except to the school itself.

(By and large, it is not in the adolescent years but in later years that, in all walks of life, there is need for academic withdrawal, periods of study and reflection, synoptic review of the texts. The Greeks understood this and regarded most of our present college curricula as appropriate for only those over the age of thirty or thirty-five. To some extent, the churches used to provide a studious environment. We do these things miserably in hurried conferences.)

We have similar problems in the universities. We cram the young with what they do not want at the time and what most of them will never use; but by requiring graded diplomas we make it hard for older people to get what they want and can use. Now, paradoxically, when so many are going to school, the training of authentic learned professionals is proving to be a failure, with dire effects on our ecology, urbanism, polity, communications, and even the direction of science. Doing others' lessons under compulsion for twenty years does not tend to produce professionals who are autonomous, principled, and ethically responsible to client and community. Broken by processing, professionals degenerate to mere professional-personnel. Professional peer groups have become economic lobbies. The licensing and maintenance of standards have been increasingly relinquished to the state, which has no competence.

In licensing professionals, we have to look more realistically at functions, drop mandarin requirements of academic diplomas that are irrelevant, and rid ourselves of the ridiculous fad of awarding diplomas for every skill and trade whatever. In most professions and arts there are important abstract parts that can best be learned academically. The natural procedure is for those actually engaged in a professional activity to go to school to learn what they now know they need; re-entry into the academic track, therefore, should be made easy for those with a strong motive.

Universities are primarily schools of learned professions, and the faculty should be composed primarily not of academics but of working professionals who feel duty-bound and attracted to pass on their tradition to apprentices of a new generation. Being combined in a community of scholars, such professionals teach a noble apprenticeship, humane and with vision toward a more ideal future. It is humane because the disciplines communicate with one another; it is ideal because the young are free and questioning. A good professional school can be tiny. In *The Community of Scholars* I suggest that 150 students and ten professionals—the size of the usual medieval university—are enough. At current faculty salaries, the cost per student would be a fourth of that of our huge administrative machines. And, of course, on such a small scale contact between faculty and students is sought for and easy.

Today, because of the proved incompetence of our adult institutions and the hypocrisy of most professionals, university students have a right to a large say in what goes on. (But this, too, is medieval.) Professors will, of course, teach what they please. My advice to students is that given by Prince Kropotkin, in "A Letter to the Young": "Ask what kind of world do you want to live in? What are you good at and want to work at to build that world? What do you need to know? Demand that your teachers teach you that." Serious teachers would be delighted by this approach.

The idea of the liberal arts college is a beautiful one: to teach the common culture and refine character and citizenship. But it does not happen; the evidence is that the college curriculum has little effect on underlying attitudes, and most cultivated folk do not become so by this route. School friendships and the community of youth do have lasting effects, but these do not require ivied clubhouses. Young men learn more about the theory and practice of government by resisting the draft than they ever learned in Political Science 412.

Much of the present university expansion, needless to say, consists in federal- and corporation-contracted research and other research and has nothing to do with teaching. Surely such expansion can be better carried on in the Government's and corporations' own institutes, which would be unencumbered by the young, except those who are hired or attach themselves as apprentices.

Every part of education can be open to need, desire, choice, and trying out. Nothing needs to be compelled or extrinsically motivated by prizes and threats. I do not know if the procedure here outlined would cost more than our present system—though it is hard to conceive of a need for more money than the school establishment now spends. What would be saved is the pitiful waste of youthful years—caged, daydreaming, sabotaging, and cheating—and the degrading and insulting misuse of teachers.

It has been estimated by James Coleman that the average youth in high school is really "there" about ten minutes a day. Since the growing-up of the young into society to be useful to themselves and others, and to do God's work, is one of the three or four most important functions of any society, no doubt we ought to spend even more on the education of the young than we do; but I would not give a penny to the present administrators, and I would largely dismantle the present school machinery.

6. LEARNING IN THE GLOBAL VILLAGE

MARSHALL McLUHAN AND
GEORGE LEONARD

Marshall McLuhan is Director of the Center for Culture and Technology at the University of Toronto and author of the widely read Understanding Media *and* The Medium Is the Massage.

George Leonard is Vice-President of the Esalen Institute of California, a Senior Editor of Look, *and the author of* Education and Ecstasy.

The time is coming, if it is not already here, when children can learn far more, far faster in the outside world than within schoolhouse walls. "Why should I go back to school and interrupt my education?" the high-school dropout asks. His question is impudent but to the point. The modern urban environment is packed with energy and information—diverse, insistent, compelling. Four-year-olds, as school innovators are fond of saying, may spend their playtimes discussing the speed, range and flight characteristics of jet aircraft, only to return to a classroom and "string some more of those old beads." The 16-year-old who drops out of school may be risking his financial future, but he is not necessarily lacking in intelligence. One of the unexpected statistics of recent years comes from Dr. Louis Bright, Associate U.S. Commissioner of Education for Research. His studies show that, in large cities where figures are available, dropouts have higher average IQ scores than high-school graduates.

This danger signal is only one of many now flashing in school systems throughout the world. The signals say that something is out of phase, that most present-day schools may be lavishing vast and increasing amounts of time and energy preparing students for a world that no longer exists. Though this is a time of educational experiments, the real reforms that might be expected have as yet touched only a small proportion of our schools. In an age when even such staid institutions as banks and insurance companies have been altered almost beyond recognition, today's typical classroom—in physical layout, method and content of instruction—still resembles the classroom of 30 or more years ago.

Resistance to change is understandable and perhaps unavoidable in an endeavor as complex as education, dealing as it does with human lives. But the status quo may not endure much longer. The demands, the very nature of this age of new technology and pervasive electric circuitry, barely perceived because so close at hand, will shape education's future. By the time this year's babies have become 1989's graduates (if college "graduation" then exists), schooling as we know it may be only a memory.

Mass education is a child of a mechanical age. It grew up along with the production line. It reached maturity just at that historical moment when Western civilization had attained its final extreme of fragmentation and specialization, and had mastered the linear technique of stamping out products in the mass.

It was this civilization's genius to manipulate matter, energy and human life by breaking every useful process down into its functional parts, then producing any required number of each. Just as shaped pieces of metal became components of a locomotive, human specialists become components of the great social machine.

In this setting, education's task was fairly simple: decide what the social machine needs, then turn out people who match those needs. The school's function was not so much to encourage people to keep exploring, learning and, therefore, changing throughout life as to slow and control those very processes of personal growth and change. Providing useful career or job skills was only a small part of this educational matching game. All students, perhaps more so in the humanities than the sciences and technologies, were furnished standard "bodies of knowledge," vocabularies, concepts and ways of viewing the world. Scholarly or trade journals generally held a close check on standard perceptions in each special field.

Specialization and standardization produced close resemblance and, therefore, hot competition between individuals. Normally, the only way a person could differentiate himself from the fellow specialists next to him was by doing the same thing better and faster. Competition, as a matter of fact, became the chief motive force in mass education, as in society, with grades and tests of all sorts gathering about them a power and glory all out of proportion to their quite limited function as learning aids.

Then, too, just as the old mechanical production line pressed physical materials into preset and unvarying molds, so mass education tended to treat students as objects to be shaped, manipulated. "Instruction" generally meant pressing information onto passive students. Lectures, the most common mode of instruction in mass education, called for very little student involvement. This mode, one of the least effective ever devised by man, served well enough in an age that demanded only a specified fragment of each human being's whole abilities. There was, however, no warranty on the human products of mass education.

That age has passed. More swiftly than we can realize, we are moving into an era dazzlingly different. Fragmentation, specialization and sameness will be replaced by wholeness, diversity and, above all, a deep involvement.

Already, mechanized production lines are yielding to electronically controlled, computerized devices that are quite capable of producing any number of varying things out of the same material. Even today, most U.S. automobiles are, in a sense, custom produced. Figuring all possible combinations of styles, options and colors available on a certain new family sports car, for example, a computer expert came up with 25 *million* different versions of it for a buyer. And that is only a beginning. When automated electronic production reaches full potential, it will be just about as cheap to turn out a million differing objects as a million exact duplicates. The only limits on production and consumption will be the human imagination.

Similarly, the new modes of instantaneous, long-distance human communication—radio, telephone, television—are linking the world's people in a vast net of electric circuitry that creates a new depth and breadth of impersonal involvement in events and breaks down the old, traditional boundaries that made specialization possible.

The very technology that now cries out for a new mode of education creates means for getting it. But new educational devices, though important, are not as central to tomorrow's schooling as are new roles for student and teacher. Citizens of the future will find much less need for sameness of function or vision. To the contrary, they will be rewarded for diversity and originality. Therefore, any real or imagined need for standardized classroom presentation may rapidly fade; the very first casualty of the present-day school system may well be the whole business of teacher-led instruction as we now know it.

Tomorrow's educator will be able to set about the exciting task of creating a new kind of learning environment. Students will rove freely through this place of learning, be it contained in a room, a building, a cluster of buildings or (as we shall see later) an even larger schoolhouse. There will be no distinction between work and play in the new school, for the student will be totally involved. Responsibility for the effectiveness of learning will be shifted from student to teacher.

As it is now, the teacher has a ready-made audience. He is assured of a full house and a long run. Those students who don't like the show get flunking grades. If students are free to move anywhere they please, however, there is an entirely new situation, and the quality of the experience called education will change drastically. The educator then will naturally have a high stake in generating interest and involvement for his students.

To be involved means to be drawn in, to interact. To go on interacting, the student must *get somewhere.* In other words, the student and the learning environment (a person, a group of people, a book, a programmed course, an electronic learning console or whatever) must respond to each other in a pleasing and purposeful interplay. When a situation of involvement is set up, the student finds it hard to drag himself away.

The notion that free-roving students would loose chaos on a school comes only from thinking of education in the present mode—as *teaching* rather than *learning*—and from thinking of learning as something that goes on mostly in classrooms. A good example of education by free interaction with a responsive environment already exists, right before our eyes. Watch a child learn to talk or, for an even more striking case, watch a five-year-old learn a new language. If the child moves to a foreign country and is allowed to play intensely and freely with neighborhood children—*with no language "instruction" whatever*—he will learn the new tongue, accent free, in two or three months. If instruction is attempted, however, the child is in trouble.

Imagine, if you will, what would happen if we set the five-year-old down in a classroom, allowed him to leave his seat only at prescribed times, presented only a few new words at a sitting, made him learn each group before going on to the next, drilled him on pronunciation, corrected his "mistakes," taught him grammar, gave him homework assignments, tested him and—worst of all—convinced him that the whole thing was work rather than play. In such a case, the child might learn the new language as slowly and painfully as do teen-agers or adults. Should an adult try to learn a language by intense play and interaction, he would probably do much better than he would in a classroom, but still fall short of a young child's performance. Why? The adult has already learned the lessons that the old schooling teaches so well: inhibition, self-consciousness, categorization, rigidity and the deep conviction that learning is hard and painful work.

Indeed, the old education gives us a sure-fire prescription for creating dislike of any type of human activity, no matter how appealing it might seem. To stop children from reading comic books (which might be ill-advised), you would only have to assign and test them on their content every week.

Learning a new language is a giant feat, compared to which mastering most of the present school curriculum should prove relatively simple. Long before 1989, all sorts of equipment will be available for producing responsive environments in all the subject matter now commonly taught, and more. Programmed instruction, for example, creates high involvement, since it draws the student along in a sort of dialogue, letting him respond at frequent intervals. Programming at its best lets the student learn commonly agreed-upon cultural techniques and knowledge— reading, spelling, arithmetic, geography and the like—in his own time, at his own pace. But present-day programming may soon seem crude in light of current developments. Computers will be able to understand students' written or spoken responses. (Already, they understand typed responses.) When these computers are hooked into learning consoles, the interplay between student and learning program can become even more intense.

When computers are properly used, in fact, they are almost certain to increase individual diversity. A worldwide network of computers will make all of mankind's factual knowledge available to students everywhere in a matter of minutes or seconds. Then, the human brain will not have to serve as a repository of specific facts, and the uses of memory will shift. In the new education, breaking the timeworn, rigid chains of memory may have greater priority than forging new links. New materials may be learned just as were the great myths of past cultures—as fully integrated systems that resonate on several levels and share the qualities of poetry and song.

Central school computers can also help keep track of students as they move freely from one activity to another, whenever moment-by-moment or year-by-year records of students' progress are needed. This will wipe out even the administrative justification for schedules and regular periods, with all their anti-educational effects, and will free teachers to get on with the real business of education. Even without computers, however, experimental schools are now finding that fixed schedules and restrictions on students' movements are artificial and unnecessary.

Television will aid students in exploring and interacting with a wide-ranging environment. It will, for example, let them see into the atom or out into space; visualize their own brainwaves; create artistic patterns of light and sound; become involved with unfamiliar old or new ways of living, feeling, perceiving; communicate with other learners, wherever in the world they may be.

Television will be used for involvement, for *two-way* communication, whether with other people or other environmental systems. It will most certainly not be used to present conventional lectures, to imitate the old classroom. That lectures frequently do appear on educational television points up mankind's common practice of driving pell-mell into the future with eyes fixed firmly on the rearview mirror. The content of each brand new medium thus far has always been the ordinary stuff of the past environment.

The student of the future will truly be an explorer, a researcher, a huntsman who ranges through the new educational world of electric circuitry and heightened human interaction just as the tribal huntsman ranged the wilds. Children, even little children, working alone or in groups, will seek their own solutions to problems that perhaps have never been solved or even conceived as problems. It is necessary here to distinguish this exploratory activity from that of the so-called "discovery method," championed by some theorists, which is simply a way of leading children around to standard perceptions and approved solutions.

Future educators will value, not fear, fresh approaches, new solutions. Among their first tasks, in fact, may be *un*learning the old, unacknowledged taboos on true originality. After that, they may well pick up a new driving style in which they glance into the rearview mirror when guidance from the past is needed but spend far more time looking forward into the unfamiliar, untested country of the present and future.

In a sense, the mass-produced student of the present and past always turned out to be a commodity—replaceable, expendable. The new student who makes his own educational space, his own curriculum and even develops many of his own learning methods will be unique, irreplaceable.

What will motivate the new student? Wide variations between individuals will make competition as we now know it irrelevant and, indeed, impossible. Unstandardized life will not provide the narrow measures needed for tight competition, and schools will find it not only unnecessary but nearly impossible to give ordinary tests or grades. Motivation will come from accomplishment itself; no one has to be forced to play. Form and discipline will spring from the very nature of the matter being explored, just as it does in artistic creation. If the student of the future may be compared with the child at play, he also resembles the artist at work.

A strange dilemma seems to arise: It appears that, with the new modes of learning, all the stuff of present-day education can be mastered much more quickly and easily than ever before. Right now, good programmed instruction is cutting the time for learning certain basic material by one-half or one-third. What will students do with all the time that is going to be gained? The problem is not a real one. With students constantly researching and exploring, each discovery will open up a new area for study. There is no limit on learning.

We are only beginning to realize what a tiny slice of human possibilities we now educate. In fragmenting all of existence, Western civilization hit upon one aspect, the literate and rational, to develop at the expense of the rest. Along with this went a lopsided development of one of the senses, the visual. Such personal and sensory specialization was useful in a mechanical age, but is fast becoming outmoded. Education will be more concerned with training the senses and perceptions than with stuffing brains. And this will be at no loss for the "intellect." Studies show a high correlation between sensory, bodily development—now largely neglected—and intelligence.

Already, school experimenters are teaching written composition with tape recorders (just as students play with these marvelous devices) in an attempt to retain the auditory sense, to recapture the neglected rhythms of speech. Already, experimental institutes are working out new ways to educate people's neglected capacities to relate, to feel, to sense, to create. Future schooling may well move into many unexplored domains of human existence. People will learn much in 1989 that today does not even have a commonly accepted name.

Can we view this future, the hard and fast of it? Never, for it will always come around a corner we never noticed, take us by surprise. But studying the future helps us toward understanding the present. And the present offers us glimpses, just glimpses: seven-year-olds (the slowest of them) sitting at electronic consoles finishing off, at their own pace, all they'll ever need in the basic skills of reading, writing and the like; eight-year-olds playing games that teach what we might call math or logic in terms of, say, music and the sense of touch; nine-year-olds joining together in large plastic tents to build environments that give one the *experience* of living in the Stone Age or in a spaceship or in an even more exotic place—say, 19th-century America; ten-year-olds interacting with five-year-olds, showing them the basics (now unknown) of human relations or of the relationships between physical movements and mental states.

In all of this, the school—that is, an institution of learning confined to a building or buildings—can continue to hold a central position only if it changes fast enough to keep pace with the seemingly inevitable changes in the outside world. The school experience can well become so rich and compelling that there will be no dropouts, only determined drop-ins. Even so, the walls between school and world will continue to blur.

Already it is becoming clear that the main "work" of the future will be education, that people will not so much earn a living as learn a living. Close to 30 million people in the U.S. are now pursuing some form of adult education, and the number shoots skyward. Industry and the military, as well as the arts and sciences, are beginning to consider education their main business.

The university is fast becoming not an isolated bastion but an integral part of the community. Eventually, nearly every member of a community may be drawn into its affairs. The university of the future could offer several degrees of "membership," from everyday full-time participation to subscriptions to its "news service," which would be received in the home on electronic consoles.

Already, though not many journalists or college presidents realize it, the biggest news of our times is coming from research in the institutions of higher learning—new scientific discoveries, new ways of putting together the webs of past and current history, new means for apprehending and enjoying the stuff of sensory input, of interpersonal relations, of involvement with all of life.

The world communications net, the all-involving linkage of electric circuitry, will grow and become more sensitive. It will also develop new modes of feedback so that communication can become dialogue instead of monologue. It will breach the wall between "in" and "out" of school. It will join all people everywhere. When this has happened, we may at last realize that our place of learning is the world itself, the entire planet we live on. The little red schoolhouse is already well on its way toward becoming the little round schoolhouse.

Someday, all of us will spend our lives in our own school, the world. And education—in the sense of learning to love, to grow, to change—can become not the woeful preparation for some job that makes us less than we could be but the very essence, the joyful whole of existence itself.

GHETTO EDUCATION: NEW DIRECTIONS

7. ALTERNATIVE PUBLIC SCHOOL SYSTEMS

Kenneth Clark

Kenneth Clark is President of the Metropolitan Applied Research Center and a professor of psychology at the City College of the City University of New York. He is the author of Prejudice and Your Child *and* Dark Ghetto: Dilemmas of Social Power *and other books. He founded and directed Harlem Youth Opportunities Unlimited (Haryou).*

It is now clear that American public education is organized and functions along social and economic class lines. A bi-racial public school system wherein approximately 90 per cent of American children are required to attend segregated schools is one of the clearest manifestations of this basic fact. The difficulties encountered in attempting to desegregate public schools in the South as well as in the North point to the tenacity of the forces seeking to prevent any basic change in the system.

The class and social organization of American public schools is consistently associated with a lower level of educational efficiency in the less privileged schools. This lower efficiency is expressed in terms of the fact that the schools attended by Negro and poor children have less adequate educational facilities than those attended by more privileged children. Teachers tend to resist assignments in Negro and other underprivileged schools and generally function less adequately in these schools. Their morale is generally lower; they are not adequately supervised; they tend to see their students as less capable of learning. The parents of the children in these schools are usually unable to bring about any positive changes in the conditions of these schools.

The pervasive and persistent educational inefficiency which characterizes these schools results in:

(1) marked and cumulative academic retardation in a disproportionately high percentage of these children, beginning in the third or fourth grade and increasing through the eighth grade;

(2) a high percentage of dropouts in the junior and senior high schools of students unequipped academically and occupationally for a constructive role in society;

(3) a pattern of rejection and despair and hopelessness resulting in massive human wastage.

Given these conditions, American public schools have become significant instruments in the blocking of economic mobility and in the intensification of class distinctions rather than fulfilling their historic function of facilitating such mobility. In effect, the public schools have become captives of a middle class who have failed to use them to aid others to move into the middle class. It might even be possible to interpret the role of the controlling middle class as that of using the public schools to block further mobility. . . .

Initially the academic retardation of Negro children was explained in terms of their inherent racial inferiority. The existence of segregated schools was either supported by law or explained in terms of the existence of segregated neighborhoods. More recently the racial inferiority or legal and custom interpretations have given way to more subtle explanations and support for continued inefficient education. Examples are theories of "cultural deprivation" and related beliefs that the culturally determined educational inferiority of Negro children will impair the ability of white children to learn if they are taught in the same classes. It is assumed that because of their background, Negro children and their parents are poorly motivated for academic achievement and will not only be unable to compete with white children but will also retard the white children. . . .

In the years 1965 to 1967 another formidable and insidious barrier in the way of the movement towards effective, desegregated public schools has emerged in the form of the black power movement and its demands for racial separatism. Some of the more vocal of the black power advocates who have addressed themselves to the problems of education have explicitly and implicitly argued for Negroes' control of "Negro Schools." Some have asserted that there should be separate school districts organized to control the schools in all-Negro residential areas; that there should be Negro Boards of Education, Negro superintendents of schools, Negro faculty, and Negro curricula and materials. These demands are clearly a rejection of the goals of integrated education and a return to the pursuit of the myth of an efficient "separate but equal"—or the pathetic wish for a separate and superior—racially organized system of education. One may view this current trend whereby some Negroes themselves seem to be asking for a racially segregated system of education as a reflection of the frustration resulting from white resistance to genuine desegregation of the public schools since the *Brown* decision and as a reaction to the reality that the quality of education in the *de facto* segregated Negro schools in the North and the Negro schools in the South has steadily deteriorated under the present system of white control.

In spite of these explanations, the demands for segregated schools can be no more acceptable coming from Negroes than they are coming from white segregationists. There is no reason to believe and certainly there is no evidence to support the contention that all-Negro schools, controlled by Negroes, will be any more efficient in preparing American children to contribute constructively to the realities of the present and future world. . . .

We cannot now permit ourselves to be deluded by wishful thinking, sentimental optimism, or rigid and oversimplified ideological postures. We must be tough-mindedly pragmatic and flexible as we seek to free our children from the cruel and dehumanizing, inferior and segregated education inflicted upon them by the insensitive, indifferent, affable, and at times callously rigid custodians of American public education.

In developing an appropriate strategy and the related flexible tactics, it must be clearly understood that the objective of improving the quality of education provided for Negro children is not a substitute for or a retreat from the fundamental goal of removing the anachronism of racially segregated schools from American life. The objective of excellent education for Negro and other lower-status children is inextricably linked with the continuing struggle to desegregate public education. . . .

Until the influx of Negro and Puerto Rican youngsters into urban public schools, the American public school system was justifiably credited with being the chief instrument for making the American dream of upward social, economic, and political mobility a reality. The depressed immigrants from southern and eastern Europe could use American public schools as the ladder toward the goals of assimilation and success. The past successes of American public education seem undebatable. The fact that American public schools were effective mobility vehicles for white American immigrants makes even more stark and intolerable their present ineffectiveness for Negro and Puerto Rican children. Now it appears that the present system of organization and functioning of urban public schools is a chief blockage in the mobility of the masses of Negro and other lower-status minority group children. The inefficiency of their schools and the persistence and acceptance of the explanations for this generalized inefficiency are clear threats to the viability of our cities and national stability. The relationship between long-standing urban problems of poverty, crime and delinquency, broken homes—the total cycle of pathology, powerlessness, and personal and social destructiveness which haunts our urban ghettos—and the breakdown in the efficiency of our public schools is now unavoidably clear. It is not enough that those responsible for our public schools should assert passively that the schools merely reflect the pathologies and injustices of our society. Public schools and their administrators must assert boldly that education must dare to challenge and change society toward social justice as the basis for democratic stability.

There remains the disturbing question—a most relevant question probably too painful for educators themselves to ask—whether the selection process involved in training and promoting educators and administrators for our public schools emphasizes qualities of passivity, conformity, caution, smoothness, and superficial affability rather than boldness, creativity, substance, and the ability to demand and obtain those things which are essential for solid and effective public education for all children. If the former is true and if we are dependent upon the present educational establishment, then all hopes for the imperative reforms which must be made so that city public schools can return to a level of innovation and excellence are reduced to a minimum, if not totally eliminated.

The racial components of the present crisis in urban public education clearly make the possibilities of solution more difficult and may contribute to the passivity and pervading sense of hopelessness of school administrators. Aside from any latent or subtle racism which might infect school personnel themselves, they are hampered by the gnawing awareness that with the continuing flight of middle-class whites from urban public schools and with the increasing competition which education must engage in for a fair share of the tax dollar, it is quite possible that Americans will decide deliberately or by default to sacrifice urban public schools on the altars of its historic and contemporary forms of racism. If this can be done without any real threat to the important segments of economic and political power in the society and with only Negro children as the victims, then there is no realistic basis for hope that our urban public schools will be saved.

The hope for a realistic approach to saving public education in American cities seems to this observer to be found in a formula whereby it can be demonstrated to the public at large that the present level of public school inefficiency has reached an intolerable stage of public calamity. It must be demonstrated that minority group children are not the only victims of the monopolistic inefficiency of the present pattern of organization and functioning of our public schools.

It must be demonstrated that white children—privileged white children whose parents understandably seek to protect them by moving to suburbs or by sending them to private and parochial schools—also suffer both potentially and immediately.

It must be demonstrated that business and industry suffer intolerable financial burdens of double and triple taxation in seeking to maintain a stable economy in the face of the public school inefficiency which produces human casualties rather than constructive human beings.

It must be demonstrated that the cost in correctional, welfare, and health services is intolerably high in seeking to cope with consequences of educational inefficiency—that it would be more economical, even for an affluent society, to pay the price and meet the demands of efficient public education.

It must be demonstrated that a nation which presents itself to the world as the guardian of democracy and the protector of human values throughout the world cannot itself make a mockery of these significant ethical principles by dooming one-tenth of its own population to a lifetime of inhumane futility because of remediable educational deficiencies in its public schools.

These must be understood and there must be the commitment to make the average American understand them if our public schools and our cities are to be effective. But it does not seem likely that the changes necessary for increased efficiency of our urban public schools will come about because they should. Our urban public school systems seem muscle-bound with tradition. They seem to represent the most rigid forms of bureaucracies which, paradoxically, are most resilient in their ability and use of devices to resist rational or irrational demands for change. What is most important in understanding the ability of the educational establishment to resist change is the fact that public school systems are protected public monopolies with only minimal competition from private and parochial schools. Few critics of the American urban public schools—even severe ones such as myself—dare to question the givens of the present organization of public education in terms of local control of public schools, in terms of existing municipal or political boundaries, or in terms of the rights and prerogatives of boards of education to establish policy and select professional staff—at least nominally or titularly if not actually. Nor dare the critics question the relevance of the criteria and standards for selecting superintendents, principals, and teachers, or the relevance of all of these to the objectives of public education—producing a literate and informed public to carry on the business of democracy—and to the goal of producing human beings with social sensitivity and dignity and creativity and a respect for the humanity of others.

A monopoly need not genuinely concern itself with these matters. As long as local school systems can be assured of state aid and increasing federal aid without the accountability which inevitably comes with aggressive competition, it would be sentimental, wishful thinking to expect any significant increase in the efficiency of our public schools. If there are no alternatives to the present system—short of present private and parochial schools which are approaching their limit of expansion—then the possibilities of improvement in public education are limited.

ALTERNATIVE FORMS OF PUBLIC EDUCATION

Alternatives—realistic, aggressive, and viable competitors—to the present public school systems must be found. The development of such competitive public school systems will be attacked by the defenders of the present system as attempts to weaken the present system and thereby weaken, if not destroy, public education. This type of expected self-serving argument can be briefly and accurately disposed of by asserting and demonstrating that truly effective competition strengthens rather than weakens that which deserves to survive. I would argue further that public education need not be identified with the present system of organization of public schools. Public education can be more broadly and pragmatically defined in terms of that form of organization and functioning of an educational system which is in the public interest. Given this definition, it becomes clear that an inefficient system of public systems is not in the public interest:

—a system of public schools which destroys rather than develops positive human potentialities is not in the public interest;

—a system which consumes funds without demonstrating effective returns is not in the public interest;

—a system which insists that its standards of performance should not or cannot be judged by those who must pay the cost is not in the public interest;

—a system which says that the public has no competence to assert that a patently defective product is a sign of the system's inefficiency and demand radical reforms is not in the public interest;

—a system which blames its human resources and its society while it quietly acquiesces in, and inadvertently perpetuates, the very injustices which it claims limit its efficiency is not in the public interest.

Given these assumptions, therefore, it follows that alternative forms of public education must be developed if the children of our cities are to be educated and made constructive members of our society. In the development of alternatives, all attempts must at the same time be made to strengthen our present urban public schools. Such attempts would involve re-examination, revision, and strengthening of curricula, methods, personnel selection, and evaluation; the development of more rigorous procedures of supervision, reward of superior performance, and the institution of a realistic and tough system of accountability, and the provision of meaningful ways of involving the parents and the community in the activities of the school.

The above measures, however, will not suffice. The following are suggested as possible, realistic, and practical competitors to the present form of urban public school systems:

REGIONAL STATE SCHOOLS. These schools would be financed by the states and would cut across present urban-suburban boundaries.

FEDERAL REGIONAL SCHOOLS. These schools would be financed by the Federal Government out of present state aid funds or with additional federal funds. These schools would be able to cut through state boundaries and could make provisions for residential students.

COLLEGE- AND UNIVERSITY-RELATED OPEN SCHOOLS. These schools would be financed by colleges and universities as part of their laboratories in education. They would be open to the public and not restricted to children of faculty and students. Obviously, students would be selected in terms of constitutional criteria and their percentage determined by realistic considerations.

INDUSTRIAL DEMONSTRATION SCHOOLS. These schools would be financed by industrial, business, and commercial firms for their employees and selected members of the public. These would not be vocational schools—but elementary and comprehensive high schools of quality. They would be sponsored by combinations of business and industrial firms in much the same way as churches and denominations sponsor and support parochial or sectarian schools.

LABOR UNION SPONSORED SCHOOLS. These schools would be financed and sponsored by labor unions largely, but not exclusively, for the children of their members.

ARMY SCHOOLS. The Defense Department has been quietly effective in educating some of the casualties of our present public schools. It is hereby suggested that they now go into the business of repairing hundreds of thousands of these human casualties with affirmation rather than apology. Schools for adolescent dropouts or educational rejects could be set up by the Defense Department adjacent to camps—but not necessarily as an integral part of the military. If this is necessary, it should not block the attainment of the goal of rescuing as many of these young people as possible. They are not expendable on the altar of anti-militarism rhetoric.

With strong, efficient, and demonstrably excellent parallel systems of public schools, organized and operated on a quasi-private level, and with quality control and professional accountability maintained and determined by Federal and State educational standards and supervision, it would be possible to bring back into public education a vitality and dynamism which are now clearly missing. Even the public discussion of these possibilities might clear away some of the dank stagnation which seems to be suffocating urban education today. American industrial and material wealth was made possible through industrial competition. American educational health may be made possible through educational competition.

If we succeed, we will have returned to the dynamic, affirmative goal of education; namely, to free man of irrational fears, superstitions, and hatreds. Specifically, in America the goal of democratic education must be to free Americans of the blinding and atrophying shackles of racism. A fearful, passive, apologetic, and inefficient educational system cannot help in the attainment of these goals.

If we succeed in finding and developing these and better alternatives to the present educational inefficiency, we will not only save countless Negro children from lives of despair and hopelessness; and thousands and thousands of white children from cynicism, moral emptiness, and social ineptness—but we will also demonstrate the validity of our democratic promises. We also will have saved our civilization through saving our cities.

8. THE COMMUNITY-CENTERED SCHOOL
PRESTON R. WILCOX

Preston R. Wilcox, formerly a professor at the Columbia School of Social Work, has more recently been involved in several ghetto education projects, including the struggle over school decentralization at I.S. 201 in Harlem, and is presently affiliated with the Bedford-Stuyvesant Development and Services Corporation.

Who controls the schools our children attend? Who *should* control them? And what is the appropriate relationship between a school and the surrounding community? These questions are increasingly being forced into the headlines today by the devastating failure of our public education systems to educate millions of Black and poor youngsters. Today in the ghettos, angry parents and community leaders are literally demanding the right to shape new educational policies.

This unprecedented demand conflicts dramatically with the vested interests of boards of education, teachers' professional associations, unions, and other groups. The resultant clash has sharpened the issues, trained a whole cadre of educational activists, and raised fundamental questions affecting not merely ghetto schools but all education. It has also drawn long-overdue attention to the concept of the community-centered school. Before examining this revolutionary concept, we need to understand why so many Negroes today are seeking to control the schools in their communities.

Much of the early controversy in New York has centered on control of I.S. 201, a public intermediate school in Harlem. There, educational activists sought to get the New York City Board of Education to implement "other way" integration—that is, the transporting of white students into a Black ghetto to attend school. When this failed, a community-controlled school was sought. These activists chose to believe that even in a racist society, organized to protect the interests of whites, one could be both Black *and* successful.

At first, the I.S. 201 activists attempted to elicit the agreement of the New York City Board of Education to conduct an experiment in community control of a school. The responses were evasive, perfunctory, or nonexistent. This is not surprising. As in most U.S. cities, the Board of Education is expected to represent *all* the people, and it has an established and unwritten policy that requires consensus. Yet, in most cases, consensus guarantees that the interests of the ghetto will be overlooked. (Until its recent expansion, only one member of the New York City Board of Education was Black and none were Puerto Rican, even though the student population was more than 50 per cent nonwhite.)

Failing to move the Board, the I.S. 201 parents had also carried their integration fight to the Mayor's office. The Mayor, in measured and somewhat professorial tones, gave them a lecture on the tax base of the city, and told them that school integration might stimulate an escalation of the white exodus. This was followed by a visit to Commissioner of Education Harold Howe. . . . [He] was cordial, concerned, committed to the principle—but apparently helpless to act.

Why do Black people seek control over their local schools? After watching the failures of the present school system, they have concluded that those in control of that system define its objectives in terms of white America. The present authorities use such phrases as "the entire system" or "Negroes aren't the only ones who need better schools." Activists, however, recognize these as euphemisms for maintenance of the degrading *status quo*. The tragic fact is that, regardless of intentions, Black Americans are treated not as full participants in the society but essentially as a group to be considered after the interests of others are attended to. So long as this remains true, school programs will continue to draw heavily on white, middle-class assumptions.

The essence of the struggle, therefore, has been to help the Black and poor residents of the ghettos understand that the present system, in the last analysis, was organized for the protection of "others"—not Black Americans. Indeed, it has been established fairly conclusively on the basis of ethnic composition, performance scores, per capita expenditures, teacher turnover and assignments, and the figures on upgrading of minority-group staff, that many large urban complexes have, in fact, dual school systems—one white and one Black, but both controlled by whites.

The minority-group student thus finds himself in the curious position of being miseducated by a system that represents everybody's interest but his. Such students are ordered to attend school under compulsory education laws seemingly for the express purpose of being convinced of their own uneducability. Those Black students who were able to negotiate the schools had to adopt the views of their oppressors. They had to listen to discussions of history that highlighted the honesty of George

Washington but not the fact that he was a slaveowner. In short, the Wasp model was substituted for one with which Black students could more readily identify.

It is this tendency to deliver *generalized* white products into *specialized* Black communities that set the stage for the thrust by Black communities to take control of the schools set up to serve their children. The issue was engaged at I.S. 201. But it quickly spread to at least four other sites in New York, and to Washington, Boston, and Columbus, Ohio. It can be expected to break into the open in the South, as well, before long.

In every instance, a confrontation has occurred between the Black and/or poor and the school system. Note the word "poor," for this thrust is quite unlike the middle-class–oriented drive for quality, integrated education outside the ghetto. It is based on the poor, not the middle class. It seeks to build a constituency among parents and community leaders who, unlike the "Black bourgeoisie," recognize that their own destiny is tied to the plight of the Black poor in a society in which it pays to be neither Black nor poor.

The new thrust for community control of ghetto schools thus represents an important shift in emphasis: from a desire to replicate that which is American to a desire to reshape it. There is in this drive less concern with social integration than with effective education. To bring about effective education, however, it is necessary to do more than simply transfer control or change the ratio of white to Black on the teaching staff. It is necessary to take a revolutionary view of the role of the school in the community.

This brings us to the concept of the community-centered school—the school that functions as an acculturation tool, an educational instrument, and a community center.

As an acculturation tool, the community-centered school serves as a life-orientation vehicle for new students and "newcomers" to the city. It attempts to make viable connections between different homes and different cultures in a climate that respects and cherishes creative differences. It also nurtures similarities. The usual school pattern is to attempt to emphasize similarities and to obliterate differences—the melting-pot approach. Moynihan and Glazer stress, however, in *Beyond the Melting Pot,* that, in fact, the melting has never really taken place.

As an educational instrument, such a school is called upon to help its charges become addicted to the idea of (1) learning for use, (2) developing a sense of functional curiosity, and (3) assuming a large part of the responsibility for developing their own intellectual resources. The skillful teacher brings knowledge to be shared and expanded upon, not just accepted. The normal pattern requires students to memorize teacher offerings and to regurgitate them upon command. The student becomes the depository for the teacher's knowledge, not the enactor, evaluator, and thinker he desires to become.

As a community center, the school takes on the coloration of a freedom school. It becomes: (1) the facility where the community begins to meet its latent needs for recreation and fun; (2) the place where the community begins to formalize its efforts to express itself through art, music, drama, etc.; (3) the locale for shaping community policy as it relates to housing, traffic, health, education, and other social issues; and (4) the arena for developing and implementing mutual-aid programs designed to aid the less fortunate in dealing with their problems.

These four functions, hopefully, are integrated into one program; they shape, and are shaped by, each other. Such a model has implications for the structure, staff roles, selection of policymakers, and methods of evaluation. More importantly, the educational philosophy must be one that views learning as being lifelong and as taking place inside the classroom and within the community. Such a philosophy accredits and rewards learning-by-doing as the present system rewards learning-by-rote. One of the early innovators of the community-centered school concept, Leonard Covello, stated it this way: "Formulation of school activities, planning of curricula, school administration, classroom techniques, and so forth, result in positive achievements only if and when all educational procedures are developed under constant awareness of the extra-school educational forces active in the background of the students."

The community-centered school is not a new concept. Covello, Principal of East Harlem's Benjamin Franklin High School until 1955, employed it as a means to enable the area's Italians to: (1) acquire the coping and elevating skills—educational, social, and others—to enable them to move into the *corporate* world; and (2) help deepen their understanding of the Italian culture as a tool for contributing effectively within their own *private* world.

According to Covello:

> The school must have a thorough understanding, not only of its aims, but of the needs and potentialities of its students. We have discarded the idea of the subject-centered school and developed, as the next step forward, the child-centered school, because we realized the futility of emphasizing subject matter instead of child development. But there is one more step forward. In the concept of the community-centered school, we have, it seems to me, the ultimate objective of all education because it deals with the child in connection with his social background and in relation to all forces, disruptive as well as constructive, that contribute to his education.

Covello's efforts were designed to enable Italian-Americans to become Americanized without experiencing ruthless assimilation. His school was built while Fiorello LaGuardia was Mayor; it was Dr. Covello who introduced Italian into the curriculum of his high school.

The community-centered school, however, has no purpose in being ethnically or racially exclusive. It builds opportunities for students to express and develop their own interests—ethnic interests included. Its thrust is in the direction of imparting citizenship skills along with those of scholarship.

The request, then, for a community-centered school by Black communities has its positive dimensions. It is an indication that they feel that they are qualified, that this is their country, too, that they want to get their concerns onto our society's agenda, and that they want to participate directly in their own social and economic elevation. Blacks themselves have made this choice against the grain of the social rhetoric; this is their right in a democracy.

Dan Dodson, Director of The Center for Human Relations at New York University, elucidates this point with greater clarity:

> No nation can maintain the distinction of being democratic if it does not make allowances for cultural diversity. Such differences cannot be "just tolerated." They must be respected and encouraged so long as they have value for any segment of the citizenry. Thus, in a real sense, this opportunity to pursue autonomous goals is a measure of "democratic." No person can make his fullest contribution to the total society with a feeling of compromise about "who he is" because he is a minority group member.

The civil-rightists have campaigned to get Negro history onto the agenda of the school; the Black Power theorists have pushed to get Afro-American history into the schools. The civil-rightists want all students—Black and white—to understand Negro history; the Black Power theorists emphasize Afro-American history as an identity-building tool for Blacks. Both fail to note that our public education system is bankrupt because it is being controlled by a group of conservative thinkers. White and Black students alike are not being taught citizenship and social responsibility. The emphasis is on "scholarship," despite its lack of social relevance in today's world.

It seems to me, for example, that an honest discussion of the attempted "castration" of Adam Clayton Powell by the U.S. Congress would make an excellent social-studies lesson. A similar critical incident would be the refusal of the press to address Cassius Clay as "Muhammed Ali," and Muhammed Ali's refusal to enter the armed forces. It is the effective teacher's role to help students to relate themselves to the context of our society and to understand their role in shaping it. This doesn't come through memorizing history. It can come, however, through helping students to engage themselves in the issues that touch upon their lives. The community-centered school, as we shall see, helps students—whether white or Black—to do precisely this.

Let us examine the special features of the community-centered school and see exactly what such a school is. We begin with the issue of control.

1. *Redistribution of power.* The community-centered school differs from the traditional public school in that it deliberately shares power with the community it serves. It attempts to define and identify those powers that belong exclusively to the local community, those that belong exclusively to the professionals, and those that should be shared. As a case in point, the community might have the ultimate decision in selecting the principal. The community ought to be able to discern such intangible factors as psychological stance, personal qualities, and commitment to uphold local community interests. The evaluation of teacher and staff performance might be shared with the community. The responsibility for implementation of the educational goals can rest solely with the professional.

The latent function of this model is to build into the local community the skill and competence to develop and establish educational policy and to acquire the skills to measure the effectiveness of the educational program. On the other side of the coin is the opportunity it affords the staff to learn of the community's interests and goals and how to help it acquire the means to achieve them.

2. *Bridging structures.* In order to carve out effective functions, local organizations can be asked to join with parents in "adopting" a piece of the school's program. All participants—organizations and individuals—should be helped to assume a specific function on which everyone else comes to depend.

One organization could spend its entire time obtaining summer camping opportunities for students, while another could assume that of securing summer employment opportunities. Another could focus its attention on securing employment for parents of students. Another could work with local, state, and national legislators to ensure that students on welfare receive decent allowances—an educable income, if you will. Other organizations might "adopt" classes to whom they become responsible for trips, visitations to local organizational headquarters, fund-raising, and the like.

Neighborhood organizations could be urged to use the school as a regular meeting place. There ought to be a "community room," supervised and controlled by the community groups.

3. *Citizen roles.* Local community residents functioning as "foster teachers" can be employed and trained. These persons should operate outside the school, perhaps in a storefront, and should be available to parents and others during nonschool hours. They can train parents to support the education of their children, put them in contact with needed resources, and find ways to relate community activities to the life of the school.

These persons also give local emphasis to the idea that education is an important elevating tool. They become "teachers" outside the school and "foster parents" within the school. An important part of their function is to help individual students in their efforts to bridge the gap between school and home. Naturally, they would expend a majority of their efforts on those students or in those situations where their roles are not already being fulfilled by an interested parent or teacher.

Unlike teacher's aides and assistants who, for all intents and purposes, are extra arms and legs for the teachers, the foster teachers carry out community-parent functions, being advocates on behalf of the community, not the school. There should be a minimum of one such person per classroom, and preferably two.

4. *Parent roles.* Parents who are not employed as teacher assistants (who will not be discussed here) or as foster teachers, or who are not serving on the policy-making school/community committee, should be formed into informal parents' clubs based on grade levels. These clubs should meet regularly to plan class trips in conjunction with the class members and to participate in parent training programs.

The latent function of this structure would be to approach the parents as adults in their own right, and to afford them the opportunity to acquire the skills with which one enhances the learning and motivation of one's own children. The parent training should emphasize (1) the transmission of skills, not just the giving of information, (2) the development of parent skills, and (3) an active concern for the personal needs of the parents.

These clubs can also meet the recreational and social needs of the parents, and should be organized by the foster teachers. Students should be expected to know about the parents' clubs. Class discussions can be held in relation to them.

5. *Parent-student linkages.* Techniques should be developed so that parents are engaged in what is going on in the classroom through a variety of ways. Most parents want to make their children feel good. How the student feels is largely a factor of the parent function.

Community service projects around local community problems should involve students and parents in data collection—interviewing, surveying, observational tours, etc. The parent and the student may find themselves discussing their communities from different perspectives but out of common experiences.

Students can be encouraged to elicit the opinions of their parents on key social issues and to write reports on their findings. An interviewing instrument might be developed for this purpose. The aim here is to stimulate intellectual exchanges between students and their parents.

Students should be asked to go on tours with their families, visit museums together, etc. Class credit should be accorded for written reports of such ventures. Prior preparation as to "what to look for" on the trip might be included.

Class pictures should be replaced by family pictures, with profits being used to support community activities. Imagine all the families in the third grade showing up at the school to have family pictures taken and then retiring to a class smorgasbord—arroz con pollo, collards, spaghetti and meatballs, Irish stew, gefilte fish, and apple pie! (Most of our schools start with the apple pie.)

6. *Mutual-aid activities.* The caste system favoring professionals in the ghettos has so effectively intervened that the key decisions are often made by them rather than the families they come to serve. The art of decision-making cannot be learned if the opportunity to learn is not afforded.

A mutual-aid committee should be established to deal with community and school problems—behavioral problems, potential suspensions and expulsions, family problems, and the like. Teachers, other staff, and families should present problems to this committee for guidance and assistance. Home visits, referrals, and special programs ought to be set up to deal with these problems.

7. *Economic development.* Credit unions, buying cooperatives, and community fund-raising should be developed as means to create a sense of economic awareness and to stimulate collective economic action. Local fund-raising styles should be employed rather than transporting the Community Chest model into the ghettos.

8. *Legislative action.* The school/community committee can establish a legislative committee that concerns itself with the resolution of those problems that lend themselves to legislative remedies. Locally elected officials can be drawn in for this purpose.

9. *Information and communication services.* A "Parents' Guide" ought to be developed as a means to help parents acquire the knowledge, and hopefully the skills, to help their children exploit the educational offerings of the school. The manual prepared by the Philadelphia Council for Community Advancement is a case in point.

Every family ought to receive or purchase a "parent notebook" emblazoned with the school name. Every insert should be numbered and dated. A history of the school and of the person after whom it is named ought to comprise the first pages. Information as to the structure and composition of the school/community committee and the school organization should be among the annual entries. Over a period of time the book should contain special reports, reading scores at the school, training tools, etc. This notebook can become a "parents' bible"—a tool for developing a continuing understanding of what is going on in the school. During the operation of the West Harlem Liberation School, when P.S. 125 in Harlem was being boycotted, daily news releases were sent to the parents, who anxiously awaited them. In addition, the content of the news releases was interpreted to the students by the teachers. Such material should be written by parents, not professionals.

Parent meetings should be held only after the students have elicited from their parents a purpose, a time, and a date for the meeting. Another stratagem is to enable parents to call such meetings. The meeting should be held to answer the questions of parents. Informational meetings should be kept small to allow parents time to raise questions and to absorb the answers. Foster teachers ought to have full access to such information so that they might interpret it and enable parents to analyze it.

Teachers, teacher assistants, foster teachers, students, and parents should form the essential horizontal communication linkages. Parents should have easy access to the school/community committee, which, in turn, should deal with the principal. Efforts should be made to encourage the principal to engage in as many nonleadership contacts with parents and community persons as possible.

10. *The school-community process.* The community-centered school depends largely for its success on the degree to which it is geared to problem-solving; citizen, student, and community development; and easy evaluation and communication.

At the beginning of each year, goals should be established as they relate to the academic program, the meeting of community needs, parent development, and program development. "Before-and-after" studies should be included in the plans so as to measure the changes that take place. These changes might be more appropriate indicators than reading levels, attendance at meetings, etc.

The annual meeting of the school/community committee must become an important community event, second only to the graduation ceremony. Tradition-building events should permeate the total community. School holidays should be made locally relevant and draw into participation as many segments of the community as possible.

Career-building ventures should be considered; that is, rela-tionships between learning and future careers should be understood. Class visitations should be made by role models, and "big brother" relationships should be established and nurtured. Leadership opportunities for local participants must be sought with the same zeal with which we decry the absence of leadership in disadvantaged areas.

11. *Student-to-student processes.* Student self-government activities can begin during elementary school years. The student government should have some real tasks to perform and real decisions to make. A focus of their attention might be community-service projects, special interest groupings, recreational activities, career-building clubs, etc.

I have listed elsewhere some techniques for helping teachers to exploit student organizational resources. They are based on the positive strengths embedded within student group relationships. Some of them are as follows:

> Permit students to sit anywhere in class they want to. Throw away the alphabetical seating system. Permit students to develop their own sociogram.
>
> Plan for group presentations, with individual responsibility for parts of total assignments to be decided upon by the group members.
>
> Encourage students to assist each other with homework assignments. Provide class time for such assignments.
>
> Encourage discussions among students, with the teacher as an observer and learner.

This has been an attempt to begin to put into one place some of the ideas I have been pulling together in relation to the community-centered school. It would probably take a book to elaborate adequately upon the ideas included herein. I have failed to touch upon the proposed structure for the school, and deliberately so. In a community-centered school, form must follow function. The opposite is true in the traditional school, where function follows form.

The qualifications and kinds of professional staff have been overlooked also. Suffice it to say that prior attention should be given to those staff whose personal interests—art, social issues, community development, and others—coincide with local community needs. The assumption here is that the staff will otherwise meet the professional qualifications for the jobs for which they apply.

The underlying aim of this statement is to restructure the relationship between the school and community by giving prior attention to addressing the parents as adults in their own right. An obvious purpose is to lessen the power of school administrators who are not educating the children, and to develop responsible parent power. The power of the teacher in the depressed neighborhood is a crucial variable. It can be used to elicit parental support of her efforts or to destroy the student because the teacher fails to respect his parents.

If we are serious, therefore, about educating Black children, it is essential to draw their parents, and the community at large, into the process. And if we are serious about the difficulties raised by the "generation gap" in the society as a whole, if we do not wish to see our society torn apart along age lines, as it has already been torn apart along racial lines, we must begin to create community-centered schools.

The fight for local control that has been waged over I.S. 201, therefore, has profound educational implications that reach far beyond a single Harlem schoolhouse. It involves the relevance of education to life.

STUDENT PARTICIPATION

9. AUTONOMY AND LEARNING
EDGAR Z. FRIEDENBERG

Edgar Z. Friedenberg, a sociologist and educational theorist currently teaching at the State University of New York at Buffalo, is a frequent contributor to magazines such as Ramparts, The New York Review of Books, *and* The Nation. *He is the author of* The Vanishing Adolescent, Coming of Age in America, *and* The Dignity of Youth and Other Atavisms.

Public education in the United States is an enormous and expanding enterprise. On any given day nearly a third of the total population—for children and "teen-agers" are people—is required by law to attend school. There are now some 12 million students in public high schools and about a million and a half in private, including church-affiliated, secondary schools. There are about 35 million pupils in elementary schools.

The younger a person is in this country, provided he has lived long enough to finish school at all, the longer he is likely to have been kept in school. Just a third of the students who entered fifth grade in 1926 completed high school; today about three-fourths of those who enter fifth grade do. Institutions of higher—or at least later—education are expanding even faster than public schools. Figures on their growth are likely to be misleading, since it is not as clear what is a college or university, or who is to be counted as a college student; but there is more truth than comfort in the familiar observation that it now takes a master's degree to confer the academic distinction provided by a high school diploma fifty years ago.

The schools are also an enormous vested interest. There are more than a million elementary school teachers and about 800,000 high school teachers, backed by myriad bureaucracies and sustained by active service staffs. Total public school expeditures for the fiscal year ending June 30, 1967, were $28 billion—about five times as much as in 1950 when enrollments were a little more than half their present size. From 1950 to 1965, employment in public education increased by 130 per cent, total U.S. employment by about 20 per cent.

This expansion of the education industry is justified by two basic, seldom questioned assumptions, neither of which seems self-evident. The first is that universal, compulsory school attendance until late adolescence is essential to the conduct of society. All modern industrial societies have adopted a similar policy in requiring school attendance. But this does not of itself tell us whether such compulsory schooling is essential or just apparently inevitable. All we can really say is that it is characteristic of modern life, like freeways and air pollution.

The second assumption is that formal instruction in school is so much more beneficial to the student—and through him, to the total society—than anything he might arrange for himself that the state is justified in making it a criminal offense for him to go about any business or pleasure of his own during school hours. The Education Code confers on the people who run schools, with the resources—internal and external—available to them, the authority to prescribe for a decade or more the only lawful path toward maturation that a young person may follow. Yet no school can do more than plan and organize experiences, arranging for some things to happen and preventing others from happening, through the days, months, and years, with the intention of insuring that life will thereby become more instructive in school than it could have been under a freer choice of alternatives.

The function of the schools is to socialize the young; and in so doing, they define "youth" as a social category, subject to special surveillance and constraint. It is rather naïve to discuss educational reform without recognizing that the schools are, in fact, the chief instrument by which young people are kept in their place, and by which that place is defined. They do so with the mandate of the adult society, which accepts, and acts on, the two assumptions I have stated. There is danger that, in discussing how education might be improved within the limits of this current social context, I may inadvertently endorse those assumptions, and the definition of youth they imply, which makes serfs of young Americans. Nevertheless, with that caveat firmly in mind, there are some suggestions for making the schools more flexible, humane, and *instructive* that are worth considering, and that are in fact under consideration by persons with a professional interest in education at the present time.

First, students might be allowed to attend any school they chose, either at state expense or under a fixed state subsidy that they or their parents could augment if necessary. Some proponents of this approach urge the abolition of the public school system as such. But this seems too drastic an action for what it would accomplish, since most public schools would simply have to learn to operate competitively as private schools, in order to fill the demand for places, until society began to grasp the idea that young people might be doing something entirely different than going to school—which would take years. A less drastic change might be made by continuing *local* support of the public schools but assigning state-aid funds now allotted on the basis of average daily attendance to the schools that pupils actually chose to attend—including, of course, their public schools if they wished to remain there.

One argument advanced against this plan is that white-racist parents would use it to achieve *de facto* segregation. But I think this is mistaken. What white parents flee to the suburbs to avoid, I am convinced, is *not* Negro children, but the often demoralized and occasionally brutal personnel who have been assigned to, or permitted to accumulate in, such schools, and the atmosphere of hostility and contempt for students that pervades them. Under a system of adequately subsidized free choice, the Black students, surely, would move, too, unless their school became a decent place. Black people have no preference for bad schools when they are afforded the means to attend better ones—the proportion of the relatively small group of middle-class Negroes who send their children to private schools is far higher than the proportion of middle-class whites who do so. But the loss of the financial support from the state that their withdrawal would occasion is a powerful sanction against schools which mistreat them.

Another device for increasing flexibility of educational opportunity, which would require less administrative revision but might encounter greater resistance from hostile adults, would be for the school to undertake to *license* off-premise educational projects. Students might then submit either a proposal for independent study or an application to participate in an ongoing extramural project; if approved, this would free them of attendance requirements for the duration of their project. They might, like grant holders, be required to submit regular progress reports for evaluation; they might also be required to report semiannually to test centers in order to demonstrate that they were learning the basic curriculum satisfactorily despite their absence from classes. During this period they should also have access to the facilities and staff of the school as, in effect, research consultants. The difficulty with this plan, however, is that one of the major functions of the school is to keep students off the streets and out of the way of adults, who really know quite well that submission to school routines, rather than the required course of study, *is* what constitutes the basic curriculum. There is, however, no way around the fact that *any* significant improvement of educational policy must reflect a corresponding improvement in the relative status of youth in society, and will therefore affront those adults whose needs are expressed in present policy.

A much more ambitious proposal now being widely considered

is that wholly publicly supported residential schools be established, especially for students whose homes provide neither the
quiet and privacy nor the basic nutrition and rest needed for
study or, what is more important, for health and a decent life.
This is a tantalizing question. The drawbacks are serious enough.
For one thing, this proposal assumes that our society cannot or
will not attack its economic problems radically enough to eliminate the slums and provide decent accommodation for the people
trapped there—whether or not they fit a social worker's conception of a stable family unit. Still, this may be true; and if so, some
children might be saved by attending boarding school. They
might also be destroyed; the possibilities for making education
really totalitarian are horrifying. School personnel, already convinced that they were dealing with the "disadvantaged" or "culturally deprived," might well treat these students the way the
teachers and staff of the boarding schools run by the U.S. Bureau
of Indian Affairs treat the children of the Oglala Sioux. These
schools, as the anthropologist and sociologist Murray and Rosalie
Wax describe them, may be the most oppressive in the world;
and the Waxes themselves point out that what makes them so is
the prevalence among their staffs of attitudes toward Indians as
dirty, shiftless, and uncouth and an enthusiastic determination to
make them clean, responsive, and middle-class, which closely
resembles the attitudes that prevail among teachers in slum
schools.

On the other hand, the very best schools I have observed are
boarding schools primarily for high school students from "disadvantaged" homes; and although—or because—they are highly
exceptional, there is a great deal to be learned from them as to
what the possibilities are. They are temporary summer programs,
held for about seven weeks on the campuses of colleges and
universities, partially or wholly funded by the Office of Economic
Opportunity, with some assistance from foundations. They are
intended to prepare students for college who almost certainly
would not otherwise get there. Those that I know at first hand—
the PREP program at Franklin and Marshall College in Lancaster, Pennsylvania, and the Yale Summer High School held on

the Divinity School campus in New Haven—have been held for several years consecutively, which makes them real pioneers in the rapidly shifting and sometimes tricky scene of educational service to the culturally deprived.

Among the lessons to be learned from them are:

1. *It is possible to cut through the stultifying mass of value judgments that accumulate in the form of a high school record and identify creative, often disaffected, intelligence underneath.* The intellectual style of these students is more aggressive than that usually found among their peers in high school; also more cogent; they stick closer to the heart of the discourse. But they readily learn the conventions of the seminar room, for what these may be worth.

They have bad academic records, both on disciplinary grounds and because their achievement is so spotty. They are likely to have been put down as either an "overachiever" or an "underachiever," depending on whether their regular school was initially impressed by their apparent brashness or their I.Q. score. To find them, therefore, one must learn to discount the academic record and turn to other sources of appraisal: persons nominated by the student himself as knowing what he is really like; or members of newer bureaucracies, with value patterns different from those of the school, with which he has had contact—OEO project directors, for example. When this is done, recruitment is so successful in attracting promising people that one can only regret that the program is directed toward college admission rather than more diverse and original educational purposes.

2. *Bureaucracy is probably as important a source of educational stultification as it is thought to be.* The Yale and PREP programs have been gifted with leadership that both "digs" and respects underclass youth. But there are people in the public schools who do, too—they write very good books about their experiences there after they get fired. What saves the summer programs is the fact that they cannot conceivably provide their staffs with a career line. Everybody who teaches there has a "real" job somewhere else which pays most of their living and defines their social identity—and which they probably do worse.

In the summer institute they are much freer to define their educational mission and work directly at it, just as temporary research teams at Arthur D. Little or SRI, unhampered by departmental lines and permanent, built-in status factors, often get more satisfaction and work more efficiently than their academic counterparts.

3. *High school students should be paid.* Students in these summer programs receive stipends of five or ten dollars a week as well as, of course, room and board. It is essential, for reasons that apply to high school students generally. Money is euphoric, psychedelic, and, though addictive, the addiction is not regarded as an offense under law. It is the most nearly universally honored claim to at least minimal dignity in our society. It provides genuine independence. At a deeper level, being paid would afford students some protection from the schools' often outrageous moral pretensions. If students were paid to go to school they would be far less implicated in the school's assumption that its demands express moral as well as social authority.

4. *Student participation in the governance of the institutions they attend is meaningful and desirable only insofar as it derives from real power.* These summer institute students participate very actively in running their program. But in any real conflict they are still regulated by adults. Some of the students at Yale Summer High School complained seriously against the regulation forbidding boys and girls access to each other's rooms—a policy the director justified simply and honestly as a necessary concession to local custom, rather than on moral grounds. His candor could not, however, prevent his actions from revealing the pretentiousness of student participation in governing the institute, since there was no process by which he could be overruled and the regulation changed, and students who disobeyed were subject to dismissal.

Persons who accept a spurious involvement in the authority that governs them must ultimately face the bitter fact that by doing so they have legitimated that authority and made themselves weaker rather than stronger with respect to it. For this reason, it seems to me especially fortunate that students now think in terms of power rather than authority, and attempt, when they are aggrieved, to counter authority with power—real power to affect the operation of the schools to which they have so long been subject. Negotiation, to be sure, is preferable to hostile confrontation; but no real negotiation takes place if either party to it is convinced that his adversary has no power to rebuke his intransigence. The question is not whether students should be permitted a voice in appointments, curriculum design, relations between school and community, and other major issues in the operation of schools and universities, but whether the entire process of education is not becoming more decent and more relevant because it is no longer possible to *deny* them a voice in matters that affect them so profoundly. Whether they should be given it I do not know—for then it might not really be theirs— but I am quite sure that they should take it if they are not given it, for their own sake and for that of the institution.

That they are doing so is, in my judgment, the most hopeful indication that education may become more decent as the decade passes. I take this position not because I impute to students wisdom superior to that of the faculty or administration, or because I believe them to be, in general, nobler and less self-seeking—though, at times, both these conclusions do indeed seem justified. But that is not the reason; even if I thought students largely fools and knaves I would still want them to have real power to influence the course of their own lives. What is most repellent about education in America and elsewhere is directly attributable to the fact that the institution has so far been able to count on social pressure and legal coercion to provide it with a captive clientele and a mandate to train that clientele in servility. Nothing so poisons a society as the prevalence within it of a petty and resentful citizenry which has been made to relinquish, through force or guile—and the schools have used both— its sense of moral authority over its own life. Education cannot be improved except in a society that respects the young; and ours respects no social group that is powerless and without resources. Yet, American society has rather consistently worked in such a way as to make it possible—difficult, but possible—for each successive discriminated group to gain enough real power to command respect and some of the elements, at least, of a decent life. With the exception of the Indians, who thought they owned the place, this has been the experience of all—even, at long last, of Black people. If—and only if—it is also the experience of youth in America, schools will become more decent, less rigid, and less *total* in their segregation from and immunity to the demands of ordinary life. Then, there may come a time when you can't even tell education from living.

10. A STUDENT VOICE

Montgomery County Student Alliance

The Montgomery County Student Alliance, a group of high school students, prepared its report and presented it to the Mcntgomery County (Maryland) Board of Education in February 1969. The students made a formal presentation at an open board hearing in March 1969, and the board listened to their criticisms but took no immediate action. The report, principally written by Norman Soloman, is one of the most impressive examples of high school student activism, and its quality exceeds most college protest documents.

From what we know to be true as full-time students and researchers of the county school system (as well as from every attempt we know of to survey student attitudes in the county), it is quite safe to say that the public schools have critically negative and absolutely destructive effects on human beings and their curiosity, natural desire to learn, confidence, individuality, creativity, freedom of thought and self-respect.

More specifically, the county public schools have the following effects which are absolutely fundamental and crucial:

1. Fear—The school system is based upon fear. Students are taught from the outset that they should be afraid of having certain things happen to them; bad grades, punishment from authorities, humiliation, ostracism, "failure," antagonizing teachers and administrators—are all things that terrify students as they enter first grade. These fears, which school officials use as a lever from elementary school through high school to establish and maintain order and obedience, have horribly destructive effects: they may be reflected in extreme nervousness, terror, paranoia, resentment, withdrawal, alienation; they may be visible, they may be submerged, but in either case these effects should be of utmost concern to those who value the human mind and spirit.

2. Dishonesty—Schools compel students to be dishonest. In order to be "successful" (the school system loses no time in providing the definition), students must learn to suppress and deny feelings, emotions, thoughts that they get the idea will not be acceptable. In the place of these honest feelings, emotions and thoughts, students are taught that to "succeed" other exteriors—dishonest though they may be—have to be substituted. The clearly defined rewards and punishments of the school system have an instructional effect on an impressionable child, and the message is clear throughout elementary school, junior high school and senior high school: "unacceptable" honesty will be punished, whether with grades, disciplinary action or a bad "permanent record"; "acceptable" responses, however dishonest, are—in the eyes of the school system and therefore according to the values it instills—simply that: "acceptable."

3. Approach to problems—It is soon clear to students what types of responses are likely to be successful at playing the school game. And so, before too long a student's approach to questions and problems undergoes a basic change. It becomes quickly clear that approaching a question on a test by saying "What is my own response to this question?" is risky indeed, and totally unwise if

one covets the highest grade possible (and the school system teaches the student that he should). Rather, the real question is clear to any student who knows anything about how schools work: "What is the answer the teacher wants me to give? What can I write that will please the teacher?"

4. Destruction of eagerness to learn—The school system takes young people who are interested in the things around them and destroys this natural joy in discovering and learning. Genuine, honest reasons for wanting to learn are quashed and replaced with an immediate set of rewards (which educators say are not ends in themselves but which nevertheless become just that). Real reasons for wanting to learn—the students' own reasons— are not treated as though they were valid. As George Leonard points out in his book *Education and Ecstasy*, and as everyone who has gone through the public school system knows, our school systems smash the natural joy in learning and make what we know as an "education" into a painful, degrading experience.

5. Alienation—With its dishonesty and premium on dutiful obedience, the school system causes feelings of resentment and alienation, whether these feelings are expressed or (as is usually the case) hidden and submerged.

6. Premium on conformity, blind obedience to authority—The school system's values and priorities *as they are practiced* ultimately become those of its students. Students—keenly aware of the rewards and punishments that can affect them—are made aware of what the school system wants most from its students on an operational, day-by-day basis. The fact that the county school system as it presently operates puts a very large premium on conformity and "knee-jerk" obedience is, we feel, indisputable; students simply know this to be true as a fact of school survival life.

7. Stifling self-expression, honest reaction—The fact that students who "step out of line" are likely to be punished for it is not lost on students, and this provides students with a basic object lesson on how to "succeed" in the public school. Once again, this

overpowering sense of rewards and punishments, which has been artificially created by the school system, has a very negative effect on the development of students.

8. Narrowing scope of ideas—The range of ideas students are exposed to by the school system is pitifully narrow, especially in the earlier grades; through use of textbooks which give only limited perspective, and through use of curriculum and teacher attitudes that are confining, students' minds are conditioned to accept what they are familiar with and reject what seems foreign.

9. Prejudice—By insisting that the schools remain pretty much isolated from ideas and cultures that do not blend in with those of the immediate community, school officials have the effect of solidifying and perpetuating local prejudices. Only with the free exchange of ideas and life-styles can students gain a broad outlook.

10. Self-hate—Perhaps most tragic is what the school system does to the emotional and mental attitudes and subconscious of its students. The system, for instance, is willing to and does label students as "failures" at age eight, twelve or seventeen. In addition to the fact that this often acts as a self-fulfilling prophecy, this has a cruelly damaging and degrading effect on students, and is inexcusable. Further, tension has been shown to be an integral part of the school experience, with very damaging effects. The self-hate which results can be directed inward or at others, but whatever the case it is extremely unhealthy; a community which says it cares about human emotions and feelings should not permit this to go on.

The extent to which school officials appear unaware or unconcerned about how students feel and the effects of the schools is frightening and disturbing. Top county school administrators' discussion of the need for relevance, sensitivity of human needs and feelings, student rights and freedom of expression and exchange of ideas seems to have little connection with the policies and priorities the administrators and teachers at the individual schools are pursuing. As for many principals and teachers, they quite often are just not concerned; their concept of the school system is that its job is to mold the behavior and attitudes of its students, and those students who balk at being molded are viewed as undisciplined annoyances, to be dealt with accordingly. The feedback in the form of grades, scores and college admissions is apparently considered adequate to prove the merit of the system; all else, it seems, must take a back seat.

The Student Alliance plans to collect feedback in these neglected but crucial, human areas. It is inexcusable that the Montgomery County School System has not made a real effort to seek this kind of feedback and enter it into the policy and organizational decision-making.

Perhaps most frustrating is the fact that leading Montgomery County school officials have criticized the schools and their inability and/or unwillingness to view and treat students as individual human beings.

The grading system is a good example, and extremely vital. Dr. James C. Craig, Assistant Superintendent for Instructional and Pupil Services, told a MCPS seminar on human relations in August, 1968: "Any school system which participates in, or suffers to continue a system of grading which by its very nature is demeaning of the human spirit, is cruel, inhumane—which approves and accepts the bright—which disapproves of and rejects those not so bright—such a school system is not worthy to be entrusted with any concerns involving differences among human beings . . ." Yet no one has been willing to make the basic changes that would be necessary to stop this "demeaning, cruel, inhumane" system from continuing to take its toll on the minds and spirits of 120,000 Montgomery County Public School students.

What it appears to come down to is a lack of a sense of urgency about these kinds of issues. If a school's heating system is found not to be working, it is quickly repaired. But say that the schools are destroying the minds and morale of its students, and administrators—perhaps even agreeing theoretically—will give you a dozen reasons why corrective action cannot be taken.

If the county school system really believes what it says about its goals, then it must devote itself to bringing the actual situation in line with these aims. If the goal of allowing students to develop as free-thinking individuals is really basic to a desirable educational setup, then it is not enough to merely say, "It would be nice . . ." If only we could give the same priority to making the schools humane and relevant that we now give to keeping computerized attendance cross-check cards and catching and punishing students who skip classes.

It is important to realize what effect all this has had on students and what their resulting responses have been.

Just about every student in Montgomery County feels the oppressiveness of the school system. Their responses, however, differ widely.

Only a fraction of the students are oriented to organizing groups, developing analyses and recommendations and approaching school officials.

Some students drop out—for varying reasons, but increasingly because school is not relevant to what they are interested in doing. (A number of county high school students have dropped out of public school to attend a "New Educational Project" founded by unhappy students from Montgomery County along with several college graduates, including an Antioch intern who taught history at Montgomery Blair for the 1967–68 school year. Other students attend the school on a part-time basis.)

Other students cut classes or skip school entirely on a consistent basis—not an intellectualized reaction, but merely an immediate, logical response: despite the attempt at "sledgehammer" motivation through grades and threats of punishment, what is going on in the classrooms is simply not worth getting involved with. These students, thousands of them, are punished; they are providing feedback that the school system does not care for.

Even for students who are not able to maintain passing grades (or who are not interested in doing so)—and "fail" or even "flunk out," it is apparent that the schools are failing by being unable to meet a wide range of needs.

But for most students, the sad result is that they take it, in fact they learn to adapt to the system and do the best they can "to succeed"—they accept (though many of them will tell you they do so reluctantly) the idea of working for the goals that have been dreamed up for them by the school system—and they learn the most successful way to play the game. The goals—high test scores, high grades—have taken on an enormous importance. And, inevitably, in pursuing these goals, students learn the usefulness—indeed the necessity—of dishonesty, conformity and yesmanship.

But the system's impersonal and authoritarian way of dealing with these students has taken its toll; submerged though the effects may be, the system has caused resentment, lack of self-respect and self-confidence, extreme nervousness, and/or behavior to compensate for such serious anxieties.

It is becoming almost a cliché to say that the public schools are not relevant, yet very little positive action has been taken to do anything about it. Every student has things that interest him; but the sad fact is that the school system very rarely gives him an opportunity to explore these interests. In many cases the student is actually hindered by the pressures and restrictions of the school system. There is no provision for giving students the chance to explore different areas of interest and follow wherever this exploration may lead them.

Knowledge is very much interrelated—math, science, history, literature and psychology, for instance, all have a great deal to do with one another, and the ways in which they have interacted have been fundamental to the development of man. Yet the school system insists on compartmentalizing these topics and creates artificial boundaries around each area. This makes learning seem narrow and confining; there is no need for it to be anything of the kind.

By the time a student reaches high school, attending school often seems to be a dull, boring and irrational experience that is viewed as something that simply has to be tolerated. This state of affairs should not exist.

Very importantly, the individual student himself, what he feels, his concerns, are ignored. How does he fit into all this?

What is important to him? What does this mean to him and his life? These questions do not fit into the school system's equation. Assisted by experience and efficiency, the county public school's operational equation seems simple; raw material (students) plus conditioning (classes, teachers, textbooks, discipline) equals products (graduates equipped to fill the necessary slots in society). The complexities of the individual, developing mind are passed over; the system is "successful," and, we are told, is among the best in the nation.

Instead of the system's being built around the needs of the students, the students are being built around the needs of the system.

WHAT NEEDS TO BE DONE

1. Establishment of an ombudsman office, responsible directly to the Board of Education, to investigate and resolve complaints from students.

If the goals and realities of the school system are ever to be brought into line with one another, it is essential that a procedure be developed to deal with instances of questionable treatment of students. Every student in county schools should be informed of the existence and purpose of the ombudsman office, and they should be made to feel free to make use of it without any fear of retaliation. It is important that the ombudsman office not be in the position of having to be defensive about the actions of school administrators and teachers. Ombudsman officials, independent of any such pressures or biases, must take a stance of neutrality and work vigorously to correct the thousands of injustices which occur every year to students who presently have no way of seeking redress.

2. The school system must put an end to intimidation of students through abuse of college recommendations, grades, secret files and "permanent record files" by school officials.

These incidents are often hard to pin down, but students are definitely being blackmailed and intimidated—with varying degrees of subtlety—through use of these documents. Students must be given access to their own files, and must have control over who can and cannot see them. The Board of Education should issue a firm memo to all teachers, administrators and counselors in the county schools emphasizing the Board's disapproval of intimidation and anything short of straightforward dealings with students in these areas. In addition, the ombudsman office for students should work to uncover and eliminate misuse of these files and documents.

3. Students must have an important role in the shaping and implementation of courses. They are also in an excellent position to provide meaningful feedback by providing continuous evaluation of the effectiveness, strengths and weaknesses of their classes.

The school system has "proclaimed" many policies and has made them stick. Teachers should be told that it is essential to have students discuss how courses and classes should be designed and operated. This continual re-evaluation will see to it that classes and courses of study are constantly improved and updated. County school officials determining courses of study must be willing to permit much more flexibility and originality than is presently allowed. Departmental faculty meetings, it should be made clear, are open to participation and input from students. On the individual class level, the successes and failures of the class can be continually evaluated by students and teachers working together and planning together.

4. Student input in teacher evaluations.

Being a good teacher involves many characteristics beyond the ability to keep accurate records, complete forms neatly, "control classes" and receive degrees from graduate school. Whether a teacher is stimulating, creates enthusiasm, is responsive to individual needs and problems of his students, can relate to students (and vice versa) and treats students with respect for their human dignity is all extremely important. Students are in the best position to provide very valuable information in these areas, and it would seem logical to construct a regular system for obtaining such feedback from students.

5. Tension and rigidity must be eliminated from the schools. Administrators must be made to stop constantly threatening students with arbitrary, almost whimsical disciplinary actions.

This implies a change in attitude; an elimination of the approach which says that to have students expressing themselves, verbally and through interaction, can pose a threat to the "authority" and "order" of the school system. Students are being pressured, threatened and suspended for skipping classes, being in the halls without passes or even possession and/or distribution of literature. A system which has an elaborate policing-system network for keeping students out of the halls and for catching students who chose not to attend classes is perpetuating tension which is absolutely unnecessary, damaging to morale and totally out of place in an institution which says it seeks to encourage learning and exploration.

6. Hiring of educators and researchers to deeply examine what effect the school system has on a student's self-concept, creativity, and desire to explore and learn.

Much of the evidence and research in this area, we feel, has already been developed (and is presently being ignored—no doubt because the findings are so very unpleasant). James Coleman's *Equality of Educational Opportunity* shows that self-concept and sense of control over one's own destiny is much more significant in the development of a child than the many other factors school administrators spend all their time worrying about. The forces which presently destroy a student's self-concept and feeling of control over his own fate must be eliminated immediately. We feel it is clear that this is going to have to mean elimination of the disciplinary threats and punishments prevailing throughout the school system, of the clockworklike class schedules and tension created by school administrators and teachers who have been encouraged to emphasize and flaunt their authority.

7. Elimination of letter grades.

This is extremely important. The use of letter grades as the basis upon which the school system is operated sets the tone and patterns of the public school experience. Its destructive effects have already been noted.

In elementary and junior high schools, grades should be abolished immediately and replaced with written evaluations by the teacher. In high school, students should simply receive credit or not receive credit for each course they have taken. In order for the students to get feedback as to how they are progressing, teachers should provide students with written and/or oral evaluations as often as necessary. Students should receive a copy of all written evaluations; a copy should be entered in students' files, but should not be released to colleges without student-parent consent.

Transition may seem rather difficult at first. But the benefits will be both immediate and increasingly apparent as students make the adjustment and begin to shake off the bad attitudes and effects of the old system. The natural joy in learning will re-emerge, and hopefully for those starting out in the system it would never be squashed in the first place.

If a complete change is made for all the schools in the county, colleges will have no choice but to consider each applicant from the county on his individual merits; they would be forced to do without grades and class rank in evaluating applicants (there are many other methods of evaluation), especially in view of the reputation Montgomery County enjoys nationally as a school system of unquestionable academic quality.

There are ways if there is the will.

8. Teachers must be encouraged and allowed to respond to the individual needs of their students. This will have to mean fewer regulatory restrictions, more flexibility.

9. Students must be given the ability to exercise control over what happens to them in school. Specifics: The right to transfer out of a course that is not satisfactory; the right to go on independent study at any time; the right to formulate their own goals and how they can best go about achieving them.

10. Rigid periods now being used in county secondary schools must be replaced with shorter and flexible modules.

Kennedy High School's use of modules—short blocks of time—make the school more flexible and open to different kinds of activities. There are now no provisions for spontaneous activities; in fact, they are absolutely prohibited. Periods which last 50 minutes or an hour are confining and should be eliminated.

11. Students must have a right to print and distribute their own publications, and restrictions should not be set up to impose obstacles—as has been the case—but rather to provide students with an orderly means of distribution, such as tables in the halls, near doors or in the cafeteria. These requirements should apply equally to all student publications. (The fact that money is involved has been used as an argument against allowing "underground" or unsanctioned papers, but money is always also involved with sanctioned, official student newspapers.)

12. Students have the right to have the freedom to decide what they want to print in student newspapers, literary magazines and yearbooks. Censorship by sponsors or principals, whatever the degree of subtlety, must not be allowed.

13. Outside speakers must be given a chance to speak to students without favoritism or discrimination.

Military recruiters, for example, address assemblies at each county high school every year, but the same right has been refused to groups presenting different or opposing viewpoints. Students must make the decisions to invite speakers and arrange assemblies.

14. The providing of the names and addresses of senior boys to the armed forces must be ended.

The county school system makes a point of its desire to protect students from businesses who get hold of mailing lists of students, yet it provides the names and addresses of senior boys in county high schools to the military. Peace and pacifist groups have been refused the same privilege. The lists should either be available to groups which disagree with the military or should not be released at all.

15. Relevant courses must be developed to meet student interests.

Students should be surveyed as to what courses they would like to see offered and the results should play a determining role in the direction of course offerings. Racism, urban life, suburban life, drugs, human relations, foreign policy, police-youth relations and civil liberties are a few topics in great need of curriculum development.

16. Students should be free to arrange voluntary seminars to be held during the school day.

If schools are really to become relevant, students must be allowed—indeed encouraged—to set up discussions, hold workshops and seminars, hear speakers who are well informed about the subjects that interest students. The students should be free to invite speakers and outside authorities to come in and give their views, without the obstacles which presently exist. Schools must come alive. The concept behind the "Experiment in Free Form Education" being tried at Whitman for one week must be integrated into the everyday functioning of the schools. With school becoming much more individualized, students should be given the flexibility of attending seminars of interest during the school day.

17. Expansion of the range of resources.

Diversified paperback books giving different perspectives should play an important part in widening the scope of thought and exposure in the schools. Textbooks alone are just too limited in coverage and perspective.

18. Informing students of their rights.

The school system should take the responsibility of informing each student of his rights in dealing with administrators and teachers. If the School Board agrees that students do have rights, then it must be willing to make these rights directly known to each student.

19. Restrictions having to do with student dress must be eliminated throughout the county.

20. County seminars in human relations, racism and progressive teaching methods should be held for teachers.

An excellent week of seminars was held by the Montgomery County Public Schools last August for about 100 county administrators. It would be very good if the same sort of program could be set up for the county's teachers.

21. Material thoroughly exploring Negro history must be integrated into classes such as U.S. History and Problems of the 20th Century. Special training should be provided to teachers in order to make them qualified to deal with this very important aspect of American history and society.

22. The School Board should launch an investigation of illegal searches of lockers in secondary schools for drugs and the recruiting by school officials of students to become narcotics informers.

School officials have been known to actively seek and encourage students to become drug informers. The unhealthy atmosphere which such a situation creates should be a matter of concern. We feel the School Board would agree that it is not a desirable situation to have students promoted to act as spies on other students in school. Such activities have no place in an institution of learning.

23. School Board hearings for students.

It is important that school officials come into contact with the concerns of students. The Board could schedule hearings every two weeks at which time students would be invited to testify and voice complaints and suggestions.

24. Student voice on School Board.

The School Board would do well to include representation of students. Every semester the School Board could supervise the election of student representatives from among county high school students, printing a special bulletin for each high school student which would give the positions of each of the students who had volunteered to run for the positions.

MAKING CONTACT: TOWARD A RELEVANT CURRICULUM

11. WHAT'S WORTH KNOWING?

NEIL POSTMAN AND
CHARLES WEINGARTNER

Neil Postman is Associate Professor of English Education at New York University and is the senior author of Holt, Rinehart and Winston's New English Series. He is former director of the New York University Linguistics Demonstration Center and is the co-author of Linguistics: A Revolution in Teaching.

Charles Weingartner is Associate Professor of Education at Queens College. He is co-author, with Postman, of Linguistics *and* Teaching as a Subversive Activity.

Suppose all of the syllabi and curricula and textbooks in the schools disappeared. Suppose all of the standardized tests—city-wide, state-wide, and national—were lost. In other words, suppose that the most common material impeding innovation in the schools simply did not exist. Then suppose that you decided to turn this "catastrophe" into an opportunity to increase the relevance of the schools. What would you do?

We have a possibility for you to consider: suppose that you decide to have the entire "curriculum" consist of questions. These questions would have to be worth seeking answers to not only from your point of view but, more importantly, from the point of view of the students. In order to get still closer to reality, add the requirement that the questions must help the students to develop and internalize concepts that will help them to survive in the rapidly changing world of the present and future.

Obviously, we are asking you to suppose you were an educator living in the second half of the twentieth century. What questions would you have on your list?

Take a pencil and list your questions on the next page, which we have left blank for you. Please do not be concerned about defacing the book, unless, of course, one of your questions is going to be, "What were some of the ways of earning a living in Ancient Egypt?" In that case, use your *own* paper. . . .

At this point it might be worth noting that our list of questions is intended to "educate" students. Contrary to conventional school practice, what that means is that we want to elicit from students the meanings that they have already stored up so that they may subject those meanings to a testing and verifying, re-ordering and reclassifying, modifying and extending process. In this process, the student is not a passive "recipient"; he becomes an active *producer* of knowledge. The word "educate" is closely related to the word "educe." In the oldest pedagogic sense of the term, this meant drawing out of a person something potential or latent. We can, after all, learn only in relation to what we already know. Again, contrary to common misconceptions, this means that, if we don't know very much, our capability for learning is not very great. This idea—virtually by itself—requires a major revision in most of the metaphors that shape school policies and procedures.

Reflect on these questions—and others that these can generate. Please do not merely react to them.

> What do you worry about most?
>
> What are the causes of your worries?
>
> Can any of your worries be eliminated? How?
>
> Which of them might you deal with first? How do you decide?
>
> Are there other people with the same problems? How do you know? How can you find out?
>
> If you had an important idea that you wanted to let everyone (in the world) know about, how might you go about letting them know?
>
> What bothers you most about adults? Why?
>
> How do you want to be similar to or different from adults you know when you become an adult?
>
> What, if anything, seems to you to be worth dying for?
>
> How did you come to believe this?
>
> What seems worth living for?
>
> How did you come to believe this? . . .
>
> At the present moment, what would you most like to be

doing? Five years from now? Ten years from now? Why? What might you have to do to realize these hopes? What might you have to give up in order to do some or all of these things?

When you hear or read or observe something, how do you know what it means? . . .

What is "progress"?

What is "change"?

What are the most obvious causes of change? What are the least apparent? What conditions are necessary in order for change to occur?

What kinds of changes are going on right now? Which are important? How are they similar to or different from other changes that have occurred?

What are the relationships between new ideas and change?

Where do *new* ideas come from? How come? So what?

If you wanted to stop one of the changes going on now (pick one), how would you go about it? What consequences would you have to consider?

Of the important changes going on in our society, which should be encouraged and which resisted? Why? How?

What are the most important changes that have occurred in the past ten years? twenty years? fifty years? In the last year? In the last six months? Last month? What will be the most important changes next month? Next year? Next decade? How can you tell? So what? . . .

What are the conditions necessary for life to survive? Plants? Animals? Humans?

Which of these conditions are necessary for all life?

Which ones for plants? Which ones for animals? Which ones for humans?

What are the greatest threats to all forms of life? To plants? To animals? To humans?

What are some of the "strategies" living things use to survive? Which unique to plants? Which unique to animals? Which unique to humans?

What kinds of human survival strategies are (1) similar to those of animals and plants; (2) different from animals and plants?

What does man's language permit him to develop as survival strategies that animals cannot develop?

How might man's survival activities be different from what they are if he did not have language?

What other "languages" does man have besides those consisting of words?

What functions do these "languages" serve? Why and how do they originate? Can you invent a new one? How might you start? . . .

What's worth knowing? How do you decide? What are some ways to go about getting to know what's worth knowing?

It is necessary for us to say at once that these questions are not intended to represent a catechism for the new education. These are samples and illustrations of the kinds of questions we think worth answering. Our set of questions is best regarded as a metaphor of our sense of relevance. If you took the trouble to list your own questions, it is quite possible that you prefer many of them to ours. Good enough. The new education is a process and will not suffer from the applied imaginations of all who wish to be a part of it. But in evaluating your own questions, as well as ours, bear in mind that there are certain *standards* that must be used. These standards may also be stated in the form of questions:

Will your questions increase the learner's *will* as well as his capacity to learn?

Will they help to give him a sense of joy in learning?

Will they help to provide the learner with confidence in his ability to learn?

In order to get answers, will the learner be required to make inquiries? (Ask further questions, clarify terms, make observations, classify data, etc.?)

Does each question allow for alternative answers (which implies alternative modes of inquiry)?

Will the process of answering the questions tend to stress the uniqueness of the learner?

Would the questions produce different answers if asked at different stages of the learner's development?

Will the answers help the learner to sense and understand the universals in the human condition and so enhance his ability to draw closer to other people?

If the answers to these questions about your list of questions are all "yes," then you are to be congratulated for insisting upon extremely high standards in education. If that seems an unusual compliment, it is only because we have all become accustomed to a conception and a hierarchy of standards that, in our opinion, is simultaneously upside-down and irrelevant. We usually think of a curriculum as having high standards if "it" covers ground, requires much and difficult reading, demands many papers, and if the students for whom it is intended do not easily get "good" grades. Advocates of "high standards" characteristically and unwittingly invoke other revealing metaphors. One of the most frequently used of these is "basic fundamentals." The most strident advocates of "high, and ever yet 'higher,' standards" insist that these be "applied" particularly to "basic fundamentals." Indulging our propensity to inquire into the language of education, we find that the essential portion of the word "fundamental" is the word "fundament." It strikes us as poetically appropriate that "fundament" also means the buttocks, and specifically the anus. We will resist the temptation to explore the unconscious motives of "fundamentalists." But we cannot resist saying that *their* "high standards" represent the *lowest possible standards imaginable* in any conception of a new education. In fact, so low, that the up-down metaphor is not very useful in describing it.

What one needs to ask of a standard is not, "Is it high or low?," but, "Is it appropriate to your goals?" If your goals are to make people more alike, to prepare them to be docile functionaries in some bureaucracy, and to prevent them from being vigorous, self-directed learners, then the standards of most schools are neither high nor low. They are simply apt. If the goals are those of a new education, one needs standards based on the actual activities of competent, confident learners when they are genuinely engaged in learning. One must be centrally concerned with the hearts and minds of learners—in contrast to those merely concerned with the "fundament." No competent learner ever says to himself, "In trying to solve this problem, I will read two books (not less than 30 pages from each). Then, I will make a report of not less than 20 pages, with a minimum of 15 footnotes. . . ." The only place one finds such "standards" is in a school syllabus. *They do not exist in natural, human learning situations, since they have nothing to do with the conditions of learning—with what the learner needs to be and to do in order to learn about learning, or indeed about anything.* Any talk about high standards from teachers or school administrators is nonsense unless they are talking about *standards of learning* (as distinct from standards for grading, which is what is usually meant). What this means is that there is a need for a new—and "higher"—conception of "fundamentals." Everyone, at present, is in favor of having students learn the fundamentals. For most people, "the three R's," or some variation of them, represent what is fundamental to a learner. However, if one *observes* a learner and asks himself, "What is it that this organism needs without which he cannot thrive?," it is impossible to come up with the answer, "The three R's." The "new fundamentals" derive from the emotional and intellectual realities of the human condition, and so "new" answers (well beyond the three-R's type) are possible in response to the question. In *In Defense of Youth,* Earl Kelley lists five such possible answers:

1. the need for other people
2. the need for good communication with other people
3. the need for a loving relationship with other people
4. the need for a workable concept of self
5. the need for freedom.

One does not need to accept all of these in order to accept Kelley's *perspective* on what is fundamental. Obviously, we would want to add to his list "the need to know how to learn," as well as some others which are suggested by our list of "standards" questions. The point is that any curriculum that does not provide for needs as viewed from this perspective—"What does the organism require in order to thrive?"—is not, by our definition, concerned with "fundamentals."

We would like to invite you now to re-examine our sample questions. They represent, after all, a possible curriculum for the new education: The What's-Worth-Knowing Questions Curriculum. This curriculum has several characteristics that require elaboration here. For example, note that all the questions are of a divergent, or open-ended, nature and that each one demands that the learner narrow its focus. Part of the process of learning how to learn is the rephrasing, refining, and dividing of a "worth knowing" question into a series of "answerable worth-knowing questions." It is a fact not easily learned (and almost never in school) that the "answer" to a great many questions is "merely" another question. This is not only true of such questions as we have listed, but even of such questions as "What is a noun?," "Who discovered oxygen?," and "What is the principal river of Uruguay?"

To illustrate the point, we have reproduced below a problem that is sometimes given to students by teachers who regard the process of question asking as basic to education:

1. Study the following questions.
    a. What is the name of this school?
    b. Are children of permissive parents more creative than children of nonpermissive parents?
    c. Who discovered oxygen?
    d. Who is the most beautiful woman in America?
    e. Are the people on Mars more advanced than the people on Earth?
    f. Will it rain tomorrow?
    g. How are you?
    h. Will you get into the college of your choice?
    i. Is *love* a noun or a verb?
    j. $8 + 6 = ?$
    k. Why do airplanes crash?

2. Answer the following questions.
   a. Which of the questions above can you answer with absolute certainty? How can you be certain of your answer?
   b. What information will enable you to answer other questions with absolute certainty? Where will you get the information?
   c. Which questions restrict you to giving factual information? Which do not? Which require no facts at all?
   d. Which questions require the greatest amount of definition before you try to answer them?
   e. Which questions require the testimony of experts? What makes one an expert?
   f. Which questions assume the answerer is the expert?
   g. Which questions may have false assumptions?
   h. Which questions require predictions as answers? What kinds of information may improve the quality of a prediction?

In working this problem through, students quite frequently discover that the question "Who discovered oxygen?" (to cite only one example) is ambiguous in that form. Usually, they rephrase it to read something like, "According to the *Encyclopaedia Britannica*, who is given credit for the 'discovery of oxygen'?" If you feel that there is no important difference between these two questions, or that "everyone knows" that the former implies the latter, may we remind you that, as a matter of fact, the answer to the question "Who discovered America?" will vary depending on whether you ask it of an Italian, a Swede, or an Irish monk.

Our Questions Curriculum, in addition to requiring the exploration of the nature of questions, has the capacity to *generate* questions that learners are not, at first, aware of. In other words, divergent questions are instruments of "consciousness expansion." They reveal to learners new and relevant areas of inquiry, permitting, quite often, the discovery that one's original question is far less significant than two or three others it has suggested. For when children are allowed to function as question askers and answer seekers, they frequently perceive relationships that others have not noticed before. Let them start with a question in "biology"—for example, "What are the conditions for sustaining life in plants?"—and they will soon start asking questions about "physics," "anthropology," "chemistry," etc. This will happen over and over again unless the teacher insists that they "stick to the subject."

And so in our Questions Curriculum, "subjects" frequently lose their "clear" and arbitrarily limiting dimensions. We will need to start talking more about the "structure of the learner and his learning" and less about the "structure of the subject."

There are two other characteristics of our Questions Curriculum that should be mentioned here. The first has to do with that recently discovered (invented?) category of human beings called "disadvantaged children." Generally speaking, these children are reputed to be "slower" learners than other types of children. If this is true, it simply means that they do not function so well as others *in the existing school environment*. It cannot be inferred from this that "disadvantaged children" would be a "problem" if the ecology of the school environment were entirely different. If we may paraphrase Heisenberg: "We have to remember that what we observe children doing in schools is not what they *are*, but children exposed to us by our methods of teaching." We are, in fact, confident that the disadvantaged child is much more likely to find the conditions which will satisfy him as a learner in the kind of environment we have been trying to describe than in any other. In a way, this statement is a tautology since the environment we are describing is devoted to making the learner "satisfied." It is based on what we know about learners, and not on what we know about what we want them to learn.

Finally, note that the questions we listed are capable of being pursued by children at every grade level. Their answers, as well as their *way* of answering, will vary, depending on their experience: where they've been, what they believe, and what their purposes are. This curriculum does not call for a single set of answers. Therefore, it does not require a single set of *answerers*. There is an old joke about a school administrator who was dismayed when he and his staff had taken great trouble to prepare a new and wonderful curriculum, only to discover that the "wrong" kids showed up. That's the trouble with the old education and its functionaries: it virtually insures an endless and increasing number of "wrong" students.

It remains for us to say here that the function of the What's-Worth-Knowing Questions Curriculum is to put two ideas into clear focus. The first is that the art and science of asking questions is the source of all knowledge.

The second idea is that question asking, if it is not to be a sterile and ritualized activity, has to deal with problems that are perceived as useful and realistic by the learners. We do not mean to suggest that a child's perception of what is relevant is an unalterable given; indeed, the thrust of the "curriculum" we have been describing is to extend the child's perception of what is relevant and what is not.

Simply said: There is no learning without a learner. And there is no meaning without a meaning maker. In order to survive in a world of rapid change there is nothing more worth knowing, for any of us, than the continuing process of how to make viable meanings.

12. MAKING CONTACT WITH THE DISADVANTAGED
MARIO D. FANTINI AND
GERALD WEINSTEIN

Mario D. Fantini is presently a Program Officer, Division of Public Education, Ford Foundation. He has taught on all levels of education and served as con-

sultant in the field of cultural deprivation to various school systems and universities.

Gerald Weinstein has served as Director of the Elementary School Teaching Project of the Fund for the Advancement of Education, and as a consultant to the National Institute for Advanced Study for Teachers of the Disadvantaged.

What is relevant? There seem to be at least four causes of irrelevance in education, and consequently, four levels on which relevance may be achieved:

1. How it is taught: Irrelevance is caused if teaching procedures and learning styles are not matched. The current literature on disadvantaged children indicates that they learn best in more concrete, inductive, kinesthetic, and less verbal situations. In view of this, their teachers should search for methodology coordinated with this learning style. Thus, if all techniques, practices and methods used by teachers are geared specifically to the pupil's own style of learning, then, regardless of content there is a degree of relevance in whatever is being taught because of *how* it is being taught. The following "from-to's" are examples of procedures geared to this match:

FROM: A curriculum that is pre-packaged, rigidly scheduled, and uniform throughout a school system.
TO: One that is flexible and geared to the unique needs of individual schools within the system.

FROM: A curriculum that is primarily symbol-based.
TO: One that is primarily experience-based.

FROM: A horizontally programmed disjointed sequence of skills.
TO: A vertically programmed small-step sequence of skills.

FROM: A curriculum that is past-and-future-oriented.
TO: One that is immediate-oriented.

FROM: A what curriculum.
TO: A why curriculum.

FROM: A completely academic curriculum (knowing).
TO: One geared to social participation (doing).

FROM: An antiseptic curriculum.
TO: One that attempts to explore reality.

FROM: Emphasis solely on cognitive, extrinsic content.
TO: An equal emphasis on affective, inner content.

2. What is taught: Irrelevance occurs if the material presented is not within or easily connected with the learner's knowledge of his physical realm of experience. If the learner is from an urban area, for instance, teaching about his neighborhood or his city may be more relevant to him and make greater contact because he is experientially familiar with the topic.

Content that is most closely connected to the learners' reality—to their experiences—will have the best possibility for engaging the learners, especially those who are disadvantaged. This "experiential content" is based on what the child learns from experiences provided by his life space, or the social contact in which he lives. It is mainly cognitive and may or may not be related to more affective or "feeling" content. For example, a child may learn how to take care of his younger brothers and sisters, or how to use the streets as a playground. He knows the latest popular songs, the "in" language, what's happening in his neighborhood, or how a leader in his group must act. The migrant child may learn the characteristics of a good worker, a good boss, or ways for picking the most strawberries with least effort.

Thus, in an effort to achieve relevance on this level, the teacher must begin by asking himself several questions: "What content does the child bring to school? What does he already know? What can he teach me? What does he talk about when no one is structuring his talk?" In other words, relevance is achieved by making *what* is being taught germane to the learner's *knowledge* of his experience.

3. Learners' feelings: The third level of irrelevance occurs if *what* is being taught and *how* it is being taught ignore the learner's *feelings* about his experiences. To be an effective teacher

on this level involves a more intrinsic operation, since it is these deeper feelings about his experiences that, if tapped, may lead to the learner's greater involvement. For instance, an urban reading series or a unit on the city policemen may be used because the learner "knows" them. But, if the learner has a fear of policemen by virtue of his particular experience with them, then, because of the content selected, learning actually may be inhibited. Until the learner's real *feelings* about his experiences are utilized, until there is an emotional connection made, the third level of relevance has not been tapped.

In order to achieve relevance on this level, one of the continuing questions a teacher must ask the learners is "How do you feel about this?" An example of the use of this type of question and of making the connection with children's feelings occurred in a situation in which a teacher told her class that a nurse was coming to the school the next day to talk to them about hospitals and how they are run. The children, who conceived of the hospital as mysterious, forbidding, and associated only with people who are injured or dying, could not get interested in such questions as how many doctors were on the staff, how many rooms it contained, how much money was needed to run it, etc. But the visiting nurse quickly excited the children in the lesson when she asked: "How do you feel when you think about a hospital?" One child put up his hand and shouted, "Scared!" Other children indicated that they, too, saw the hospital as an object of fright. The nurse, who apparently had been used to dealing with the fears of young patients, immediately started from that point—the children's feelings in regard to the subject matter (the hospital)—and developed it. By the time she finished the lesson, she managed to explain a good deal about the real world of the hospital for the children as patients or as relatives of patients. The key to it all was her having started from their ground—in this case, a feeling of fear.

4. Learners' concerns: The fourth level of irrelevance occurs if the *concerns* of the learners are ignored. Concerns also involve feelings and emotions but at a much deeper level than those

described in the third level. Concerns are the most persistent, pervasive threads of underlying uneasiness the learners have about themselves and their relation to the world. The distinction between this level and the third level may be stated this way: Concerns always engage feelings, but feelings do not always involve concerns. For example, a person may have an immediate, spontaneous feeling about listening to a symphony orchestra or about another person, without having a concern (as defined above) about either. Feeling anger at having one's toe stepped on would be an immediate feeling; whereas, becoming angry *every* time someone criticized a particular group to which one belonged would represent a more pervasive feeling which probably reflects a concern. Relevance is achieved on this fourth level if the teacher attempts to deal with the questions that people most consistently ask themselves, such as, "Who am I? What can I do about things? Who am I really connected to or how do I fit into the scheme of things?" The difference between this level and the previous one is a difference in kind as well as degree.

Some cues to children's concerns that may assist teachers in selecting relevant content that deals with these concerns may be found in the following statements made by children:

Cues indicating self-rejection that reflects a concern for self-identity

> "Why Do I Live In The Slums?"
> "I May Be Brown But I'm Not Black!"
> "How Can You Like Me When I Don't Like Myself?"
> "We're The Dumb Special Class!"

These last two statements could easily occur across socio-economic lines while the first two contain the added variables of class and caste.

Cues indicating disconnectedness that reflect a concern for greater connectedness

> "Whenever I Leave Harlem I Feel Like A Fish Out Of Water."

"Why Should I Listen To My Parents? Look At The Way They Live!"
"In Order For Me To Get Educated I Gotta Be Like You? What About Me?"
"You Can't Trust Nobody, White Or Negro."

Cues indicating powerlessness that reflect a concern for greater control over what is happening to them

"It's No Use Trying There's Nothing You Can Do."
"I'm Hercules—I Can Do Anything."
". . . what the hell can I do? This is the attitude; we can do nothing, so leave it alone. People think you're always going to be under pressure from the white man and he owns and runs everything, and we are so dependent on him that there's nothing I can do. This is the general impression I've gotten from most of the adults in Harlem."

These statements are significant to us, because they are questions with which children are grappling which are rooted in the core of their being. They are questions that all humans face, but which for the disadvantaged have been so compounded and powerful that they have become the essence of their disadvantage. Such concerns lie at the core of what we term relevance, for very little could be more relevant to groups of children than what they actually *feel* most about.

Effective teaching utilizes all four levels of relevance. Educators are beginning to use the first two levels. What they are not meeting adequately are the third or fourth levels which constitute two different levels of the "affective" or feeling domain. Educators are not answering the spoken and more often unspoken questions children ask themselves: "Why do I feel the way I do? What makes me do that? Do they think I'm any good?" Rather than try to supply insights to these questions, the school, instead, asks children, "What do we mean by the Common Market?" "How are animals and people different?" Ignored in the process is one of the child's most persistent questions: "What does it have to do with *me?*" Unless there is this connection with the child's experiential and emotional framework, the knowledge he gains will be of little significance and may not be manifested in the types of behaviors spelled out by the aims of education.

It is our general hypothesis that what makes the most contact is that which is the most "relevant" to them and which makes a connection between the affective or feeling aspects and the cognitive or conceptualizing aspects of the learner.

13. ORGANIC TEACHING
Sylvia Ashton-Warner

Sylvia Ashton-Warner has gained equal fame and respect for her work as a novelist (Spinster, Incense to Idols, Greenstone) *and her extraordinary work with Maori children in New Zealand described in her book* Teacher, *which dramatically explores the techniques and benefits of organic teaching.*

I can't disassociate the activity in an infant room from peace and war. So often I have seen the destructive vent, beneath an onslaught of creativity, dry up under my eyes. Especially with the warlike Maori five-year-olds who pass through my hands in hundreds, arriving with no other thought in their heads other than to take, break, fight and be first. With no opportunity for creativity they may well develop, as they did in the past, with fighting as their ideal of life. Yet all this can be expelled through the creative vent, and the more violent the boy the more I see that he creates, and when he kicks the others with his big boots, treads on fingers on the mat, hits another over the head with a piece of wood or throws a stone, I put clay in his hands, or chalk.

He can create bombs if he likes or draw my house in flame, but it is the creative vent that is widening all the time and the destructive one atrophying, however much it may look to the contrary. And anyway I have always been more afraid of the weapon unspoken than of the one on a blackboard.

With all this in mind therefore I try to bring as many facets of teaching into the creative vent as possible, with emphasis on reading and writing. And that's just what organic teaching is; all subjects in the creative vent. It's just as easy for a teacher, who gives a child a brush and lets him paint, to give him a pencil and let him write, and to let him pass his story to the next one to read. Simplicity is so safe. There's no occasion whatever for the early imposition of a dead reading, a dead vocabulary. I'm so afraid of it. It's like a frame over a young tree making it grow in an unnatural shape. It makes me think of that curtailment of a child's expansion of which Erich Fromm speaks, of that unlived life of which destructiveness is the outcome. "And instead of the wholeness of the expansive tree we have only the twisted and stunted bush." The trouble is that a child from a modern respectable home suffers such a serious frame on his behavior long before he comes near a teacher. Nevertheless I think that after a year of organic work the static vocabularies can be used without misfortune. They can even, under the heads of external stimulus and respect for the standard of English, become desirable.

But only when built upon the organic foundation. And there's hardly anything new in the conception of progress from the known to the unknown. It's just that when the inorganic reading is imposed first it interferes with integration; and it's upon the integrated personality that everything is built. We've lost the gracious movement from the inside outward. We overlook the footing. I talk sometimes about a bridge from the pa[1] to the European environment, but there is a common bridge for a child of any race and of more moment than any other: the bridge from the inner world outward. And that is what organic teaching is. An indispensable step in integration. Without it we get this one-

---

[1] Pa: Maori village.

patterned mind of the New Zealand child, accruing from so much American influence of the mass-mind type. I think that we already have so much pressure toward sameness through radio, film and comic outside the school, that we can't afford to do a thing inside that is not toward individual development, and from this stance I can't see that we can indulge in the one imposed reading for all until the particular variety of a mind is set. And a cross-section of children from different places in New Zealand provides me with an automatic check on the progress of the one-patterned mind. (I own seventy fancy-dress costumes which I lend.) All the children want the same costumes. If you made dozens of cowboy and cowgirl costumes, hundreds of Superman and thousands of Rocket Man costumes and hired them at half a guinea a go, you'd get every penny of it and would make a fortune vast enough to retire on and spend the rest of your life in the garden. As for my classics—Bo-Peep, the Chinese Mandarin, Peter Pan and the Witch and so on—they so gather the dust that they have had to be folded and put away. It's this sameness in children that can be so boring. So is death boring.

To write peaceful reading books and put them in an infant room is not the way to peace. They don't even scratch the surface. No child ever asked for a Janet or a John costume. There is only one answer to destructiveness and that is creativity. And it never was and never will be any different. And when I say so I am in august company.

The noticeable thing in New Zealand society is the body of people with their inner resources atrophied. Seldom have they had to reach inward to grasp the thing that they wanted. Everything, from material requirements to ideas, is available ready-made. From mechanical gadgets in the shops to sensation in the films they can buy almost anything they fancy. They can buy life itself from the film and radio—canned life.

And even if they tried to reach inward for something that maybe they couldn't find manufactured, they would no longer find anything there. They've dried up. From babyhood they have had shiny toys put in their hands, and in the kindergartens and infant rooms bright pictures and gay material. Why conceive

anything of their own? There has not been the need. The capacity to do so has been atrophied and now there is nothing there. The vast expanses of the mind that could have been alive with creative activity are now no more than empty vaults that must, for comfort's sake, be filled with non-stop radio, and their conversation consists of a list of platitudes and clichés.
I can't quite understand why.

From what I see of modern education the intention is just the opposite: to let children grow up in their own personal way into creative and interesting people. Is it the standard textbooks? Is it the consolidation? Is it the quality of the teachers? Is it the access to film and radio and the quality of those luxuries? Or is it the access to low-grade reading material infused through all of these things? I don't know where the intention fails but we end up with the same pattern of a person in nine hundred ninety-nine instances out of a thousand.

I said to a friend of mine, a professor, recently, "What kind of children arrive at the University to you?" He said, "They're all exactly the same." "But," I said, "how can it be like that? The whole plan of primary education at least is for diversity." "Well," he answered, "they come to me like samples from a mill. Not one can think for himself. I beg them not to serve back to me exactly what I have given to them. I challenge them sometimes with wrong statements to provoke at least some disagreement but even that won't work." "But," I said, "you must confess to about three per cent originality." "One in a thousand," he replied. "One in a thousand."

On the five-year-old level the mind is not yet patterned and it is an exciting thought. True, I often get the overdisciplined European five, crushed beyond recognition as an identity, by respectable parents, but never Maoris; as a rule a five-year-old child is not boring. In an infant room it is still possible to meet an interesting, unpatterned person. "In the infant room," I told this professor, "we still have identity. It's somewhere between my infant-room level and your university level that the story breaks. But I don't think it is the plan of education itself."

I think that the educational story from the infant room to the university is like the writing of a novel. You can't be sure of your beginning until you have checked it with your ending. What might come of infant teachers visiting the university and professors visiting the infant room? I had two other professors in my infant room last year and they proved themselves to be not only delightfully in tune but sensitively helpful.

Yet what I believe and what I practice are not wholly the same thing. For instance, although I have reason to think that a child's occupation until seven should not be other than creative in the many mediums, nevertheless I find myself teaching some things.

With all this in mind, therefore, the intent of the infant room is the nurturing of the organic idea,
the preservation of the inner resources,
the exercise of the inner eye and
the protraction of the true personality.

I like unpredictability and variation; I like drama and I like gaiety; I like peace in the world and I like interesting people, and all this means that I like life in its organic shape and that's just what you get in an infant room where the creative vent widens. For this is where style is born in both writing and art, for art is the way you do a thing and an education based on art at once flashes out style.

The word "jalopy" made its fascinating appearance the other day. Brian wrote, "I went to town. I came back on a jalopy bus." This word stirred us. The others cross-questioned him on the character of such a bus. It turned out to mean "rackety" and although the word was picked up at once nevertheless they still ask for it to go up on the spelling list. We haven't had "jalopy" for spelling lately, Brian says. He loves spelling it, which is what I mean when I say that the drive is the children's own. It's all so merciful on a teacher.

Organic reading is not new. The Egyptian hieroglyphics were one-word sentences. Helen Keller's first word, "water," was a one-word book. Tolstoy found his way to it in his peasant school, while, out in the field of UNESCO today, it is used automatically as the only reasonable way of introducing reading to primitive people: in a famine area the teachers wouldn't think of beginning with any words other than "crop," "soil," "hunger," "manure," and the like.

Not that organic reading is exclusively necessary to the illiterate of a primitive race. True, it is indispensable in conducting a young child from one culture to another, especially in New Zealand where the Maori is obliged to make the transition at so tender an age; but actually it is universal. First words are different from first drawings only in medium, and first drawings vary from country to country. In New Zealand a boy's first drawing is anything that is mobile; trucks, trains and planes, if he lives in a populated area, and if he doesn't, it's horses. New Zealand girls, however, draw houses first wherever they live. I once made a set of first readers on these two themes. But Tongan children's first drawings are of trees, Samoan five-year-olds draw churches and Chinese draw flowers. What a fascinating story this makes!

How can anyone begin any child on any arranged book, however good the book, when you know this? And how good is any child's book, anyway, compared with the ones they write themselves? Of course, as I'm always saying, it's not the only reading; it's no more than the *first* reading. The bridge.

It's the bridge from the known to the unknown; from a native culture to a new; and, universally speaking, from the inner man out.

Organic reading is not new: first words have ever meant first wants. "Before a nation can be formed," says Voltaire,

> it is necessary that some language should be established. People must doubtless have begun by sounds, which must have expressed their first wants. . . . Idioms in the first state must have consisted of monosyllables. . . .
>
> We really find that the most ancient nations who have preserved anything of their primitive tongue still express by monosyllables the most familiar things which most immediately strike the senses. Chinese to this very hour is founded upon monosyllables.
>
> The Chaldeans for a long time engraved their observations and laws upon bricks in hieroglyphics: these were speaking

characters. . . . They therefore, at first, painted what they wanted to communicate. . . . In time they invented symbolic figures: darts represented war; an eye signified divinity.

Children have two visions, the inner and the outer. Of the two the inner vision is brighter.

I hear that in other infant rooms widespread illustration is used to introduce the reading vocabulary to a five-year-old, a vocabulary chosen by adult educationists. I use pictures, too, to introduce the reading vocabulary, but they are pictures of the inner vision and the captions are chosen by the children themselves. True, the picture of the outer, adult-chosen pictures can be meaningful and delightful to children; but it is the captions of the mind pictures that have the power and the light. For whereas the illustrations perceived by the outer eye cannot be other than interesting, the illustrations seen by the inner eye are organic, and it is the captioning of these that I call the "Key Vocabulary."

I see the mind of a five-year-old as a volcano with two vents; destructiveness and creativeness. And I see that to the extent that we widen the creative channel, we atrophy the destructive one. And it seems to me that since these words of the key vocabulary are no less than the captions of the dynamic life itself, they course out through the creative channel, making their contribution to the drying up of the destructive vent. From all of which I am constrained to see it as creative reading and to count it among the arts.

First words must mean something to a child.

First words must have intense meaning for a child. They must be part of his being.

How much hangs on the love of reading, the instinctive inclination to hold a book! *Instinctive.* That's what it must be. The reaching out for a book needs to become an organic action, which can happen at this yet formative age. Pleasant words won't do. Respectable words won't do. They must be words organically tied up, organically born from the dynamic life itself. They must be words that are already part of the child's being. "A child," reads a recent publication on the approach of the American books, "can be led to feel that Janet and John are friends." *Can be led to feel.* Why lead him to feel or try to lead him to feel that these strangers are friends? What about the passionate feeling he has already for his own friends? To me it is inorganic to overlook this step. To me it is an offense against art. I see it as an interruption in the natural expansion of life of which Erich Fromm speaks. How would New Zealand children get on if all their reading material were built from the life of African blacks? It's little enough to ask that a Maori child should begin his reading from a book of his own color and culture. This is the formative age where habits are born and established. An aversion to the written word is a habit I have seen born under my own eyes in my own infant room on occasion.

It's not beauty to abruptly halt the growth of a young mind and to overlay it with the frame of an imposed culture. There are ways of training and grafting young growth. The true conception of beauty is the shape of organic life and that is the very thing at stake in the transition from one culture to another. If this transition took place at a later age when the security of a person was already established there would not be the same need for care. But in this country it happens that the transition takes place at a tender and vulnerable age, which is the reason why we all try to work delicately.

Back to these first words. To these first books. They must be made out of the stuff of the child itself. I reach a hand into the mind of the child, bring out a handful of the stuff I find there, and use that as our first working material. Whether it is good or bad stuff, violent or placid stuff, colored or dun. To effect an unbroken beginning. And in this dynamic material, within the familiarity and security of it, the Maori finds that words have intense meaning to him, from which cannot help but arise a love of reading. For it's here, right in this first word, that the love of reading is born, and the longer his reading is organic the stronger it becomes, until by the time he arrives at the books of the new culture, he receives them as another joy rather than as a labor. I know all this because I've done it.

Out press these words, grouping themselves in their own wild order. All boys wanting words of locomotion, airplane, tractor, jet, and the girls the words of domesticity, house, Mummy, doll. Then the fear words, ghost, tiger, skellington, alligator, bulldog, wild piggy, police. The sex words, kiss, love, touch, *haka*.[2] The key words carrying their own illustrations in the mind, vivid and powerful pictures which none of us could possibly draw for them—since in the first place we can't see them and in the second because they are so alive with an organic life that the external pictorial representation of them is beyond the frontier of possibility. We can do no more than supply the captions.

Out push these words. The tendency is for them to gather force once the fears are said, but there are so many variations on character. Even more so in this span of life where personality has not yet been molded into the general New Zealand pattern by the one imposed vocabulary for all. They are more than captions. They are even more than sentences. They are whole stories at times. They are actually schematic drawing. I know because they tell them to me.

Out flow these captions. It's a lovely flowing. I see the creative channel swelling and undulating like an artery with blood pumping through. And as it settles, just like any other organic arrangement of nature it spreads out into an harmonious pattern; the fear words dominating the design, a few sex words, the person interest, and the temper of the century. Daddy, Mummy, ghost, bomb, kiss, brothers, butcher knife, goal, love, dance, cry, fight, hat, bulldog, touch, wild piggy . . . if you were a child, which vocabulary would you prefer? Your own or the one at present in the New Zealand infant rooms? Come John come. Look John look. Come and look. See the boats? The vocabulary of the English upper middle class, two-dimensional and respectable?

Out pelt these captions, these one-word accounts of the pictures within. Is it art? Is it creation? Is it reading? I know that it is integral. It is organic. And it is the most vital and the most sure reading vocabulary a child can build. It is the key that unlocks

[2] *Haka:* Maori war dance.

the mind and releases the tongue. It is the key that opens the door upon a love of reading. It is the organic foundation of a lifetime of books. It is the key that I use daily with my fives, along with the clay and the paint and amid the singing and quarreling.

It is the key whose turning preserves intact for a little longer the true personality. It is the Key Vocabulary.

The Key Vocabulary and the creative writing have shown me into every corner of a Maori five-year-old mind. I feel I know it inside out. I've got books and books written by these small brown people on the subject of themselves. Sentence-length and story-length captions of the pictures within. Not that their writings are the only evidence. Working with them every day as we do we learn their moods, their tragedies and their desires whether we wish to or not. From this soil the Maori Transitional Readers have grown. . . . It was the *temperament* of the pa that had to be got into these books. The instinctive living, the drama, the communal sympathy and the violence. Life in the pa is so often a sequence of tears, tenderness, brawls, beer, love and song. I know because I have been part of it all. In the pa tears still hold the beauty and the importance that the European has long since disclaimed.

Why is sorrow in such disgrace in infant-room reading fare? Where are the wonderful words "kiss" and "cry"? The exciting words "ghost" and "darling"? Everyday words in European homes as well as Maori ones. Kingsley's water-baby, Tom, had his despair, Alice in Wonderland found herself in tight corners, and David Copperfield had occasion enough to weep. Why then is the large part of infant-room reading so carefully and placidly two-dimensional? Is there any time of life when tears and trouble are not a part of living? I think sometimes of the children in the slums faced with these happy smooth books, and feel the same about them as I do about Maori primers. Do the word experts who assemble these books assume that by putting peaceful books into the hands of children they will be an influence for peaceful living? When I see children turning from the respectable, rhythmless stories that parents think it wisest to give them to the drama and violence of comics I think it might be the other way.

The distance between the content of their minds and the content of our reading books is nothing less than frightening. I can't believe that Janet and John never fall down and scratch a knee and run crying to Mummy. I don't know why their mother never kisses them or calls them "darling." Doesn't John ever disobey? Has the American child no fears? Does it never rain or blow in America? Why is it always fine in primer books? If these questions are naïve it must be because of the five-year-old company I keep. Heaven knows we have enough lively incident in our Maori infant rooms. The fights, the loveships, and the uppercuts from the newcomers. I see the respectable happy reading book placed like a lid upon all this—ignoring, hiding and suppressing it.

Into the text and pictures of these transitional books I have let a little of the drama through. A few of the tears. A good bit of the fears, some of the love, and an implication of the culture. From the rich soil of the Key Vocabulary and the creative writing I can do no less. Even if I did deplore dramatic living, which I don't. To me it is life complete with its third dimension and since Beethoven and Tchaikovsky see it the same way, I am this time in more august company.

Inescapably war and peace wait in an infant room; wait and vie.

True the toy shops are full of guns, boys' hands hold tanks and war planes while the blackboards, clay boards and easels burst with war play. But I'm unalarmed. My concern is the rearing of the creative disposition, for creativity in this crèche of living where people can still be changed must in the end defy, if not defeat, the capacity for destruction. Every happening in the infant room is either creative or destructive; every drawing, every shaping, every sentence and every dance goes one way or the other. For, as Erich Fromm says, "Life has an inner dynamism of its own; it tends to grow, to be expressed, to be lived. The amount of destructiveness in a child is proportionate to the amount to which the expansiveness of his life has been curtailed. Destructiveness is the outcome of the unlived life."

I believe in this as passionately as the artist in his brush and the roadman in his shovel. For every work, and first of all that of a teacher, must have its form, its design. And the design of my work is that creativity in this time of life when character can be influenced forever is the solution to the problem of war. To me it has the validity of a law of physics and all the unstatable, irrepressible emotion of beauty.

Part Three

SOMETHING ELSE: PRACTICE

The reports in this section show some of the principles of radical school reform in practice. The schools described vary greatly: freedom and relevance mean one thing to a Black child in a Boston ghetto and quite another to a farm boy in Colton, Oregon. The schools represented include private and public, elementary and secondary, urban and rural. A number are in slums and ghettos, because it is from there that are coming many of the most interesting attempts at radically different schools.

In the first group—the British Infant Schools, the Responsive Environments Laboratory, and the First Street School—the focus is on greatly enlivening the child's school experiences through a program that is flexible enough to meet his individual pace and style of learning. The environment is greatly enriched, either through diverse materials, electronic technology, or other means. At the same time, the teachers get out of the way of the youngsters' innate curiosity and energy. In the last of this group, the children's emotional lives were matters of central concern; the First Street School thereby overlaps with the second group in this section.

The schools in the second group explore the outermost limits of freedom. Here it is the child who leads the teacher, the child who, with support given only when requested, will resolve his own psychological problems, determine the best learning environment, and follow his interests only as far as he, himself, desires. Whereas teachers in the first two schools vary the program and the approach to entice the child and encourage him to learn, Neill, Drews, and Long feel that the real subject is life itself and that doing nothing is just as "productive" as actively working.

In the ghetto schools, a rich environment combined with other strategies, including creative expression in the arts and ego-strengthening study of Black culture, proves more effective than the conventional forms of "remedial" education. Especially notable here are the initiative and creativity displayed by these children when the constraints and compulsions of regular schooling are removed.

GETTING OUT OF THEIR WAY: ENVIRONMENTS FOR LEARNING

14. THE BRITISH INFANT SCHOOLS

JOSEPH FEATHERSTONE

Publicly supported primary education in Britain has changed drastically in recent years, moving toward a freedom and flexibility matched by few American schools. The classroom atmosphere of the British Infant Schools is well sketched by Joseph Feather-stone, associate editor of The New Republic.

My wife and I spent a month in England visiting classes in primary schools, talking to children and teachers. Friends told us about good things happening in British classrooms, but we were scarcely prepared for what we found; in recent decades there has been a profound and sweeping revolution in English primary education, involving new ways of thinking about how young children learn, classroom organization, the curriculum and the role of the teacher. We saw schools in some good local educational authorities: Bristol, Nottingham, Leicestershire, Oxfordshire and a few serving immigrant areas in cities like London.

Primary schools divide into "infant" and "junior" schools. Much of this report will focus on the infant schools, which take children from the age of five to seven, and in some authorities eight. (As in Israel, children begin compulsory schooling at the early age of five in England.) It is in the infant schools that people learn to read and write and to work with numbers. Junior schools take children from seven or eight to 11, when they go on to secondary school. Infant and junior schools sometimes occupy the same building, and some authorities—Oxfordshire, for example—have a policy of putting them together in one unit, like an American elementary school.

It is important to understand that what goes on in the good infant schools is much the same. The approach is similar, though the quality of teaching and children's work varies greatly.

Westfield Infant School is a one-story structure, like any of a thousand American buildings, on a working-class housing estate in Leicestershire. If you arrive early, you find a number of children already inside, reading, writing, painting, playing music, tending to pets. Teachers sift in slowly, and begin working with students. Apart from a religious assembly (required by English law) it's hard to say just when school actually begins, because there is very little organized activity for a whole class to do together. The puzzled visitor sees some small group work in mathematics ("maths") or reading, but mostly children are on their own, moving about and talking quite freely. The teacher sometimes sits at her desk, and the children flock to her for consultations, but more often she moves about the room, advising on projects, listening to children read, asking questions, giving words, talking, sometimes prodding.

The hallways, which are about the size of those in our schools, are filled with busy children, displays of paintings and graphs, a play grocery store where children use play money and learn to count, easels, tables for collections of shells and plants, workbenches on which to pound and hammer nails and boards, big wooden boxes full of building blocks.

Classrooms open out onto the playground, which is also much in use. A contingent of children is kneeling on the grass, clocking the speed of a tortoise, which they want to graph against the speeds of other pets and people. Nearby are five-year-olds, finishing an intricate, tall tower of blocks, triumphantly counting as they add the last one, "23, 24." A solitary boy is mixing powders for paint; on a large piece of paper attached to an easel, with very big strokes, he makes an ominous, stylized building that seems largely to consist of black shutters framing deep red windows. "It's the hospital where my brother is," he explains, and pulls the visitor over to the class-library corner, where a picture book discusses hospitals. He can't read it yet (he's five), but says he is trying. And he is; he can make out a number of words, some pretty hard, on different pages, and it is clear that he has been *studying* the book, because he wants badly to know about hospitals. At another end of the hall there is a quieter library nook for the whole school. Here two small boys are reading aloud; the better reader is, with indifferent grace, correcting the grateful slower boy as he stumbles over words.

The rooms are fairly noisy—more noisy than many American teachers or principals would allow—because children can talk freely. Sometimes the teacher has to ask for quiet. With as many as 40 in some classes, rooms are crowded and accidents happen. Paint spills, a tub overflows, there are recriminations. Usually the children mop up and work resumes.

The visitor is dazed by the amount and variety and fluency of the free writing produced: stories, free-verse poems, with intricate images, precise accounts of experiments in "maths" and finally, looking over a tiny little girl's shoulder, he finds: "Today we had visitors from America. . . ."

After a time, you overcome your confusion at the sheer variety of it all, and you begin making more definite observations. The physical layout of the classrooms is markedly different from ours. American teachers are coming to appreciate the importance of a flexible room, but even in good elementary schools this usually means having movable, rather than fixed, desks. In these classes there are no individual desks, and no assigned places. Around the room (which is about the size of one of ours) there are different tables for different kinds of activities: art, water and sand play, number work. (The number tables have all kinds of number lines—strips of paper with numbers marked on them in sequence on which children learn to count and reason mathematically—beads, buttons and odd things to count; weights and balances; dry and liquid measures; and a rich variety of apparatus for learning basic mathematical concepts, some of it homemade, some ready-made. The best of the commercial materials were familiar: Cuisenaire rods, the Dienes multibase material, Stern rods and attribute or logical blocks. This sort of thing is stressed much more than formal arithmetic.)

Every class has a library alcove, which is separated off by a room divider that also serves as a display shelf for books. Some library corners have a patch of carpet and an old easy chair. Every room has a "Wendy House," a play corner with dolls and furniture for playing house. Often there is a dress-up corner, too, with different kinds of cast-off adult clothes. The small children love the Wendy houses and dress-up corners, but you see older ones using them as well. Some classes have puppet theaters for putting on improvised plays with homemade puppets—although many make do with the legs of one table turned upside down on top of another for a makeshift stage. Often, small children perform dance dramas involving a lot of motion and a minimum of words.

Gradually it becomes clear how the day proceeds in one of these rooms. In many infant and some junior schools the choice of the day's routine is left completely up to the teacher, and the teacher, in turn, leaves options open to the children. Classes for young children, the visitor learns, are reaching a point in many schools where there is no real difference between one subject in the curriculum and another, or even between work and play. A school day run on these lines is called, variously, the "free day," the "integrated curriculum," or the "integrated day." The term scarcely matters.

In a school that operates with a free day, the teacher usually starts in the morning by listing the different activities available. A lot of rich material is needed, according to the teachers, but the best stuff is often homemade; and, in any case, it isn't necessary to have 30 or 40 sets of everything, because most activities are for a limited number of people. "Six children can play in the Wendy House," says a sign in one classroom. The ground rules are that they must clean up when they finish, and they mustn't bother others.

A child might spend the day on his first choice, or he might not. Many teachers confess they get nervous if everybody doesn't do some reading and writing every day; others are committed in principle to letting children choose freely. In practice, a lot of teachers give work when they think it's needed. In this, as in any other way of doing things, teachers tailor their styles to their own temperament and the kind of children they have. But the extent to which children really have a choice and really work purposefully is astonishing.

How they learn reading offers a clear example of the kind of individual learning and teaching going on in these classrooms, even in quite large ones. Reading is not particularly emphasized, and my purpose in singling it out is purely illustrative, though the contrast between English classes and most American ones, where reading is a formidable matter, is vivid and depressing.

At first it is hard to say just how they do learn reading, since there are no separate subjects. A part of the answer slowly becomes clear, and it surprises American visitors used to thinking of the teacher as the generating force of education: children learn from each other. They hang around the library corners long before they can read, handling the books, looking at pictures, trying to find words they do know, listening and watching as the teacher hears other children's reading. It is common to see nonreaders studying people as they read, and then imitating them, monkey doing what monkey sees. Nobody makes fun of their grave parodies, and for good reasons.

A very small number of schools in two or three authorities have adopted what they call "family," or "vertical," grouping, which further promotes the idea of children teaching children. In these schools, each class is a cross-section of the whole school's population, all ages mixed together. This seems particularly successful in the early school years, when newcomers are easily absorbed, and older children help teach the young ones to clean up and take first steps in reading. Family grouping needs smaller classes, teachers say, because it requires close supervision to make sure small children don't get overshadowed and big ones are still challenged. Teachers using it swear by the flexibility it provides.

Teachers use a range of reading schemes, sight reading, phonics, and so forth, whatever seems to work with a child. (Only about five per cent of English schools use the Initial Teaching Alphabet, an improved alphabet, not a method of reading, that has proved successful with poor readers and adults both in England and in this country; heads of good schools we visited thought that ITA was unnecessary with a truly flexible reading program, but that in a rigid scheme, it gave the slow reader another chance, and thus a break.)

Increasingly in the good infant schools, there are no textbooks and no class readers. There are just books, in profusion. Instead of spending their scanty book money on 40 sets of everything, wise schools have purchased different sets of reading series, as well as a great many single books, at all levels of difficulty. Teachers arrange their classroom libraries so they can direct students of different abilities to appropriate books, but in most classes a child can tackle anything he wants. As a check, cautious teachers ask them to go on their own through a graded reading series—which one doesn't matter.

However a child picks up reading, it will involve learning to write at the same time, and some write before they can read; there is an attempt to break down the mental barrier between the spoken, the written and the printed word. When a child starts school, he gets a large, unlined notebook; this is his book for free writing, and he can put what he wants in it. On his own, he may draw a picture in it with crayon or pencil, discuss the picture with the teacher, and dictate a caption to her, which she then writes down for him: "This is my Dad." He copies the caption, writing just underneath. In this way he learns to memorize the look and sound of his dictated words and phrases, until he reaches a point where, with help, he can write sentences. Often his notebook serves as his own first reading book.

He also gets a smaller notebook, his private dictionary, in which he enters words as he learns them. "I got a new word," a five-year-old brags to the visitor. Children are always running to the teacher for words, as they find they have more and more to write. Good teachers don't give in without a struggle; the children have to guess the first letter and sound the word out before they get it. Thus they pick up phonetic skills informally, although some teachers do use sight cards at the outset with their children. Gradually as a child amasses a reading and writing vocabulary, he reaches a fluent stage and you see six-year-olds writing stories, free-verse poems, accounts of things done in class, for an audience that includes other children as well as the teacher.

As a rule, teachers don't pay much attention to accuracy or neatness until a child is well on in his writing. They introduce grammar and spelling after a time, but not as separate subjects or ends in themselves: they are simply ways to say what you want better and more efficiently. Under these methods, where the children choose the content of their writing, there seems in fact to be more attention paid to content than externals, such as punctuation, spelling and grammar. In the good schools, these are presented as what they are, living ways to get a meaning across, to be understood. Even some unimaginative teachers, who quibble with children about other work, can respect the content of the free writing books and take it seriously. This emphasis on self-chosen content has produced a flowering of young children's literature in schools working with many kinds of teachers and children. There is growing recognition that different people flourish on different kinds of writing; storytellers and poets are not necessarily the same as those who can do elegant and graceful writing about mathematics. Impressive examples of free writing and poetry similar to what we saw are contained in the West Riding Education Committee's anthology, *The Excitement of Writing*. Samples of "maths" writing are included in the Schools Council's *Mathematics in the Primary Schools*, a wonderfully instructive book on many accounts. Books made and illustrated by the children are coming to be a regular part of the curriculum in some schools.

I've focused on reading, although of course children spend their time doing other things, and the teachers in the schools we saw would be annoyed at the manner in which I've singled out one academic subject. The very best often argued that art was the key. Miss Nash, the head of Sea Mills School in Bristol, said firmly that if the art is good, all else follows. All else does follow, richly, at Sea Mills, where the infants sat us down and performed a concert of skillful poetry and songs they made up on musical instruments.

But my purpose was to show not reading, but the changed role of the classroom teacher. Formal classroom teaching—the instructor standing up front, talking to the group, or even the first-grade room divided up into reading groups which the teacher listens to separately as she tries desperately to keep order—has disappeared from many infant and a number of junior schools. It has disappeared because it is inflexible, because it imposes a single pattern of learning on a whole group of children—thus forcing the schools to "track," or to group classes by ability—because it ignores the extent to which children teach each other, and because in many workaday schools other methods are working better. Ordinary teachers, trained formally, take to the new role when they can see with their own eyes that the result is not chaos.

These methods mean more work for the teacher, not less. In informal conditions, it is essential for the teacher to keep detailed and accurate accounts of what a child is learning, even though at any given moment she might not know what he's up to. Children help by keeping their own records: in some schools, they have private shelves where they store writing books, accounts of experiments and work in "maths," lists of the books they've read, and dates when they checked in with the teacher to read aloud. If American parents could ever see some of the detailed histories kept of each child's separate path, including his art work, they would feel, quite rightly, that a report card is a swindle.

When the class seldom meets as a unit, when children work independently, discipline is less of a problem. It does not disappear as a problem, but it becomes less paramount. The purposeful self-discipline of these children is, we were told, just as surprising to middle-aged Englishmen as it is to Americans. It is a recent development, and by no means the product of luck: much hard work and thought go into the arrangement of these classrooms and their rich materials. When they work at it, teachers find they can make time during the day for children who need it. "I can give all my attention to a child for five minutes, and that's worth more to him than being part of a sea of faces all day," said a teacher in an East London school overlooking the docks. Other teachers say they can watch children as they work and ask them questions; there is a better chance of finding out what children really understand.

What we saw is no statistical sample. The practices of the good schools we visited in different kinds of communities are not universal; but there are reasons for thinking that they are no longer strikingly exceptional. The schools we saw are, for the most part, staffed by ordinary teachers; they are not isolated experiments, run by cranks and geniuses. A government advisory body—the Plowden Committee—published a massive, and to American eyes, a radical report early this year, in which it indicated that about a third of England's 23,000 primary schools have been deeply influenced by the new ideas and methods, that another third are stirring under their impact, and that the remaining third are still teaching along the formal lines of British schools in the thirties, and of American schools now.

The change is most widespread and impressive in the infant schools, and becomes more scattered on the junior level. Junior schools in some authorities are playing stunning variations on the free themes developed by the infant schools; but, in general, change in the junior schools is slower; more diffident and faces more problems.

Many formal schools—English and American—are probably doing a more effective job, in conventional terms, than many of these schools. It doesn't do to dogmatize. For example, by and large, in terms of measurable achievement on conventional tests, children in traditional, formal classes in England do slightly better than children from the freer classes. (The survey is submitted by the Plowden Report.) The difference is greatest in mechanical arithmetic, and least in reading. These are facts, but there are reasons for discounting them, apart from evidence that the differences disappear in later school years. Formal schools teach children to take conventional tests; that is their function, and it would be surprising if all their efforts didn't produce some results. In view of the lack of test training in the freer schools, the students' results seem to me surprisingly high. It is perfectly clear that the mathematics taught in the informal schools—mathematical relationships in which process of thought counts for more than arithmetical skill—and the English—free writing, rather than grammar and so on—put their students at a disadvantage on achievement tests, whose authors would probably be the first to admit this. England and America badly need new kinds of tests. My own very strong impression is that in areas easy to define and probably not hard to test—ability to write, for example, or understanding of the math they were doing—the children in the good schools I saw, including slum schools, were far ahead of students in good schools in this country.

The external motions teachers go through in the schools matter less than what the teachers are and what they think. An organizational change—the free day, for example, or simply rearranging classroom space—is unlikely to make much difference unless teachers really believe that in a rich environment young children can learn a great deal by themselves and that most often their own choices reflect their needs. But when you see schools where teachers do believe in them, it is easy to share the Plowden Report's enthusiasm for informal, individual learning in the early years of school. (The Plowden Committee is in a sense the official voice of the primary school revolution.) The infant schools are a historical accident—nobody years ago gave much thought to why children should begin school at five—but British teachers are now realizing their advantages. With kindergarten and the first few years fused together, children have an extended time in which to learn to read and write and work with numbers. This is especially effective if the pattern of learning is largely individual;

if the teacher is important, but she doesn't stand in the way or try to take over the whole job. Many of the difficulties that plague formal first-grade classes disappear; children aren't kept back from learning, nor are they branded as problems if they take their time.

A few American kindergartens and Head Start classes have tried to alter the rigid rules of the game, but they are just voices in the wilderness. And the cry doesn't carry very far. An Englishman told me of a good Head Start class run on individual lines; when he peeked into the next room it was the first-grade class and there were the children, sitting in rows, all copying the letter "E."

15. THE RESPONSIVE ENVIRONMENTS LABORATORY
Omar Khayyam Moore

O. K. Moore's "talking typewriter" uses technology to create a completely free environment in which anything the child does is educationally relevant. Although it has won renown for teaching preschool children to read and write, the machine's underlying purpose is to stimulate the child to a freer style of learning. This report describes an installation which no longer exists, but the "talking typewriter" has been applied in many other classrooms in the past few years. Dr. Moore is presently Professor of Social Psychology and Senior Research Associate of the Learning Research and Development Center of the University of Pittsburgh.

For a number of years my staff and I have been conducting studies of early learning in prenursery, nursery, kindergarten, and first grades, where children are in the process of acquiring complex symbolic skills. In the course of this work I formulated the notion of a responsive environment and decided to act on the assumption that an *autotelic responsive environment* is optimal for acquiring such skills. I will now try to make clear just what this assumption means.

I have defined a *responsive environment* as one which satisfies the following conditions:

1. It permits the learner to explore freely.

2. It informs the learner immediately about the consequences of his actions.

3. It is self-pacing, i.e., events happen within the environment at a rate determined by the learner.

4. It permits the learner to make full use of his capacity for discovering relations of various kinds.

5. Its structure is such that the learner is likely to make a series of interconnected discoveries about the physical, cultural, or social world.

My colleague, Alan Anderson, and I have defined a responsive environment as *autotelic* if engaging in it is done for its own sake rather than for obtaining rewards or avoiding punishments that have no inherent connection with the activity itself.

The Responsive Environments Laboratory is located at Hamden Hall Country Day School, Hamden, Connecticut, a few yards from the Hamden Hall preschool classrooms. It consists of two adjoining prefabricated metal sheds, each 20′ x 40′, set on concrete foundations.

In Shed 1 are five portable soundproofed booths, 7′ x 7′ x 7′, arranged along two 40-foot walls, leaving a middle aisle as well as small aisles between booths for observation through windows with one-way glass. One booth has camera ports and built-in lighting equipment so that sound motion pictures can be made on a semi-automatic basis. Shed 1 also contains a conference table and two desks (one for a secretary).

Shed 2 is divided into three areas separated by natural wood partitions: a small classroom, an office conference room which also contains a booth for testing, and a bathroom. From the standpoint of construction the 16′ x 20′ classroom is an oversized booth. Like the booth, it is soundproof, air-conditioned, equipped with one-way glass, finished in natural wood (exterior) and natural wood and sound-absorbent tile (interior). Again there is provision for the making of motion pictures on a semi-automatic basis. A central two-way communication system permits the staff to speak or listen either at the main console or at the booths themselves.

With respect to the Responsive Environments Laboratory, every effort is made to maintain a setting in which "kibitzing" by parents and friends of the children is virtually impossible (there is a rule against their visiting, and the physical arrangement ensures privacy vis-à-vis the "significant persons" in the child's life).

The staff seeks to make the laboratory a child-centered milieu. Even the introduction of a child to the laboratory is done by another child rather than an adult. A child guide takes the newcomer through the laboratory (equipment is turned off—the introduction to its operation is made later). Sometimes three introductory visits are needed before a newcomer seems to be at ease—although one visit is sufficient for most children. The guide also explains some of the relevant rules: (1) that he need not come to the laboratory unless he wants to, (2) that he can leave whenever he wishes, (3) that he must leave when his time is up (thirty minutes maximum stay), (4) that he need not explain his coming or going, (5) that he go to the booth to which he is assigned for the day, (6) that if he says he wants to leave, or starts to leave, he *can* come back again the next day (but not the same day). Newcomers have the opportunity to explore every nook and corner of the laboratory. The guide watches this activity but does not interfere. After a while newcomers seem to feel satisfied that they have seen everything and are ready to leave.

It should be obvious that the role of the guide requires the ability to communicate clearly and to exercise self-restraint. The task of being a guide is assigned to gifted children; this is but one of many special tasks which they are given.

The laboratory staff is carefully instructed about treating the children. The import of the rules is that we want children to initiate activities. The staff is to respond to them rather than to teach them. Those who are in daily interaction with the children are not permitted to see the background information gathered by the project's professional staff; for example, the operating personnel do not know I.Q. test scores. Operating personnel are randomly assigned to booths every day. (There are two kinds of booths, automated and nonautomated. In nonautomated booths an adult is with the child. Since these adults do not teach, we prefer to call them "booth assistants." . . .)

The Hamden Hall children leave their classrooms (nursery, kindergarten, and first-grade) to come to the laboratory every school day. When it is a child's turn to come, his classroom teacher lets him know. He then either accepts or rejects his turn for the day. If he decides to come he takes his "pass" and goes by himself the few yards to the laboratory, where he is checked in and goes to the booth assistant to whom he has been assigned. One of the most remarkable things about this environment is that, day in and day out, children elect to come to it—sometimes several months go by without one child of the current group (which numbers sixty) refusing his turn. However, it frequently happens that a child does not want to leave when his time is up—in which case he is gently picked up and told that another child is waiting.

From what has been said it should be clear that the adults the child encounters in the laboratory are *not* the significant adults in his life—they are *not* his mother, father, grandmother, etc. Those significant adults who ordinarily are in the best position to reward or punish him have no way of knowing how he spends his time in the laboratory on a day-to-day basis. It is therefore unlike Little League baseball, with relatives and friends observing from the sidelines; the laboratory time represents thirty minutes *away from* the significant persons in his life. . . .

I should like to make it clear (once and for all, I might add) that the Responsive Environments Laboratory is *not* just a place where children learn to read: approximately equal emphasis is given to speaking, writing, listening, and reading. . . .

Speaking and writing are active processes and listening and reading are passive ones. An attempt is made to tie each of these four activities (or passivities) to the others, not only maintaining a balance between active and passive processes, but also avoiding the pitfalls of underemphasizing or overemphasizing any one of them at the expense of the others. . . .

In order to determine whether such overall abilities are developing and, at the same time, to facilitate their development, it is necessary to set some task for the children which involves all four of the processes. There are many jobs which would do the work. The one which was chosen as a part of the laboratory curriculum was publishing a newspaper. The first-grade class publishes its own newspaper (there are also contributions by nursery and kindergarten children), and the four processes (speaking, writing, listening, and reading) are subordinate to the superordinate skill of *publishing a newspaper*. A child may begin a newspaper story by speaking into a microphone; later, he will type his own story from dictation—this means that he goes directly from the spoken word to the written word. After he has completed his transcription he may then read it critically before turning it over to one of the other children who is an editor. The editor first proofreads the copy, perhaps reading it aloud to a fellow editor, and then the suggested changes are discussed with the author. Then the children type it on stencils along with other stories. Finally, they mimeograph, collate, staple, and distribute the paper. If they wish to discuss the newspaper in their regular classroom, they may do so (with their teacher's permission). It is also permissible to take the newspaper home, where it is sometimes subject to further discussion.

It can be seen, then, that publishing a paper, as the children do it, is an achievement which embraces speaking, writing, listening, and reading. This activity provides guide lines on the basis of which the children set standards for spelling, punctuation, intelligibility, general relevance, and interest. The emergence of such a higher-order skill helps give to reading and writing the same kind of direction and meaning that listening and speaking have by virtue of their ordinary social uses.

Publishing a newspaper is an activity which ordinarily would be beyond the ability of a first-grade class. Permitting the children themselves to set the standards for the newspaper seems like a risky educational practice; however, here again is another vital role for gifted children to play. They are capable of serving as editors and coordinating the efforts of the other children, which allows them to make extensive use of their intellectual abilities within the social context of their peer group.

By the time the laboratory children are able to publish a newspaper the subordinate skills have been learned well enough so that the *learning* problem has been replaced by the *practicing* problem. There are many intrinsic rewards and punishments associated with turning out a newspaper. To be sure, when the proud parents get copies there may be additional extrinsic rewards and punishments—but by this time it is too late for anyone to interfere with the learning of the subordinate skills.

The actual work of turning out the newspaper is done under the supervision of a teacher, who introduces the children to the equipment (copy aid, mimeograph, thermofax, etc.) and guides their first efforts. This takes place within [a] small classroom in the laboratory. . . . This classroom is called the "transfer room." What this name connotes is the *transfer* of skills acquired individually within the privacy of the booths to social activities. Just as we make explicit provision for the introduction of children to the laboratory with the help of gifted child guides, we also make explicit provision for relating laboratory activities to outside interests through the help of our more precocious children who serve as editors. The children are very proud of their newspaper—everyone contributes in his own way and, most importantly, it really is *theirs*. . . .

Phase 1. Free Exploration

Let us turn our attention now to the interior of a booth and imagine that a child, already introduced to the laboratory in the manner previously explained, is ready for his first booth session. For convenience of exposition pretend that he is to begin learning in an automated booth. The booth assistant helps him get into the elevated chair (because some children do not like to sit in a *high chair,* in the laboratory we call it an "elevated chair"), turns one switch, tells the child to enjoy himself and to raise his hand if he wants anything. Without further comment the assistant leaves the booth, closes the booth door, and then goes to a control panel mounted on the exterior wall of the booth, presses appropriate buttons, and begins to watch the child through a one-way window located just below the control panel.

The child is alone in the booth confronted with what may appear to him to be a typewriter with colored keys. (Prior to entering the booth his fingernails have been painted with non-toxic water colors. There is a match between the nail colors and the colored typewriter keys so that striking keys with matching fingers constitutes correct fingering. Also, there is a noticeable difference in pressure between the left-hand and the right-hand keys to help the child orient his hands. Behind the keyboard is a lucite housing which permits him to see everything in front of him, but which keeps his fingers out of the moving parts of the typewriter.) Whether or not he believes that the object in front of him is some kind of typewriter, as a matter of fact he is in charge of much more than an electric typewriter—he is at the controls of a computer in-put and read-out device, three distinct memory systems, an audio-recording system, and two visual exhibition systems, all of which are integrated by a central electronic logic and control system. Nevertheless, the operation of this complex instrument is under his management.

Of course, not all of the abilities of the instrument are needed for the child's first session. The booth assistant has set the instrument, which is called the Edison Responsive Environment

(E.R.E.), in what is called Phase 1, Free Exploration, i.e., the instrument is set so that the child can explore the keyboard freely. Whenever a key is struck, E.R.E. types the letter (in large type) and pronounces the name of the character that has been typed. (The "reaction time" of E.R.E. to a key operation averages one-tenth of a second.) When a key has been depressed and released no key can be operated for about one second—this gives E.R.E. time to pronounce the name of the character. No two keys can be depressed simultaneously—this makes it impossible to jam or to garble pronunciations. The moment any given pronunciation is completed, the keyboard is automatically unlocked so that the child can go on exploring. The keyboard of E.R.E. is, essentially, a full, standard one. Because the standard keyboard has both upper and lower cases, and the young child probably does not know this, there are small lights next to the upper- and lower-case keys to show which case is operative. If the child were to play by himself with an ordinary typewriter he might get "stuck" at the end of a line because he does not know about the carriage return. E.R.E. automatically returns the carriage at the end of a line even though there is a carriage-return key whose function the child will catch on to sooner or later. His exploration will not be interrupted by using up a sheet of paper—E.R.E. has a fan-folded tape of paper several thousand feet long. It should also be mentioned that E.R.E. is rugged—it withstands the pounding it sometimes receives.

Returning to the hypothetical child, the intriguing question is: What will he do when he is alone at the keyboard of the "talking typewriter"? Until he strikes the first key he does not even know that the typewriter talks. One thing we can say with near certainty about our hypothetical child is that he will not sit there for a half an hour simply looking at the instrument. Only one child out of the 102 children I have studied sat for as long as ten minutes before striking a key. Most children begin immediately using fingers, fists, elbows, and an occasional nose—if the instrument were not jam-proof, the game would be halted in less than a minute, or if the keyboard were not locked during pronunciations, E.R.E. would babble. There are children who proceed in a very thoughtful way; looking, listening, repeating what the instrument says, reflecting—in brief, they explore systematically. Some notice at once the relation between their colored fingernails and the colored keys and painstakingly match fingers to keys. If, at first, a finger is wayward, they use their other hand to guide it. Some children go on exploring for their full thirty minutes; others raise their hands and want to leave after a few minutes.

In order to guess what our hypothetical child is likely to do, it would be necessary to posit a great deal more about him. I will make one overall comment based on my experience with the laboratory children—he will like his first session, and he will want to return to play with this fascinating "toy."

A daily record is kept of each child's performance in the laboratory. Some parts of this cumulative record are quite objective—E.R.E., for example, keeps track of the time the child spends in the booth and his stroke count, i.e., the number of times he depresses keys. Other aspects of the record are less objective—for instance, booth assistants' notes about a child's attitude. There is a daily staff conference at which each child's performance is reviewed. It is the laboratory supervisor's responsibility to decide when a child is beginning to lose interest in any given phase of the curriculum. There are children who will go on happily in Phase 1, Free Exploration, for a number of weeks, whereas others' interest in this phase declines rapidly after as few as two sessions. Sooner or later every child's interest in Phase 1 will wane (at least every child the laboratory has encountered behaved this way), and before his interest completely disappears, he must be shifted to the next phase. If a child were permitted to completely exhaust his interest, he might very well not return to the laboratory. Quite clearly, the decision as to when to shift a child from one phase to another still is a matter of experience and judgment. In the early days of this research I had to make this decision. Later I trained supervisors who now are fully capable of performing this task. For the most part, the more objective indicators of declining interest are a sufficient basis for judgment—for example, a child's sessions become markedly shorter and his stroke count drops off. Sometimes a child will simply say that he is tired of what he is doing—his opinion counts! As a general rule, it is safer to err on the side of shifting the child too soon. It will be made clear below that explicit provision is made for regressing from advanced phases to more elementary ones, and since no significant persons in his life are there to see this regression, there is little stigma attached to it. All the children whom I have studied have regressed from time to time. The children call Phase 1 (Free Exploration) "plain typing." It is not unusual for even a gifted child to say with a little laugh, "Today I just want to plain type."

Phase 2. Search and Match

When the laboratory supervisor makes the decision to shift a child from Phase 1 to the next phase, the learner receives no warning—he has to discover for himself that he is playing a new game with new rules. Phase 2 is called Search and Match.

In this phase, unlike Phase 1, E.R.E. takes the initiative in starting the game. All typewriter characters appear in the rectangular exhibitor window one at a time in random order. When a character appears with the red arrow pointing to it. E.R.E. automatically locks the keyboard, with the exception of the appropriate matching key, and pronounces the name of the character. If the child wants to get a response from E.R.E., he must find the right key. As soon as he strikes the matching key which causes the character to be typed, E.R.E. repronounces the character and then covers it up before exposing a new one. The game becomes a little more difficult when the new character is in a different case—under this circumstance, E.R.E. first says "upper case" or "lower case" (as the case may be), the appropriate case light flickers, and the keyboard must be changed to the proper case (when this is done it repronounces it) before the matching character is named by E.R.E. and can be struck by the child. It should be mentioned that if a child is fast enough at pressing the appropriate key, he can cause E.R.E. to speed up by omitting redundant pronunciations. If a child's attention has wandered so that he missed the first pronunciation, or if he has forgotten it, there is a repeat cycle which the booth assistant can start, using a delay appropriate for the given child. A dial can be set which will delay E.R.E.'s repronunciation in order to give the child a chance to speak first. E.R.E. is not restricted to pronouncing the names of characters—it also can give phonetic values for them (or, for the linguistic purist, hints as to phonetic values).

What has just been described is the simplest version of Phase 2, Search and Match. As interest wanes in this first version of Phase 2, the booth assistant (following the laboratory supervisor's instructions) can make the game more challenging in many ways. For example, the assistant can cause (by pushing buttons or setting dials) E.R.E. to omit its first pronunciation of characters, or the second, or both. The window display can be changed to show characters cumulatively, one line at a time, or four lines at a time. A blank card can be used in the window so that the match is solely between pronunciations and keys.

I have found that adults, as well as children, like to play with E.R.E. in both Phase 1, Free Exploration, and the various versions of Phase 2, Search and Match. These activities are especially interesting to adults when E.R.E. is switched to a foreign language—one unfamiliar to the players. Of course, for children who are learning to read, the written form of English is a new language. Both children and adults discover that they always can succeed in finding the appropriate key in Search and Match by the simple-minded expedient of trying each key. This is a tedious and boring way to go at it on a continuing basis; both children and adults prefer to learn the characters.

Phase 3. Word Construction

When a child has eliminated nearly all of the "search" from the Search and Match game, it is time to shift to a new phase of the curriculum. Phase 3 is called Word Construction. There are two forms of this game. One form leads to reading, the other to writing, i.e., writing in the sense of composing original stories. We will designate the former as "WC-R" (Word Construction-Reading) and the latter as "WC-W" (Word Construction-Writing). When a child has been shifted to Phase 3 he alternates in his booth sessions between these two forms of the game. Let us take up WC-R first.

Phase 3. WC-R. Up to this point, the child has been dealing exclusively with the building blocks, or primitive elements, of the written language (notice that punctuation marks have not been neglected)—he has been exposed to and can discriminate among the basic set of elements from which all meaningful written expressions are formed. He is in a position to begin to get some sense of the formation rules of the written language. Now other of E.R.E.'s abilities can be brought into play.

Imagine that a child who has become quick at finding individual characters is confronted without notice with several of them at a time, isolated either by a margin and a space or by spaces. For instance, the first letters might be *b-a-r-n*. So, the child types *b-a-r-n*. E.R.E. pronounces these letters before and after each is struck and then, following the pronunciation of *n*, it calls for a space. A light flickers just under the space bar, and after the bar is pressed, E.R.E. says, "Space, *b-a-r-n*, barn." E.R.E. may also exhibit a barn on the projector. . . .

From the standpoint of planning the curriculum, WC-R offers an indefinitely large number of choices with respect to the selection of a beginning or basic vocabulary. The question is: What words should come first? There are a great many plausible criteria which have been offered by reading experts, linguists, and others who have concerned themselves with this topic. For example, (1) word frequency, (2) letter frequency, (3) pronounceableness, (4) word length, (5) familiarity, (6) stimulus similarity, (7) grapheme-phoneme correspondence, etc. . . .

For my own part, faced with the problem of selection, I preferred a direct solution, namely, to choose those words which are constituents of interesting stories—that is, stories which have proved to be intriguing to children and adults over a long period of time, for example, *Aesop's Fables*. Many children can be expected to have lost interest in WC-R long before they have mastered a vocabulary large enough to enable them to read a wide variety of stories. Therefore, it is essential to be able to shift them to at least some stories, and they can do this only if they have mastered enough of the words to get started reading them. If the stories are of some intellectual and aesthetic value, it is highly probable that the words out of which they are composed will offer a sufficient basis for making sound inferences about the relations between letters and sets of letters, on the one hand, and appropriate verbalizations, on the other.

Phase 3. WC-W. The form of the Word Construction game explained above is somewhat arbitrary from a child's standpoint. The experimenter has decided, in advance, what is good for him. It is especially important, from the point of view of sustaining children's interest, to let them take the initiative. It is also important to see to it that at times there is an almost perfect correspondence between their verbal skills and the written symbols with which they will be dealing. WC-W serves these purposes. The first step in this activity is to have the child go to the Transfer Room (the small classroom described earlier) where he is encouraged to talk—he may talk about anything he pleases—and everything that he says is recorded. Later, an analysis is made of his utterances and a list is compiled consisting of those words which are constituents of coherent statements on some topic in which he was engrossed. Sometimes it has taken weeks with a child to elicit such material. The next step is to program this word list in E.R.E. (E.R.E. is easily programed—it is not necessary to translate material into a machine language; hence, there are no technical difficulties to get in the way.) The child is virtually certain to find some of his own words meaningful.

An alternative version of WC-W involves the use of a standard recording-reproducing unit attached to E.R.E. or to an electric typewriter. This version does not require programing. The child simply talks into a microphone and then takes his own dictation, word by word. In this version of the game, he responds to his own voice. Interestingly enough, from a social-psychological perspective, some children reject their own voice, but will type other children's dictation. Some three-year-olds have learned to be very skillful in taking dictation.

Phase 4. Reading and Writing

Anyone who has followed children's progress from Free Exploration to Search and Match and on through Word Construction easily can see that the shift to Phase 4 comes very naturally. E.R.E. is at its best here. It can read a sentence, a paragraph, or tell a story before or after a child types, while at the same time it can continue to respond to individual characters and words. In sum, it can deal with higher-order units while exercising all of the abilities previously described with reference to the earlier learning sequences.

E.R.E., of course, can ask questions, just as teachers do. The questions may pertain to what is visually exhibited in the rectangular window or on the projection screen. The questions may call for subtle interpretations. Answers can either be typed out or expressed verbally on E.R.E.'s own recording-reproducing unit.

The material programed for E.R.E. can be as banal as the dullest courses in school or it can be as stimulating as the best of new programs, for example, some in modern mathematics or science. (It should be noted that E.R.E. can handle many aspects of mathematics and of science programs—numbers and some arithmetic symbols are on the keyboard.)

When children go to first grade, having reached Phase 4 both in reading and in composing original stories, a new curriculum is needed. Most of the things which ordinarily are taught in first grade lie far behind them. (In 1962 at the end of first grade, the Hamden Hall Country Day School children who had been in the program at least two years, read, on the average, according to the Metropolitan Achievement Test, at the beginning sixth-grade level. Their competence in composing original stories can be judged by examining their newspaper. For second grade they again will require a totally new curriculum.) The half-hour a day the children can spend in the laboratory is certainly not a substitute for the rest of the school day. Fortunately, at Hamden Hall there has been strong administrative support for curriculum revision. However, an adequate curriculum is not the whole answer either—competent teachers are equally necessary. Teachers find that they have independent students on their hands—students who are accustomed to solving problems on their own or in cooperation with their peers.

Handwriting

One of the five booths is reserved for learning to write by hand. The writing equipment in this booth is primitive—it consists of a lined blackboard, chalk, and eraser. On a random basis children spend about one-tenth of their time in this booth after they have completed Phase 1. I assumed that after children had been exposed to the characters on the typewriter they would begin to reproduce them manually if they had the opportunity. Children begin by scribbling or drawing pictures on the board, but it would appear that some would go on doing this indefinitely if they were not subtly guided by a patient booth assistant. The difficulty lies in the fact that the environment is not sufficiently responsive. (Automated equipment could be devised for facilitating the development of this skill.)

The children are exposed to cursive or manuscript writing, as opposed to printing, through the use of typewriters with cursive type. This serves to familiarize them with this form of writing. Even two- and three-year-olds, including retarded children, can learn to print and write in the cursive style.

At present, four of the five laboratory booths are nonautomated; thus there is a human instructor with the child on an average of four sessions out of five. . . . It is not known whether children would continue to come to the laboratory on a daily basis over a long period of time if they were interacting with automated equipment only. Even if they were able to go through all phases on automated equipment this might produce undesirable psychological or social-psychological side effects. No one knows now the optimal mixture of automated and nonautomated equipment. It is reasonably certain, however, that a one to four mix will work—at least it has worked with the children who have come to the laboratory.

One of the interesting consequences of having a fully automated booth has been its effect on assistants. Before such equipment was available, it was difficult to explain to new personnel what was expected of them. Also, some of them apparently did not believe that children would work out problems for themselves—so they tended to be too *helpful*. . . . Like E.R.E., well-trained booth assistants do not intrude. In my opinion, in too many situations in everyday life adults rush to the aid of children, thus depriving them of the opportunity of making discoveries and consequently undermining their confidence in their own resourcefulness.

CHILDREN IN A RESPONSIVE ENVIRONMENT

Before a child enters the laboratory for his introductory session quite a bit is known about him. Each child is given a general physical examination, an eye examination, and a hearing test. A speech evaluation is made, with special attention paid to a child's ability to produce utterances in conformity with the phonemic structure of the language. A clinical psychologist obtains a developmental history from the mother and gives the child an intelligence test as well as projective tests. A sociological analysis is made of the family in terms of socio-economic variables. . . .

A daily record is kept of each child's behavior in the laboratory, and the child is examined periodically to determine his level of skill.

Let us now consider a child who has gone through the phases presented in the preceding section.

Billy

Billy's mother enrolled him in an integrated public school kindergarten when he was five years old. After a few weeks his teacher reported to her supervisor that he was unable to follow directions and that he disrupted the classroom—for instance, he rolled on the tables and stubbornly refused to move. Nothing was done about her complaints until a month later when she delivered an ultimatum—"Either Billy goes or I go." At this point the school psychologist was called in and Billy was given a

Stanford-Binet intelligence test with the result that he was classi-fied as an educable retardate with an I.Q. of 65. It was recom-mended that he be placed in a nursery group for the mentally retarded. The mother, a former special-class student herself, was irate about this recommendation—she caused so much difficulty over it that the school, in self-defense, sent Billy to an outside expert, who confirmed the prior evaluation. (This second exami-nation was slightly more hopeful in that it placed him on the borderline between the educable retardate and the dull normal.) With great reluctance, Billy's mother acquiesced to his removal from public school at mid-term and to his placement in a nursery group for educable retardates.

When Billy was six years old, he came to the laboratory under the auspices of a state agency. The laboratory's initial evaluation of Billy's intelligence (I.Q. 72) agreed with the more promising of the two prior reports. However, it was obvious at once that there were at least two sides to Billy in terms of his ability to get along with adults; for example, the examiner commented, "In the testing situation, Billy was a pleasant child, friendly and respon-sive and anxious to please." This judgment says something about both Billy and the examiner. This examiner is very skillful in establishing rapport with children, and it is a difficult child indeed who does not respond positively to her.

So we have Billy, age six, already out of the mainstream of education. He either could not or would not take directions: what is more, he was willing and able to cause disturbances.

Billy, a light-colored Negro, is always neatly dressed. His appearance is normal, but his physical movements are somewhat clumsy, although he has an alert manner. He always has been in excellent health; his vision and hearing are normal. However, his speech was very difficult to understand, even at six; the speech evaluation showed, for instance, that he omitted most final consonants. Also, there were many repetitions and hesitations in his speech, and his mother said that he, unlike her other children, did not talk until he was four. Billy had not done a very good job of mastering his native tongue—he had not developed the requi-site verbal skills to express his needs or interests.

The eight members of Billy's family share five rooms in a low-income row house—a reasonably large living room (with a record player and a monstrous TV set), a large kitchen, and three bedrooms. There are three older boys in their middle teens and Billy and his younger brother and sister, ages five and four. The family is crowded, but the apartment is spotless and tastefully decorated. There is a large bookcase nearly full of books, topped by a complete set of supermarket encyclopedias. At present, the family is wholly self-supporting, though off and on in the past it has been on welfare. Billy's father, a small, meek, self-effacing person, is an unskilled day laborer who generally works in construction. A social worker, who has known the family for years, classifies the whole family as dull normal.

Billy's mother is the dominant figure around whom everything turns—she is a heavy-handed, strict disciplinarian who can wither her husband and children with a glance. In or out of the family she is a formidable woman who is articulate about her ambitions for her children, but she lacks knowledge about how to advance them. She had hoped that the older boys would be able to go to college, but their academic records are so poor (she is forcing them to stay in school) that the guidance counselor has told her that college is out of the question. Though the older children are disappointing to her—she still has great hopes for her two youngest children, who are developing more rapidly than any of the others did—Billy is the only child who has her worried. He was later than the others in standing, walking, talking, and toilet training—toilet training must be a nightmare for Billy, because, as his mother says, "Whenever he goes in his pants, I whack him in front of everybody." (Billy still has accidents quite frequently.) The other members of the family are very fond of Billy, baby him, and try to cover up his many mistakes before they are discovered by his mother. His mother says that Billy is not dumb, he is "stubborn and lazy." When Billy does something that really pleases her, she picks him up and enfolds him in her enormous arms while smothering him with kisses.

Billy's introductory session was calm—he quietly followed the guide around. He could not be drawn into conversation. Once in a while he smiled and in general was wide-eyed. In his second introductory session he explored some on his own but spent most of the time holding the guide's hand. By the end of this session he was becoming curious about the equipment and seemed quite relaxed, and so he was scheduled for the automated booth the following day. The third day he came in—noisy and confident— he permitted the booth assistant to help him into the elevated chair, he watched her leave, and then turned his attention immediately to the keyboard. What happened next is best described as an attack upon the instrument. In thirty minutes he typed 1,302 characters. The booth assistant had to turn off the instrument and lead him out of the booth when his time was up. For the next nine sessions he continued to "machine gun" the instrument at a gradually slowing pace. In his eleventh session there was a sharp drop in strokes. The booth assistant wrote, "He seems to be getting interested in looking at what he has typed." The laboratory supervisor shifted him from Phase 1, Free Exploration, to Phase 2, Search and Match. Billy was startled and angry. He put up his hand over and over to call the booth assistant in—he evidently thought the instrument was broken and that the assistant would not fix it. All previous sessions had lasted thirty minutes, but Billy stopped this one after nine minutes. He had made five matches by accident (he had not come up with a way of systematically trying all keys). The laboratory supervisor switched him back to Phase 1 for his next session, and he was very pleased, although he proceeded more cautiously than he had before—looking, listening, and occasionally repeating what was said. After another five days his time dropped to fifteen minutes and the supervisor again switched him to Phase 2 for the following session.

This time he was calmer about the change. After five minutes he was pressing every key with his thumb. He clapped his hands when he made a match. At the end of this thirty-minute session he said he wanted to take the "typewriter" home. For the next sixty days he played Search and Match in its increasingly difficult versions. There seemed to be no diminution in his interest. This was the game for Billy. He made it more complex for himself by shutting his eyes while finding keys, by "dive bombing" the keyboard, by first using one hand and then the other. He was still not using the color coding of fingers to keys, however. The supervisor switched him to Phase 3, Word Construction, R and W, even though his interest had not waned. He could find the characters to make words but he did not want the words—he told the instrument to "shut up." His time dropped down to three minutes after five days. He was shifted back to Phase 2. In WC-W he had been nearly mute—he kept mumbling something about, "It's not broken." Billy continued in Phase 2 for another thirty days, still eager and interested. His refusal to go on to words was perplexing because by this time he was very expert at finding all characters and was using the color-coding system. Also, he had learned to print all the characters in the handwriting booth.

An interviewer was sent to Billy's home to find out if something unusual was going on there. His mother said that she had caught Billy "playing with himself," and that she had whipped him and told him he would hurt himself. This made it much clearer what Billy was mumbling about. In WC-W the assistant pointed to his penis when he said, "It's not broken." She said the word "penis" and spelled it. It was put on the dictation equipment for him in a nonautomated booth. He typed the word "penis" twelve times with manifest enjoyment. In his next WC-W storytelling session he said, among other things, "When my dad took the prayers away, my mother got sick and died." The constituent words of this story were made into a word list for the next WC-W typing session. Billy liked these words and now was willing to accept word lists in WC-R.

Billy was shifted to Phase 4 in his 130th session. At the end of his laboratory experience (172 sessions) he was reading pre-primer and beginning first-grade stories, he could print nicely, and he could type five words a minute with correct fingering on the automated equipment. His typing was comparable to that exhibited by other children classifiable as educable retardates.

When Billy was transferred from public school to the nursery for educable retardates at mid-year, he established a satisfactory relation with the skillful teacher in charge of this group. However, he would not accept her assistant. The end-of-the-term report stated, "When he is helped or scolded by the assistant he becomes very belligerent and disrespectful." Billy began his laboratory sessions in late spring while still in this nursery class. Public school officials were invited to watch Billy in his booth sessions. They were so impressed by his good manners and by his ability to concentrate that arrangements were made to re-admit him to public school kindergarten in the fall. Given this second chance he managed to get on with his new teacher, and at the end of the year she passed him to first grade.

Billy entered first grade with 172 laboratory sessions behind him as well as with the benefits of a constructive experience in the nursery group and kindergarten. The laboratory, of course, was interested in following his progress even though he was no longer in its program.

Billy was placed in a "combined" first grade—this is, a class with a reading-readiness group and a first-grade group. He was assigned to the latter section on the basis of a reading-readiness test. His teacher wrote,

> When we began our work, Billy was ahead of the other children. He could write and recognize his numbers to 10 and count up to 29. He knows his colors, alphabet, and his knowledge of phonics is very good in that he knows the sounds of each isolated consonant and can tell with what various words begin. What he needs now is to develop his comprehension not only in reading words but in picture interpretation. As you know, to get the idea of a story in the pre-primers and primers, the child should understand the picture. Billy's reasoning and associations are ofttimes far-fetched. I must ask him many questions before he gets the point of the picture. He finds it hard to follow directions, but he will ask many questions in order to get the direction correct. There are now children who have caught up to Billy but he still has an edge on them because he has a better background and the work I am doing now is not completely new to him. The proof of the pudding must wait until I begin to teach in completely new areas, for example, addition and subtraction.

Billy finished first grade successfully and will be in second grade next year—he did have trouble with arithmetic.

Billy was retested by the laboratory at the end of first grade. His I.Q. score is now 79. The appraisal of his speech placed him in the normal range with respect to the making of phonemic discriminations in speech production—the repetitions and hesitations have disappeared. Billy now can express his needs and interests verbally in a much more adequate way and, as his teacher mentioned, he is able to ask many questions in order to understand directions. One year of first grade did not improve Billy's reading significantly—for all practical purposes, he was held back, though his skill at picture interpretation undoubtedly improved. It is my overall impression that Billy is still a vulnerable dependent child who will rebel if he is not skillfully handled. A second year in the laboratory would have afforded him a good deal of protection—it would have been especially helpful if his introduction to arithmetic could have been carried out within the context of a responsive environment.

Billy's family is proud of him, and now they let him work more things out for himself. His mother feels completely vindicated—all the psychologists, social workers, and teachers were wrong—Billy is not dumb, he is simply a "stubborn and lazy" child who needs a good whack.

It was the purpose of this paper to describe an autotelic responsive environment which facilitates the learning of complex symbolic skills. It was suggested initially that no one aspect of the environment should be thought of as constituting its essence. In part it is a mechanical system; in part it is a social system; and in part it is a cultural system. All of these parts are constituents of the total system—all of them must be taken into account if the laboratory is to be understood. The task of designing optimal environments for learning is in its infancy, and the theoretical problems of understanding what is going on in the laboratory are staggering. One would have to be very insensitive to its research possibilities not to imagine quickly a hundred and one experiments that could be carried out within it which might increase our understanding of human beings.

16. THE FIRST STREET SCHOOL
GEORGE DENNISON

How can the ideals of freedom and autonomy be preserved in a city school with culturally diversified students? The First Street School, described by George Dennison, writer and teacher, pointed the way.

The First Street School was founded in 1964 by Mabel Chrystie, on the lower east side (or East Village), handling twenty-three children, mostly under ten years of age. The school was conceived of more or less as an antidote to the dehumanization of the public school system. Where the latter is huge, impersonal, and bureaucratic, the First Street School is small and informal and is oriented entirely toward the personalities of the students, the teachers, and the parents. Administration is handled directly by the teachers, who in all respects are absolutely free agents. This arrangement not only produces a high teacher morale but has proven to be marvelously economical: the cost per pupil, in classes of seven and eight, compares favorably to that of the public schools with classes of thirty. The school's choice of facilities is also an important factor in economy of operation. We leased classrooms, a playroom, a gymnasium, an art room, and a woodworking shop at the Emanu-El Midtown YMHA on East Sixth Street. The Y itself had been lying idle during school hours. There are many such facilities in New York, and it is worth mentioning that nothing is needed to start a school but space, teachers, and students. Financing is a variable thing. First Street is very much in need of funds, but this is partly because one of the aims of the school was to bring quality education and experimental methods into an area which has seen very little of either. This means that almost all the children have been granted full-tuition scholarships. The school has survived so far on a loan made available by a private donor. We have been accredited by the New York City Board of Education and were granted a provisional charter by the New York State Board of Regents. Racially the school is integrated in exactly the way that the neighborhood is: about one third Negro, one third Puerto Rican, and one third "white." Some of the families are college-educated, though most are not. The children range from slow-normal to bright. Several of them came to us with learning problems. I would like to say a few words now about the philosophy of the school and its methods, and then describe the results we have achieved so far.

I

From the point of view of standard education, the First Street School is radical and experimental. There are no grades, no graded report cards, no competitive examinations. No child is compelled to study or answer questions when he does not want to. The children are free to consult each other, examine each other's work, leave the room, leave the school building itself, talk to each other and to the teachers at will. Several rules have been established by the students themselves meeting as a parliament (a parliament in which some very fine distinctions have been drawn by tots of six), and the parliamentary method is used frequently to decide upon outings and special activities. These are not common practices, even in private schools. Readers who are familiar with the writings of A. S. Neill, however, will have heard of this in a more radical form than we are able to ex-emplify at First Street. And perhaps from their point of view we are running a relatively conventional school. The differences are not so much ideological, however, as immediate functions of personalities and of the exigencies of operating a day school in New York. But let me give an example here, since only an example from life is capable of introducing the kind of irony that really obtains.

We believe—with Neill and many others—that going to school should be entirely voluntary; and that young boys, from say nine through twelve, should have access to school as to a clubhouse, but should ideally spend their time roving about the city, observing, helping, annoying, adventuring—whatever they wish. Last year we had a group of five such boys. All five had been chronic truants and vandals in the public schools, and in varying degrees all five were on the route to Youth House. Now the ideological convictions of the teachers indicated that these boys should be given a great deal of freedom; and we felt compromised because we did not actually *want* them to go venturing, first because they would be fair game for truant officers, and second because we, in case of injury, would be fair game for lawsuits. But in fact the issue never came up. These chronic truants came to school devotedly and never once suggested a venturesome outing among themselves. After a few months we decided to risk our misgivings. The school had been donated bicycles. Each boy was given one, and each boy was given money for lunch: and then with a great deal of encouragement, they were turned loose. Rather, we tried to turn them loose. The fact is, they would not go. And we came to realize that for these particular boys—who had been characterized by the violence of the fearful—there was nothing in the city quite as attractive or as supportive as their own school. I do not say this to praise the school (it would be a foolish kind of praise, since school at best is only school) but to indicate the extreme needs and dependencies of these boys, not one of whom had developed the kind of independence normal to a boy of twelve. All the idealized hopes and practical misgivings of the teachers had been beside the point. It did not matter what our *policy* was regarding freedom—we were obliged to answer the needs of these particular boys. And as a result of doing just that, we have come to see that we do not exemplify policies at all. Some children are given great freedom (i.e. will accept it and use it), others are treated more strictly (i.e. demand the kind of firm guidance characteristic of very early childhood). Obviously there is a policy of sorts behind all this, an ideal of ego-growth and of supportive, broadly therapeutic responsibilities on the part of the teachers. But we have never spelled this policy out and see no need to. To the best of our ability we meet every child on his own terms. But conversely, the children must meet the teachers on *their terms*. There could be no reality of encounter if this were not the case. And in fact one of the familiar sights of the school is that of a six-year-old with his hands on his hips arguing heatedly with a teacher who towers over him. No child can be given more freedom than this—or can be given it only at the risk of entering an unreal environment in which teachers are not persons but are merely exemplifications of some desirable utopia. It follows, of course, that all but everything depends upon the choosing of the staff. But this is always the case. Ideals, in the abstract, count for very little. Much as we admire Neill—and I think we do not disagree with him on anything—we have made no effort to recruit teachers from his disciples, who all too often use his ideas as metaphoric expressions of their own needs. We have gone to great pains, however, to find teachers of ability, and of personal warmth and kindliness, bearing in mind always that the child's desire to learn is nothing less than his total attraction to the world and that therefore teachers who are vividly *in* the world in their own right are the best persons for the children to associate with. There are considerable differences, then, from classroom to classroom. One room will be relatively orderly, relatively quiet, another relatively noisy and messy. This is the way it should be. Given the general agreement that coercion is pointless, competitive learning a violation of nature, and bureaucratic manipulation the high road, or low road, to slavishness, there is no need to unify the techniques of the various teachers. And since the students, the teachers, and the parents are all in close contact and make their opinions known, there is no possibility of incompetence going unnoticed.

The students are divided into three classes, and each class "belongs" to a particular teacher, though there are frequent regroupings for special activities like dance instruction, music, gym, and so forth. Age, of course, is the chief criterion in the forming of classes, but other factors play a part. One little girl, for instance, a bright and boisterous Jewish-Italian girl of eight, wanted to spend time both with the younger children of five and six and with the children in the eight-to-ten-year group. It was extremely beneficial for her to do this, since she was precocious and capable but also suffered many unresolved problems of early childhood. She behaved quite differently in the two groups, tending to be cooperative and affectionate among the younger children and disruptive among the older. She obviously needed both, and we ourselves could not have devised anything better than the arrangement she brought about simply by expressing her own desires. The self-corrective, health-seeking powers of the young are enormous, and wherever possible we have tried to follow the clues given us by the children. Vincente, a diminutive, panicky, intelligent Puerto Rican of nine, was torn between wanting to be an infant and wanting to be one of the boys. It was essential to him that he identify with the older boys, and so this was the group he "belonged" to, but we allowed him to join the younger children pretty much at will—again, with great benefit to himself, not only because of his association with the children (who were his true peers in an important way), but because of the relationship he established with their teacher, who was a woman, whereas the teacher of the boys was a man. In his home life Vincente was not only without a father but was alienated from his half-brothers and sisters because he was the child of a love-affair—for which reason, also, his mother alternately pampered and denied him. . . .

What I would really like to convey—though it is almost impossible—is the simplicity and downright homeliness of the real events: Vincente's wrinkled forehead straightening out as he comes to understand some vital little fact; the teachers laughing at the witticisms of the children; one child intently studying the behavior of another and thereby learning an entire process the teacher had been powerless to teach him. We are so flooded these days by the elaborate formulations of Experts that we have lost sight of the underlying simplicity of things, such as, for instance, that school is not *primarily* the relation of teachers and students, but of adults and children, and of course of children and children. The very phrase "natural powers" is enough to bring a skeptical look into (especially) sophisticated faces, though these same powers, once they are described in the jargon of academic psychology (they are presently the objects of vast inquiry) will be fully accepted by our sophisticates, who will now believe, however, that they have been invented by the Experts. . . .

On the basis of what is known about learning at this very moment, vast, vast improvements in the lives of our young could be achieved immediately simply by applying available monies toward the alleviation of conditions already recognized as critical. But the mandarins of the universities speak the language of the bureaucracy. Furthermore, they staff the foundations. They have claimed the money for themselves—and we are being treated to the sickening spectacle of "more research" in the teeth of an avalanche of remediable catastrophes.

I would like to give some examples of what I mean by *improvement,* and then later show that the methods involved are quite simple and the amounts of money very modest. The one really necessary thing is to pay attention to the *big* problems by which children are beset. You cannot bypass these central issues and expect to accomplish much simply by improving the internal structure of the curriculum. In his *Aims of Education* Whitehead raises the question of whether any subject can be considered difficult in itself. The most difficult process, he points out, is the one that children accomplish without instruction, namely learning to talk. In my own experience I have found it to be invariably true that if a child is having difficulty learning, it is because something is impeding the natural activity of his faculties. This something is frequently the teacher himself, the teacher's methods, the school itself; usually it is all these things plus emotional dilemmas originating outside the school. And yet it is not really difficult to alter these circumstances. At the First Street School we have done *no remedial teaching as such,* and yet some very striking improvements have occurred. And it is not as if we were a staff of extraordinarily dedicated teachers. We are not. I am sure that the same methods, in other hands, would yield results as good or better.

Here are some comments that were solicited from teachers and parents to be included in a fund-raising brochure.

A Twelve Year Old Girl

TEACHER: This child from a Spanish-speaking home entered the school generally doing first grade work. She spoke adequate "school English" but did not know the vocabulary for common household objects. Her school failure had given her a resentful conviction that she was "stupid." Actually she was quite intelligent. She used to settle all disputes with her fists, steal, and wantonly destroy property. When she transferred to a public school in the Bronx, after a year and a half, she could be trusted with large sums of money, showed respect for other people's possessions, and had stopped trying to beat everybody up. During the year and a half that she was with us, she progressed to advanced fourth grade work in all subjects. Her English vocabulary had increased a hundredfold and she was expressing a desire to go to college.

MOTHER (Does not speak English): The teacher used to make her do things she didn't want to. She was scared and didn't do anything.

A Six Year Old Girl

TEACHER: She was silent and frightened when she came to school. She jumped when she was spoken to, ran to the teacher when approached by other children, and was unable to express any of her own wishes and choices. Now, six months later, she plays with other children, makes her opinions known, and talks animatedly. I think her progress has been the most spectacular I've ever seen in a child over a short period.

A Twelve Year Old Boy

TEACHER: He comes from a Spanish-speaking home. He came to school at the age of eleven—from the fourth grade in public school—and could read only twenty words in English, though he spoke it fairly well. He was so inured to failure that he seemed to have no conception of the experience of learning. It was as if he believed that other people simply knew things and he did not. The greatest discovery he made at school was that by talking, listening, looking, trying, and especially by failing and trying again, he could actually acquire new skills and knowledge. His personality changed a great deal—from a kind of stupid belligerence to amiability and even eagerness. At the end of the first year he was still terribly behind his age level, but he no longer failed at the things he attempted. During the last two months he went through a year and a half in the graded reading. . . .

The kinds of changes referred to in these comments—changes in learning, in performance, and in personality—were not brought about by particular methods of instruction (many different methods have been used) but by granting the children the consideration due them as persons, by giving them free access to each other, and by removing irrational, that is to say bureaucratic, demands, so that the day's activities could be modified by the energies and interests of the persons involved. In order to give a concrete notion of what this means, I would like to quote from the journal I kept while I was teaching at the school last year.

II

At regular times during the week, special instructors come to the school to conduct classes in music, dance, and singing. The following excerpt from my journal refers to one of these occasions.

Barney, the folk-singer, came today with his guitar and autoharp. It was a marvelous session and the best demonstration possible of what the freedom in the school is really all about. He came at the end of the lunch period . . . and lunch itself was

unusually pleasant today, the usual roaming around and shouting, everyone sitting where they liked and changing seats often,
sometimes to sit by favorite teachers and sometimes to sit by
friends and sometimes to sit alone. Ramon and Maxine are up on
their feet every two minutes, doing dance steps—or Ramon
expanding his chest and making like a wrestler, Maxine flaunting
herself. . . .

After most of the food was consumed, everyone became very
noisy and active. Ramon began juggling with apples, and Maxine
tried first to imitate him and then to interfere with him. The
teachers were all just trying to relax, i.e., there was never any
pressing reason to interfere with the growing pandemonium.
Which is to say that no one was becoming hysterical or being
injured. And all that noise, when you really listen to it, turns out
to be a boiling mixture of very specific meanings and relations.
Timmy steals Marilyn's lunchbox. Marilyn yells for it, but is also
pleased. Timmy inveigles Ramon into helping him hide it—and
the two boys rush from the room, followed by Marilyn. Now
there is a great squabbling in the hall. Marilyn can't find it.
Timmy comes skipping into the room, whizzes past me, flicks my
hair with his hand, and with a beaming face shouts the one word,
"Cooperation!" Maxine runs about among the boys, shouting and
pushing—but her reign as sex queen has been ended by Marilyn,
who didn't even try to end it—and Maxine gives up the boys for
a while and goes to sit beside her friend Donna, the sweet-
natured charmer of six. Then Maxine takes Donna out into the
hall, and now almost all the children are in the hall or running
from room to room, and the shouting has reached a tremendous
pitch—at which point Barney arrives . . . and that great volume
of energy, without losing its head of steam, modulates into a
series of shouts—"Barney is here! Barney is here!"—and several
of the kids, especially the young ones, come back into the room
and cluster around him. The other kids are still howling in the
hall. One of the teachers tells them it's time for singing, and
comes into the room herself. Barney is greeting all the children
and forming the chairs into a circle. The howling continues in the
hall. Ramon runs into the room, runs out again. Marilyn runs in,

gets interested and stays. Suddenly the howling is all over and everyone is sitting in a great circle, swinging their legs and chattering, some of them doubling up in the chairs and leaning against each other (the little girls, especially, and Nora, who mothers them with real affection). Barney asks several of the children which verses they would like to sing of the *Michael* song. Maxine has the verses on the tip of her tongue and immediately jumps into the center of the circle and flaunting herself Twist style shouts out the verses so loud that no one can hear what Barney is saying. The corners of her lips are turned up and she keeps one eye cocked on Barney. So Barney is forced to concentrate on Maxine for a while. But several of the children join in on Barney's side: "Come on, Maxine! Hey Maxine! Shut up, Maxine!" And so the verses are parceled out. Barney strums the guitar. The children are smiling and wiggling and swinging their legs against the chairs. Ramon jumps up and does a dance step and sits down again. Dodie is supposed to sing the first verse, but she is bashful—and while she sits there blushing, Maxine hollers out the verse and jumps into the center of the ring. Dodie's big smile turns into a frown. Now she refuses absolutely to sing the verse. But it's time for the chorus anyway and everyone knows the words and sings them with marvelous full-throated voices, retaining all the zest of their scampering and squabbling in the hallway. When Maxine is invited now to stand in the center and sing her own verse, she suddenly becomes bashful. But she leans against the desk and sings it and everyone listens. Then the thunderous chorus again—and the song goes straight through with the greatest animation and pleasure. When it's over, Maxine asks Barney to play *Glory, Glory Hallelujah,* adding, "It's a very sad song." "That's funny," says Barney, "the one I know is not sad." "Oh yes," says Maxine, and she begins to howl "Gloooooory glooooooory hallelujah . . ." just as it might be howled at the Volunteers of America. Barney accompanies her and soon all the kids join in. Now Maxine has become inspired. She jumps into the center of the ring and cracks everybody up by her stylization. She puts her hand on her hip, looks utterly bored, and in the dry, abrupt voice of a stock clerk reading an inventory, speaks the words "Glory . . . glory . . ."—then jumping up and down like a maniac yells "Hallelujah!" Then abruptly bored again—"Glory . . . glory . . ."—and jumping wildly again, "Hallelujah!" The teachers, especially, are howling with laughter. When this is over, Jenny, who is ten, thoughtful and quiet, tells Barney she knows a song. Barney asks her what it is . . . and Dodie says she knows it too. Barney asks them to sing it together. But Dodie is sitting all the way across the room and is too bashful to walk through the center of the circle. So Ramon yells, "You have to bring her!"—and he goes over and pushes her chair across the room, Dodie grinning and blushing and enjoying the ride. So Barney plays and Jenny and Dodie, in timid voices, sing the song. Here again, everyone listens. Now comes a Catalan folk song with lots of hand gestures—the sea, the mountains, the sun, the bull, the wineskin—with a shouted chorus of *Olé!* Everyone makes the gestures and roars the *Olé!* with gusto. Becho, an eleven year old Puerto Rican, instead of making the big circle to indicate *sun,* makes the gesture of a woman's curves and grins at Ramon. Donna has come running across the room and is sitting in my lap. Whenever *toro,* the bull, is named in the song and everyone makes horns, Donna, holding her fingers at her head, charges all the way across the circle and gores Barney very gently in the knee, then runs back smiling to sit in my lap until the word *toro* is shouted again. This song has a dancing rhythm and Maxine leaps into the center and makes up a kind of folk dance, throwing her legs out and hopping. The next song is Spanish, a real dance song, and suddenly Ramon, Becho, and Nora are out in the center dancing a graceful approximation of the Hat Dance, their hands behind their backs and their bodies swaying with the music. Several of the children join them, and since the floor is crowded with dancers now, Barney swings into a lively Twist number and everyone changes to the Twist. Ramon and Timmy are both very good at it and they pair off and do some fancy steps. A couple of the teachers have joined the dancing. Even little Donna is doing the Twist, which she varies from time to time by putting her fingers at her head and charging into me. Betsy is carried out of her usual reserve and does a few fancy steps (leaving out all the simple ones). She goes around in a circle with one arm held high and loose. Dodie, too, is carried away. She executes a step and tries to end it with a full-extension split on the floor. She gets stuck in the split and stays there a few moments looking around with a long face. Then she gets up and tries it again. Everyone is dancing, Barney singing and strumming. Timmy and Ramon look happier than I have ever seen them, and Nora, who very frequently is joyous, looks joyous, twisting and whirling in her big Christmas boots. Only Alberto has been unable to participate. He leaves the room for extended intervals. A teacher goes with him and they play in the gym.

After the dancing, the older children gather around Barney and he gives each one a little lesson on the guitar, one or two chords, and a little lesson on the auto-harp. Ramon and Becho are especially interested, pay close attention and put themselves into it. . . .

Readers who have worked with children under the institutionalized conditions of the ordinary school will realize at once what inferences can be drawn from this description of the folksinging. I would like to go the other way for a moment and use these little examples of behavior to clarify some of the principles we have been following. There are three things I would like to comment on, first, the effect of the children on each other; second, the orderly structures which emerge more or less spontaneously from what appears to be chaos; and third, the relation between unhampered movement and learning.

Maxine, who comes from a Jewish-Italian family, was brought to First Street because she was in trouble at the public school and was falling behind in her work. Some visitors who saw her when she arrived and then saw her again a year and a half later, were amazed at the change that had come over her, and naturally they asked us what we had done. To an important extent the question should have been addressed to the other children, though their answers would have been infinitely complicated, since their treatment of Maxine varied subtly with the changes in her treatment of them. This interchange can be accomplished only by the forbearance of the teachers, not by their guidance, though this sort of thing is hard to state as a rule, since the teachers are by no means passive. Nor can "judicious forbearance" be defined without examples. When Maxine stole Dodie's soda pop, she was not immediately reprimanded by a teacher, but by Dodie, to whom the soda pop belonged and who had a right to be angry. Similarly, when Maxine took Nora's cookies, it was Nora who chastised her, not a teacher. No one interfered with Nora, even when she was kicking Maxine. Certainly it takes an experienced, or at least an observant, teacher to know where to draw the line so as to prevent injury. But this case was similar to almost every case that I have seen: the children themselves, even when angry, are subtly responsible toward each other with regard both to inflicting pain and to the justice of their own actions. They are more accepting of each other, and are more forgiving than adults can ever hope to be. They distinguish between the person and his actions more accurately and generously. They do not reject their antagonists out of hand, but exert a steadily civilizing influence upon each other, the more so since in the simplicity of their wants and pleasures there is always an evident rationality, a manifest relation of cause and effect. Maxine was basically a robust person, yet in certain ways she was fearful and resentful, and was therefore aggressive. She needed to know the true limits in all of her relationships—both with children and adults—and by acquiring this knowledge she obtained a security she could trust. This security would have been unobtainable if we had obscured those relationships by enforcing a uniform discipline "from above." Most important, Maxine would have been deprived of all that multiform give and take with her peers—the simple anger which is so much more instructive than teachers' homilies, and the forgiveness and acceptance which are so much brighter inducements to sociability than adult rewards for "good behavior."

It is worth mentioning, in connection with this question of the children's effect upon each other, that where few children will take it on trust that they *should* be interested in what their elders place before them, *every* child is affected by the interests shown by another child. By interests and by abilities. Ramon, who was a poor reader, was a good dancer. No one asked him to dance. He danced because he loved it. No one asked the bashful children to brave their embarrassment and try to dance. They were impressed by Ramon, and so they jumped up and tried to dance. Similarly, they listened when Jenny, whose memory was good, sang verses they themselves had not yet learned.

All of this leads directly into the question of order—into what might be called the internal sources of order. (There are external sources, too, and we use them, though in a minimal way—there are no bells, no supervisors, no punishments, no threats.)

The day is alternately noisy and quiet. How do those quiet periods come about? The question is somewhat misleading, for the truth is that the noise is not chaos, it possesses the same elements that are observable during a period of calm when the children are bent over their books or are talking with their teachers. What seems like chaos is nothing but a multiplicity of actions, each one of which is highly rational and purposive. As much as the children enjoy these wild, sometimes merry, sometimes conflictive episodes, there is a built-in principle of transformation-into-calm. This principle is simply the fact that all creatures tend toward the completion of purposive actions, and progress from less defined toward more defined situational structures. The noisy periods are not the opposites of the quiet ones, but are the background out of which the quiet ones emerge. When this cycle is given its natural place in the routine of the school, the children tend to bring the vividness of their noisy play into the quiet of the more simply structured "lessons" (those too are social exchanges). The calm is not the oppressive silence of the disciplined classroom, but the electric ease of organic order.

Which brings me to the third thing that I wanted to mention, the relation between unhampered movement and the process of learning. Those folk-song sessions were so lively and enjoyable that I myself was unaware of them as teaching/learning episodes. I tended to be more impressed by the happiness I saw on the faces which had come to us looking so worried. It was not until the end of the year that I discovered how much the children had learned. We were all driving back from a picnic in the bus, and the children began to sing. They went through song after song, verse after verse, absolutely flawlessly. I was touched and surprised—and I was embarrassed, too, for when I tried to join them I discovered that they had learned far more than I, though I had been exposed to the very same songs.

III

I have been talking about the learning and behavioral advantages of freedom. I would like to give an example now—a game period in the gym with the ten to twelve year old boys—of the moral effect of non-intervention.

My presence in the gymnasium was not that of a supervisor, teacher, or coach. I held sweaters, stayed in the background, became nothing more than the authentication of the *place*, i.e., I could be relied upon to keep people out. This sounds like almost nothing, as indeed it was, but if one calls to mind the ordinary conditions of a boy's life in New York, not only at school, but on the streets, in the playgrounds, and at home, these little interludes of protected freedom will sound more like the rare occasions they really were. This will be all the more evident if it is borne in mind that four out of the six boys belonged to self-protective gangs, which tend to be as stifling as the organizations imposed by adults. Too, the non-intervention of an observant adult has a powerful effect on children who are used to prohibitions and supervision. It is not merely that they feel free to do and express things otherwise inhibited, but that they sense, quite directly, that the moral reality has been shifted from the person of authority into the situation as a whole, of which they themselves are the most important parts. Let me make this clear by describing their behavior, since it may sound like a large claim. I would like to make clear, too, that non-intervention is a very active kind of collaboration.

The boys are playing dodgeball. One of them repeatedly breaks the rule about stepping over the center line. That is, he *sort of* observes the rule by anchoring one foot on the boundary line, but then when he throws the ball he allows the other foot to come a full stride into enemy territory. His opponents have been complaining and yelling, and now they lose patience. They know they are in the right, but they are afraid of being punched by the rule-breaker, who is also a bully. And so they appeal to me to arbitrate. "He keeps steppin' over the line!" This is quite true, and I nod. "Well it's against the rules, man!" Again I nod. "Well tell 'im to quit it, man!" I shake my head and shrug, conveying pretty clearly, "It's your affair, not mine." And so the boy who is angriest, the best player on the losing side, cries, "Shit, man, I quit!" and starts to walk off the court. The bully runs up to him with a raised fist and says, "You gonna quit, huh? Well I'm gonna break your ass." The other cringes, but stands his ground to the extent of saying, "I don't care, man." The bully is glaring at him, and he, mopingly, is staring at the bully. They are not only sizing each other up, but they are weighing the situation with great nicety and one can almost see the relevant wishes and fears in their faces. Both boys want to keep playing. The game was exciting—otherwise the argument would not have arisen. The rivalry was intense—otherwise the cheating would not have been so blatant, so much a deliberate insult. The bully knows very well that he cannot force the other boy to play. Even if his threats are successful, the boy will play half-heartedly, and the bully, who is a good thrower, is especially dependent on this boy, who is a good dodger. And so the bully sees his own pleasure in the game evaporating. He knows too that if he beats him up the whole game will be destroyed, partly because the excitement of competition really does depend on prior agreements and a fight would destroy the agreements, and partly because the loser's teammates, though they are not fond of him, will be forced to show their loyalty, not only to a teammate but to a fellow Puerto Rican, and they will certainly walk out. All of this is more or less visible on the quite intelligent face of the bully. And so after narrowing his eyes and sticking out his chin silently for a while, he punches him on the arm. The other boy mumbles, "Fuck you" and walks off the court. He hesitates a moment, and then leaves the gym. His teammates yell to him to come back, and then they curse him, and then they yell, "Throw the ball, man! We can beat you anyway!"—though they had been losing from the beginning. And so the game goes on, but it is woefully lacking in excitement. The bully's teammate, who is also his buddy, says nothing to him, but it is evident by his silence that his pleasure has been spoiled; and though the bully blusters and yells, as if the game were still at its peak, his face is wooden. The ball flies back and forth. The losing side is put out too quickly. The next round commences. The boy who walked out appears in the doorway and watches. One of his teammates yells, "Shit, man, come *on!*" He shakes his head and mumbles, "No, man." And then the bully's teammate yells, "Come on, Becho, he won't cheat no more!" And the bully, who is holding the ball, yells, "That's right, chicken! Come on, chicken!" and hurls the ball at him. The boy catches the ball and hurls it back. The bully catches it, and screaming, "Come on, chicken, come on, chicken!" charges up to the line and hurls the ball at him. This time the boy dodges the ball—but he dodges onto the field of play, and immediately one of his teammates cups his hands at his mouth and yells at the bully, "Come on, chicken, quawk, quawk, quawk" and in a moment the game is in full swing and all three Puerto Ricans, who are masters of derision, are flaunting themselves as targets and are yelling in unison through their cupped hands, "Quawk, quawk, quawk, quawk." The bully is grinning. He charges up to the line again—not stepping over—and yells, "Buncha fuckin' chickens over there"—and hurls the ball. The boy who had walked out dodges the ball, puts his hand at his groin and yells, "Yeah, man . . . you want a worm!" Once again the game is merry, obscene, and intense. And this time there is no cheating. It is worth mentioning, too, that the boys left the gym as one gang, talking back and forth.

Now what was their sense of me, their teacher? I had refused to arbitrate their quarrel—and by this very act I had put myself into relation with everything that transpired. Everything, in effect, was sanctioned—the cheating, the walking away—everything. But then what was I collaborating with? It seems to me that the boys were aware, each one—not conceptually, but with immediate intuition—that I was collaborating with his own attempt to make a workable union of egocentric and social needs, a union which is not possible when either of the two kinds is slighted. Each boy was able to experience the *necessary relation* between his own excitement and the code of conduct which joined him to others in a social group, and his sensing of this introduced a moral element into his play, for at bottom this is what morality is: the necessity of the relation between conduct and individual fulfillment. It is the indwelling of the *all* in the *one*—in the end a biological demand. When this relation ceases to be a necessary one, "right action" is no longer demonstrably good—and we are in the familiar quandary of empty forms, bankrupt laws, etc. Games and play, not only among children but adults as well, could not be so lovely and exciting if they did not refer our standards of conduct backward toward their deeper biological and passional bases. . . .

It can be stated axiomatically that whenever a child has trouble with reading, it is invariably a symptom of some deeper problem in his life. It is never "a reading problem." The reason for this lies simply in the fact that the written word is an extension of speech.

Certainly the ability to read is founded on the acquisition of certain skills, but these are such (Tolstoy points this out repeatedly) that one child can teach another and it need take no longer than six or eight weeks. True reading begins as soon as the child can read the words aloud with appropriate animation, which is nothing but the music of ordinary speech. At this point the child will have made a kinesthetic identification with the written words. Even when he reads them silently he will begin to experience the totality of eyes, throat, and ears, for though the sense data are visual he will to some extent be "saying" the words and "hearing" them. At this point there will be no doubt in his mind that the written words are a form of speech. He will find in the act of reading the same properties that he finds in other social acts: challenge, response, growth, gratification, etc. If one wanted to destroy this inherent organic integrity, one could do no better than adopt the techniques ordinarily used to teach reading: 1) proceed as if it were merely a skill, 2) create artificial

separations between reading and speech. Let me make clear
what I mean.

At the age of seven, shortly after arriving in this country,
Ramon was able to read Spanish. At the age of twelve he could
read neither English nor Spanish. The social *life* of reading had
been destroyed for him.

A boy who can read will say, with regard to the printed words,
"This is talk, like all talk. The words are yours and mine. To see
them is to hear them. To understand them is to possess them. To
possess them is to use them. To use them is to belong ever more
deeply to the life of the world." Ramon, staring at the printed
page, his forehead lumpy, his lip thrust out resentfully—anger,
neurotic stupidity, and shame written all over him—seemed to be
saying, "This belongs to the school teachers, not to me. It is not
speech, but a task. I am not meant to possess it, but to perform it
and be graded. And anyway, it belongs to the Americans, who
kick me around and don't want me getting deeper in their lives.
Why should I let them see me fail? I'll quit at the very beginning." And—to make matters worse—at the same time that these
thoughts were tormenting him, he remembered quite clearly
reading the postcards from his father at the age of seven—a little
fact he refused to divulge to me until I had thoroughly won his
confidence. Our problem with Ramon, then, was to create a
situation in which reading might once again assume its true
nature as an extension of speech. . . . We used no books until
the end of the year—at which time, in two months, Ramon went
through a year and a half in the "graded readers." He was still
woefully behind the other boys his age—but he no longer failed
in everything he attempted; and in fact was no longer blankly
terrified of failure.

I am afraid that I have given a sketchy and unbalanced picture
of the school. While Ramon, for instance, was years behind in his
work, other children were impressively ahead. Yet from class to
class, certain things remain constant, and perhaps they can be
glimpsed in the episodes I have described. They are chiefly
these: honesty and directness in relationships; the absence of
academic rivalry; the proprietary feeling of the children ("It's *our*

school"); the abundance of individual attention; the importance given to ordinary conversation, which is always the primary way in which a child communicates and enlarges his sense of the world; the cheerfulness, the noise, the quiet.

There is much else that I would like to talk about—that the children do not "dress up" for school, but wear their play clothes, an important consideration in poor families, since it is no light matter to get paint on a dress-up dress, or tear it playing hide-and-seek—the children are a raggedy bunch, and are all the livelier and freer because of it; that the day does not begin with a bell, but with a sociable milling around, teachers and children talking of the night's events, a courteous and desirable way to launch another six-hour episode together. . . .

Rather than give more details of this kind, however, I would like to simply stress the fact that the rapid spurts in learning, and the great changes in personality and happiness were not dependent on teaching equipment, elaborate methods of instruction, or an imposing architectural facade. All that is needed is a little space, good teachers, and abundant consideration for the children. These don't cost much money. They don't require more research. They are available all over the city of New York.

FOLLOWING THEIR LEAD: EXPLORING THE LIMITS OF FREEDOM

17. SUMMERHILL:

REPORT OF THE
BRITISH GOVERNMENT INSPECTORS*

Summerhill, the most famous experimental school in the world, was founded in the year 1921. This report is the best objective description of its theory and practice.

MINISTRY OF EDUCATION
CURZON STREET
LONDON, W. I.   IND: 38B/6/8.

This School is famous throughout the world as one in which educational experiment is conducted on revolutionary lines and

---

* MINISTRY OF EDUCATION: *Report by H.M. Inspectors on the Summerhill School, Leiston, Suffolk East, inspected on 20th and 21st June, 1949*

NOTES

1. This Report is confidential and may not be published save by the express direction of the School. If published it must be published in its entirety.
2. The Copyright of the Report is vested in the Controller of H. M.

in which the published theories of its Head Master, widely known and discussed, are put into practice. The task of inspecting it proved to be exacting and interesting, exacting because of the wide difference in practice between this School and others with which the inspectors were familiar, and interesting because of the opportunity offered of trying to assess, and not merely to observe, the value of the education given.

All the children in the School are boarders and the annual fee is £120. In spite of the low salaries paid to the staff, which will be referred to later, the Head Master finds it difficult to run the School at this figure which he is reluctant to increase in view of what he knows about the financial circumstances of the parents. Although the fee is low, compared with that at many independent boarding schools and the staffing ratio is high, the inspectors were a little surprised at the financial difficulties of which the Head Master complained. Only a close scrutiny of accounts and expenses could show whether costs could be cut without loss and it might be a good plan to invite such a scrutiny from some independent and experienced source. In the meantime it may be said that whatever else is deficient, the children are well and plentifully fed.

The principles upon which the School is conducted are well known to the readers of the Head Master's books. Some have gained wide acceptance since they were first declared, some are exerting a widening influence in schools generally while others are regarded with suspicion and abhorrence by the majority of teachers and parents. While the inspectors tried to follow their normal custom of assessing what is being done in an objective manner, it appears to them impossible to report fairly on the School without some reference to its principles and aims, whether they accept them personally or not.

The main principle upon which the School is run is freedom. This freedom is not quite unqualified. There is a number of laws concerned with safety of life and limb made by the children but approved by the Head Master only if they are sufficiently stringent. Children, for instance, cannot bathe except in the presence of two members of the staff who are lifesavers. The younger children cannot go out of the school grounds without the escort of older ones. These, and similar regulations, are categorical, and transgressors are punished by a system of fines. But the degree of freedom allowed to the children is very much greater than the inspectors had seen in any other school, and the freedom is real. No child, for instance, is obliged to attend any lessons. As will be revealed later, the majority do attend for the most part regularly, but one pupil was actually at this School for 13 years without once attending a lesson and is now an expert toolmaker and precision instrument maker. This extreme case is mentioned to show that the freedom given to children is genuine and is not withdrawn as soon as its results become awkward. The School, however, is not run on anarchist principles. Laws are made by a school parliament which meets regularly under the chairmanship of a child and is attended by any staff and child who wish. This assembly has unlimited power of discussion and apparently fairly wide ones of legislation. On one occasion it discussed the dismissal of a teacher, showing, it is understood, excellent judgment in its opinions. But such an event is rare, and normally the parliament is concerned with the day-to-day problems of living in a community.

The inspectors were able to attend a session on the first day of the inspection. The principal matters under discussion were the enforcement of the bedtime regulations made by the parliament and the control of entry into the kitchen at unauthorized times. These problems were discussed with great vigor and freedom of comment, in a reasonably orderly fashion and without respect of persons. Although it seemed that a good deal of time was spent on some rather fruitless lines of argument, the Inspectors were disposed to agree with the Head Master that the experience of learning how to organize their own affairs was more valuable to the children than the time lost.

It is evident that the majority of parents and teachers would be most hesitant to grant complete freedom in the matter of sex. Many who would agree with the Head Master up to a point would part company with him there. They would, perhaps, have no difficulty in accepting his view that sex knowledge should be freely given, that sex should be separated from guilt and that many long-accepted inhibitions have done infinite harm, but they would, in a mixed school, take more precautions than he does. It is, obviously, exceedingly difficult to comment fairly upon the results of not doing so. In any community of adolescents sexual feelings must be present and they will certainly not be removed by being surrounded by taboos. They are, in fact, likely to be inflamed. At the same time, as the Head Master agrees, complete freedom to express them is not possible even if it is desirable. All that can safely be said here is that it would be difficult to find a more natural, open-faced, unself-conscious collection of boys and girls, and disasters which some might have expected to occur have not occurred in all the twenty-eight years of the School's existence.

One other highly controversial matter must be mentioned here, the absence of any kind of religious life or instruction. There is no ban on religion, and if the school parliament decided to introduce it, it would presumably be introduced. Similarly, if an individual wanted it, nothing would be done to hinder him. The children all come from families which do not accept ortho-dox Christian doctrines, and in fact no desire for religion has ever been expressed. Without doing any violence to the term it may safely be said that many Christian principles are put into practice in this School and that there is much in it of which any Christian can approve. The effects of the complete absence of religious instruction could obviously not be judged in a two days' in-spection.

It seemed necessary to write this introductory account of the School before proceeding to the more usual material of a report.

It is against this background of real freedom that the organization and activities of the School must be viewed.

ORGANIZATION

There are 70 children between the ages of 4 and 16. They live in four separate buildings which will be described in the section on premises. In this section their education in the narrower sense of the word will be described. There are six Forms organized very loosely according to age but with considerable weighting according to ability. These Forms meet according to a quite ordinary and orthodox timetable of five 40-minute periods on five mornings a week. They have definite places of meeting and definite teachers to teach them. Where they differ from similar Forms in ordinary schools is that there is not the slightest guarantee that everyone, or indeed anyone, will turn up. The inspectors were at much pains to discover what in fact happened, both by attending classes and by inquiry. It appears that attendance increases in regularity as the children grow older and that once a child has decided to attend a particular class he usually does so regularly. It was much more difficult to discover whether the balance of work and subjects was a good one. As many of the children take the School Certificate, their choice is controlled by examination requirements as the examination approaches; but the younger ones are completely free to choose. On the whole the results of this system are unimpressive. It is true that the children work with a will and an interest that is most refreshing, but their achievements are rather meager. This is not, in the inspectors' opinion, an inevitable result of the system, but rather of the system working badly. Among its causes appears to be:

1. The lack of a good teacher of juniors who can supervise and integrate their work and activities.

2. The quality of the teaching generally. The teaching of infants is, as far as could be judged, enlightened and effective and there is some good teaching in the upper Forms, but the lack of a

good junior teacher who can inspire and stimulate the 8, 9 and 10 year olds is most apparent. Some surprisingly old-fashioned and formal methods are in use, and when the children reach the age at which they are ready for advanced work they suffer from considerable disadvantages and present their teachers with severe problems. The teaching of the older children is a good deal better and in one or two cases really good.

3. The children lacked guidance. It is commendable that a fifteen-year-old girl should decide that she would like to learn French and German, two languages that she had previously neglected, but to allow her to attempt this task in two periods for German and three for French a week is surely a little irresponsible. The child's progress was slow in spite of her admirable determination and she ought to have been allowed much more time. It appears to the inspectors that some kind of tutorial system might be developed to assist children in planning their work.

4. Lack of privacy. "Summerhill is a difficult place in which to study." The words are the Head Master's. It is a hive of activity and there is much to capture the attention and interest. No child has a room to himself and there are no rooms specifically set apart for quiet study. A determined person could no doubt always find somewhere, but the necessary degree of determination is rare. Few children remain in the School beyond the age of 16 though there is nothing to prevent them. There are and have been some extremely able and intelligent children at Summerhill and it must be doubted whether, academically, it is giving them all that they need.

At the same time there is some excellent work done wherever the quality of the teaching is good. The Art is outstanding. It was difficult to detect any significant difference between the painting of Summerhill children and that of children from many much more traditional schools, but by any standard the work was good. Some good craft work in great variety was to be seen. The installation of a kiln was going on during the inspection and the pots awaiting first firing were excellent in form. The provision of a treadle-loom would allow another craft which has made promising beginnings to develop.

A good deal of creative written work is done, including a Wall Newspaper, and plays which are written and acted every term. A good deal was heard of these plays, but it is apparently not customary to preserve the scripts so it was not possible to judge of their quality. Recently a performance of *Macbeth* was given in the small School theater, all the sets and dresses being home-made. It was interesting to learn that this was decided upon by the children against the wishes of the Head Master who prefers them to act plays of their own writing.

Physical Education is carried on in accordance with the prin-ciples of the School. There are no compulsory games or physical training. Football, cricket, and tennis are all played with enthusi-asm, football it is understood with considerable skill owing to the presence on the staff of an expert. The children arrange matches with other schools in the town. On the day visited there was a cricket match against the neighboring modern school, in which Summerhill had decided not to play their best player having learned that their opponents' best player was ill.

A great deal of time is spent out of doors, and the children lead an active, healthy life and look like it. Only a close and expert investigation could reveal how much, if anything, they lose from the absence of more formal Physical Education.

PREMISES

The School is situated in grounds which give ample scope for recreation. The main building, which was formerly a private house, provides for school purposes a hall, a dining room, sick rooms, an art room, a small craft room and the girls' dormitories. The youngest children sleep in a cottage, where their classroom is also situated. The dormitories for the other boys and the remain-ing classrooms are in huts in the garden, where are also the bedrooms of some members of the staff. All these rooms have doors opening directly to the garden. The classrooms are small, though not unsuitable, as the teaching is done in small groups. One of the dormitories represents a notable building effort by the boys and staff: it was built as a sanatorium for which apparently no use has arisen. The sleeping accommodation is somewhat primitive when judged by normal standards, but it is understood that the health record of the School is good, and the provision may be regarded as satisfactory. There are sufficient bathrooms available.

While these garden premises are at first sight unusually primitive and public, they do in fact seem to be eminently well suited for creating the atmosphere of a permanent holiday camp which is an important feature of the School. Moreover they gave the opportunity of seeing how the children pursued their studies entirely undisturbed by the many visitors, who were present on the day of the inspection.

STAFF

The staff are paid £8 a month with board and lodging. To find men and women who not only believe in the principles of the School but are sufficiently mature and well balanced to be able to live on equal terms with children, who are well qualified academically and highly skilled as teachers and then to persuade them to work for £8 a month, must be a considerable task for the Head Master. Service at Summerhill is not a recommendation in many quarters, and the necessary combination of conviction, disinterestedness, character and ability is rare. It has already been pointed out that the staff are not equal to all the demands, yet they are very much better than the staff of many independent schools paying much higher salaries. They include an M.A. (Hons.) Edinburgh in English, an M.A. and B.Sc. of Liverpool, a Cambridge Wrangler, a F.A. (Hons.) London in French and German, and a Cambridge B.A. in History. Four have teacher's qualifications. This does not include the teachers of arts and crafts who have foreign qualifications and are among the best on the staff.

While they need strengthening here and there, the present staff is far from being weak and if, by attendance at courses and visits of observation, they could widen and refresh their experience and bring themselves up to date, they could give a very good account of themselves. At the same time it is too much to hope that a salary of £96 a year can go on attracting to this School the teachers that it needs and it seems clear that this difficulty will have to be squarely faced.

The Head Master is a man of deep conviction and sincerity. His faith and patience must be inexhaustible. He has the rare power of being a strong personality without dominating. It is impossible to see him in his School without respecting him even if one disagrees with or even dislikes some of his ideas. He has a sense of humor, a warm humanity and a strong common sense which would make him a good Head Master anywhere, and his happy family life is shared with the children who are presumably as capable of profiting by example as any others.

He takes a broad view of education as the means of learning how to live abundantly and, though he would admit the force of some at least of the criticisms in this Report, he would feel that his School must stand or fall rather by the kind of children that it allows its pupils to grow into, than by the specific skills and abilities that it teaches them. On this basis of evaluation it may be said:

1. That the children are full of life and zest. Of boredom and apathy there was no sign. An atmosphere of contentment and tolerance pervades the School. The affection with which it is regarded by its old pupils is evidence of its success. An average number of 30 attend the end-of-term plays and dances, and many make the School their headquarters during the holidays.

It may be worth noting at this point that, whereas in its early days the School was attended almost entirely by "problem" children, the intake is now from a fairly normal cross-section of the population.

2. That the children's manners are delightful. They may lack, here and there, some of the conventions of manners, but their friendliness, ease and naturalness, and their total lack of shyness and self-consciousness made them very easy, pleasant people to get on with.

3. That initiative, responsibility and integrity are all encouraged by the system and that, so far as such things can be judged, they are in fact being developed.

4. That such evidence as is available does not suggest that the products of Summerhill are unable to fit into ordinary society

when they leave School. Information such as follows does not of course tell the whole story but it indicates that Summerhill education is not necessarily hostile to worldly success. Old pupils have become a Captain in the R.E.M.E. [Royal Electrical/ Mechanical Engineers], a Battery Q.M.S. [Quartermaster Sergeant], a bomber pilot and Squadron Leader, a Nursery Nurse, an Air Hostess, a clarinet player in the Grenadier Guards Band, a Beit Fellow of the Imperial College, a ballet dancer at Sadler's Wells, a radio operator and contributor of short stories to an important national daily newspaper, and a market research investigator with a big firm. They have taken the following degrees etc., among others: F.A. Hons. Econ. Cambridge; Scholar Royal College of Art; B.Sc., 1st Class Hons. Physics, London; B.A. Hons. History, Cambridge; B.A. 1st Class Hons. Modern Language, Manchester.

5. The Head Master's educational views make this School an exceptionally suitable place for the type of education in which such fundamental work is based on children's interests and in which class work is not unduly governed by examination requirements. To have created a situation in which academic education of the most intelligent kind could flourish is an achievement, but in fact it is not flourishing and a great opportunity is thus being lost. With better teaching at all stages, and above all the junior stage, it might be made to flourish, and an experiment of profound interest be given its full chance to prove itself.

There remains in the mind some doubts both about principles and about methods. A closer and longer acquaintance with the School would perhaps remove some of these and possibly intensify others. What cannot be doubted is that a piece of fascinating and valuable educational research is going on here which it would do all educationists good to see.

NOTES ON HIS MAJESTY'S INSPECTORS' REPORT

We were indeed lucky to have two broad-minded inspectors sent to us. We dropped "mister" straightaway. During the two days' visit, we had quite a few friendly arguments.

I felt that school inspectors were accustomed to picking up a French book in front of a class and quizzing the class to find out what the pupils knew. I reasoned that that kind of training and experience would be of little use in inspecting the worth of a school in which lessons were not the prime criterion. I said to one of the inspectors, "You really can't inspect Summerhill because our criteria are happiness, sincerity, balance and sociability." He grinned and said they'd have a go at it anyway. And both our inspectors made a remarkable adaptation, and obviously enjoyed themselves in the process.

Odd things struck them. Said one, "What a delightful shock it is to enter a classroom and find the children not taking any notice of you, after years of seeing classes jump to attention." Yes, we were lucky to have the two of them.

But to the report itself: "the inspectors were a little surprised at the financial difficulties. . . ." The answer lies mostly in bad debts, yet that is not the whole story. The report mentions an annual fee of £120, but since then we have tried to cope with high prices throughout the years by raising the average annual fee to about £250 (about $700). This does not allow anything for repairs to the buildings, for purchasing new apparatus, and so on. For one thing, damages are heavier in Summerhill than in a disciplined school. Summerhill children are allowed to go through their gangster period, and consequently more furniture is destroyed.

The report says that we have seventy children. Today, we are down to forty-five, a fact that offsets to some extent the rise in fees.

The report speaks of the poor teaching of our juniors. We have always had that difficulty. Even with an excellent teacher, it is difficult to get through the ordinary public school work if only for the reason that the children are free to do other things. If children in a public school at the age of ten or twelve could climb trees or dig holes instead of going to lessons, their standards would be like ours. But we accept the fact that our boys and girls will have a period during which there must be a lower standard of learning, because we think that play is of greater importance during this period in their lives than learning.

Even if we assume that the backwardness in lessons of our juniors is important, it is still true that a year later these same juniors, then turned seniors, passed the Oxford exams with very good grades. These pupils were examined in a total of 39 subjects, an average of 6½ subjects for each pupil. The results were 24 *Very Good*, which is better than 70 per cent. In all the 39 exams, there was only one failure. The handicap of not being up to regular school standard when a boy is a junior in Summerhill does not necessarily mean that such a pupil will be at a low standard when he is a senior.

For my part I have always liked late starters. I have seen quite a few bright children who could recite Milton at four blossom forth as drunkards and loafers at twenty-four. I like to meet the man who at the age of fifty-three says he doesn't quite know what he is to be in life. I have a hunch that the boy who knows at seven just what he wants to be may be an inferior who will have a conservative attitude to life later on.

The report says: "To have created a situation in which academic education of the most intelligent kind could flourish is an achievement; but in fact, it is not flourishing and a great opportunity is thus being lost." That is the only paragraph in which the two inspectors did not rise above their academic preoccupations. Our system flourishes when a child *wants* an academic education, as our exam results show. But perhaps the inspectors' paragraph means that better junior teaching would result in more children *wanting* to take matriculation exams.

Is it not time that we put academic education in its place? Academic education too often tries to make a silk purse out of a sow's ear. I wonder what an academic education would have done for some of our old Summerhill pupils—a dress designer, a hairdresser, a male ballet dancer, some musicians, some children's nurses, some mechanics, some engineers, and half a dozen artists.

Yet it is a fair report, a sincere one, a generous one. I am publishing it simply because it is good that the reading public should see a view of Summerhill that is not my own. Note that the report does not carry any form of official recognition by the

Ministry of Education. Personally, I do not mind; but recognition would have been welcome because of two factors: the teachers would have come under the State Superannuation Scheme, and parents would have a better chance of getting aid from local Councils.

I should like to put on record the fact that Summerhill has never had any difficulty with the Ministry of Education. Any inquiry, any visit of mine to the Ministry, has been met with courtesy and friendliness. My only setback came when the Minister refused permission for a Scandinavian parent to import and erect prefabs, free of charge, just after the war.

When I think of the authoritative interest taken by European governments in private schools, I am glad I live and work in a country that allows so much scope to private venture. I show tolerance of children; the Ministry shows tolerance of my school. I am content.

18. FERNWOOD
Elizabeth Monroe Drews

Fernwood was probably the most radical experiment ever undertaken in American public education. The idea on which it was based came from Professor Elizabeth Drews of Portland State University, a distinguished humanistic psychologist and educational researcher. In 1966 Professor Drews translated into educational practice some of the humanistic psychologists' new theories about self-actualization. Along with two respected teachers from the community, she submitted the plan for Fernwood to local school authorities in Colton, Oregon, and together they obtained a small grant from the Northwest Regional Educational Research Laboratory, a conduit for federal funds.

Fernwood was a free school, differing from other schools much in the sense that a free university differs from the usual institution. There was no schedule at Fernwood for the twenty-four adolescent boys and girls who were randomly selected from volunteers for the experiment from grades seven, eight, and nine at the Colton Consolidated School (Colton, Oregon). All but four of those selected chose to participate throughout, i.e., September through December 1966. At the beginning of the school year the large room was almost empty, just chairs and tables and these in no set order. The two young men, Roger Bishop and Bill Monroe, who were to be the teacher-counselors set the stage very simply the first day of school. They announced to the young people as they sat in the bare classroom that the students could make this the kind of school they wanted. They could find out what was important to them and then work on what was important. Both teachers and students would learn together.

The way the room was to be organized, what the room was to contain, and how the furniture would be used and added to was up to the youngsters. Since it was early fall, the out-of-school environment—including the extensive school grounds, the wooded areas, and a large pond 20 minutes away—proved irresistible. When it at last became clear to the students that they were free to choose, they reveled in their liberty. At these early stages the teachers would prepare what they felt to be the best that they could, as they put it, of "their usual dynamic presentations," only to find that after teacher talk was under way the students would begin to disappear. Realizing that they could, in truth, come and go as they pleased, only one or two students ever would sit through even a better-than-ordinary lesson or lecture.

The Colton area where the children lived is one of great natural beauty, although the houses are often shabby and many of the residents are somewhat impoverished. Wild flowers, ferns and shrubs, dozens of bird species, wild animals, and towering Douglas firs invite budding botanists and biologists, naturalists and ecologists to look and listen carefully and sometimes study in depth. (In the run-of-the-week activities most Colton young people did none of this. They knew little or nothing of nature, watched TV instead of birds; and seemed generally unaware of the intellectual and esthetic possibilities in the natural world around them.) Houses are generally set apart from one another, often small, and privacy is at a premium or nonexistent. Many of the young people have little space to claim as their own beyond a spot in bed. Thus it seemed only natural in the free environment of Fernwood that, as days passed, they sought out personal refuges, sometimes in groups but often singly. A boy or girl would lay claim to a corner or a nook and "nest" there.

These claims to space and privacy—inside and out-of-doors— seemed to give security and peace of mind just as did the long, deep personal conversations. One boy made daily trips to the pond, where he stretched out on a raft he had put together. Another who sought solitude, one of the most confirmed low achievers and general misfits, was a boy of sixteen—a nonreader with a tested I.Q. that placed him in the moron category. Generally belligerent, he was mean to younger students and had been thrown out of school repeatedly and always bounced back —more inured each time against learning. In the course of these abrasive confrontations, he had become a habitual truant, but at Fernwood his attendance record became perfect. At first he lay claim to the merry-go-round, where he would lie for hours watching the clouds or waving at the occasional bewildered taxpayer who drove by. Gradually he gained peace of mind and overcame his aversion to school to the extent that he could cross the threshold and enter the classroom. By dint of alchemy or miracle (and perhaps with the aid of a stack of some 200 comic books) he learned to read. His next venture was to become social. As a beginning, he learned to play chess, occasionally beat his teachers at the game they taught him, and finally became an excellent conversationalist who could speak on war and peace as well as on the vagaries of the weather. Now, a year after the program's end, he spends half of each day helping mentally retarded children in a special room. He is known for his gentleness and loving ways.

From early September until the Christmas recess, the young inhabitants of Fernwood and the often bewildered teacher-counselors lived together from 8 A.M., when the school bus arrived, until 3 P.M., when the bus came again and redistributed the children throughout the wooded slopes and on the meadows where their homes were. The foundation of the program was love. Love which came to mean a delight in mutual discovery, and a sense of well-being and pleasure in finding out about themselves. There was time to look for Indian artifacts and to visit the old settler who had been hunting arrowheads since he was a boy and now had them mounted in picture frames and sorted in jars. There were hours to listen to music, to build things, to plan trips and go on them, and to read books. And most importantly, there was time to form relationships that were natural and meaningful.

Few of these children had ever found a time or a place to make friends. They lived miles away from potential friends and often there was much work—endless chores—to be done. When in school at Colton there had been the relentless bells dictating when the mind was to be turned on and off and what words the eyes were to focus upon. The curriculum in this consolidated school was text-centered and fact-oriented. Talk, other than recitation, was generally thought to be idle chatter—discouraged in the classrooms and forbidden in the halls. Fernwood freed the students from onerous rules and arbitrary judgments, allowing them to discover and accept themselves. There was time for each to dream and envision what he might be and become. And time, as well, to talk for the hours on end that made friendships possible.

The teacher-counselors played an important role in this new relationship which allowed the young to bridge generation gaps. The warmth and trust expressed by the teachers, and the integrity which they demonstrated by not coercing the students when they had promised freedom, finally won over the more reluctant students. The teachers set the stage and then merged with the setting.

However, it gradually became clear that gentle teachers with unobtrusive ways could become models for many of the students. Both men were leaders in the community, had taught in the area for a decade, were well educated, and had rich personal resources. They were hopeful, joyful at times, and quietly confident—committed to serving youth. How they served was often improvisational but rarely unrewarding either for them or their students. Mr. Monroe reports:

> I'd stalk groups of youngsters like I might stalk coveys of quail. I'd follow along on the trail as though I was out nature hunting on my own and stay within distance so I could see them out of the corner of my eye. After several days I could get close enough so I could actually hear them talking. This was very exciting. I can imagine that anthropologists who go to some strange culture might have the same feeling that I had—perhaps someone studying animals. I thought of that girl who studied the chimpanzees in Africa.
>
> Gradually I was allowed to come into one of these groups— to walk right along with them and not have them scatter and run or leave me. Later they allowed me to say something— now and then. To say something without their turning and walking away. And one day I was even allowed to change the subject. And they listened—and they asked me questions—and I was part of the group—and I felt exhilarated that finally I had become part of the group.
>
> Other groups were formed the same way and Roger and I became friends of the students. Then the conversation really began to roll. In the classroom on rainy days we'd sit around and talk by the hour—talk about books, war, peace, birth— talk about dying—talk about anything. People listened— people shared and the relationships between individuals grew deeper than any relationships I have ever known.

Equally as important as the attitudes of love and helpfulness was the vision of the future that the teachers expressed. Mr. Bishop read J. R. Platt's article "Diversity," in his book *The Step to Man,* and discussed it with the students and put down his own feelings about the new image of man as follows:

TEMPLATE FOR NONTECHNOLOGICAL TERRESTRIANS

Third Force psychologists, many theologians and philosophers, some educators, and even Marxist theoreticians are defining a new image of man and saying he can choose, strive for, and achieve this image in an evolutionary step with tools he has in his possession today.

The "new" man will become a transcendent version of himself:

Man, not coping with a future that happened accidentally, but consciously creating—planning and achieving—the world in which he wants to live.

Man, not passing hostility and fear from generation to generation, but helping satisfy in his children, neighbors, and colleagues the basic needs of love, respect, trust, and safety; filling the physiological needs; and starting a cycle of growth as infinite as the universe. Growth motivated by human capabilities insisting on fulfillment.

Man, not trapped and bound by his culture, but able to examine himself and his society with undistorted perceptions; aware of intercultural truth; able to respect and value an ecology of the universe.

Man, not afraid to be sensitive to his feelings, but aware; cultivating the awareness of emotions, of being, of beauty, of living in the "here and now."

Man, not lost in apathy or living in meditation, but functioning in and contributing to his world; knowing his capabilities and committing them to his convictions. An exciting man.

Man, honest with himself and others. A self-directed man satisfying himself and transcending himself—altruistic.

Man, with the courage to venture; the courage to stand, alone if necessary, for a principle he believes to be unalterable.

Man, filled with an understanding—trustful, compassion-
ate, accepting, nonjudging, open. A valuing, loving spirit
that permits the communication of his values and allows him
to be the paradox that is self-actualizing man.

BEYOND CURRICULUM

Fernwood was an effort by two dedicated teachers to translate
concepts that were important to the author and to them (and
that were basic as well to theories of self-actualization and
intrinsic learning) into educational practice. Prior to beginning
the venture the author talked for many hours with these teachers
and then spent several weeks reading Third Force psychological
literature to develop a statement of aims entitled "Beyond Curriculum." (Dorris Lee, Professor of Education, Portland State
College, was an inspiration to all of us in these early stages. Later
she served as our consultant.) The major emphases of this
statement and selected happenings at Fernwood which illustrate
"Beyond Curriculum" concepts follows:

Item 1: Each individual is different. The range of these differences extends far beyond the reach of textbook levels and the
intelligence derived from testing. Each is unique as to rate, style,
tempo, and pattern of learning. Each chooses his own values and
interests and develops personal tastes. By honoring these directions of growth and allowing them to flourish naturally, we found
that students could master what had been difficult topics and
material and do this easily. As we have seen, a nonreader began
to read without the pressure of applied methods and scheduled
class periods. Students who habitually failed English found they
could speak fluently and well when they could talk about something of interest rather than on an assigned topic. Just as the
school came to a close, a boy who had been an indifferent
mathematics student did four months' work in three days and
ended up six weeks ahead of his former classmates.

*Item 2: Only a fraction of the potential of each is developed and
used.* This is true in life at large as well as in the conventional
classroom. School learning is narrowly cognitive (usually lower-

order, i.e., facts). Socialization processes often force constriction of interests and conformity. However, when there is a climate of mutual trust and freedom, democratic processes often emerge in natural and effective ways. A group of boys decided they wanted to transform the woodshed into an industrial-arts center. They had begun to level the floor for pouring concrete when they became aware of interlopers in one end, separated only by a thin partition. These turned out to be a group of four girls who had located a study center in the eight-by-twelve space and equipped it with shelves and books. In the ensuing melee the boys threw dirt and rocks against the wall and did their best to dislodge the girls and their artifacts. Words of color ranging into deep blue were exchanged and the Fernwood version of a town meeting was called by someone who rang the bell. The boys claimed that the decision had been made in an earlier meeting that they were to have the entire woodshed for their industrial-arts center and the girls claimed that no such decision had been made. The boys called for a reading of prior notes by the secretary only to be informed that the group had neglected to elect a secretary. The denouement was that the meeting was stopped then and there to elect a secretary, one of the most literate among the twenty-four. But the boys were not able to effectively oust the girls from their quick claim.

Affective, esthetic, altruistic, and ethical growth is rarely encouraged or even allowed in our schools. As one boy commented when the first snow fell in December and the students raced outdoors to revel in it, "You know what is so wonderful? There is no teacher to say 'Now sit down and get to work—you've all seen snow before'"! The students came to see changes in themselves and toward the end of the term commented that they had not destroyed property at Fernwood—not even those who had habitually scraped and gouged their ways through the Colton corridors. As one of the most hardened of the former marauders commented, "I was not closed in at Fernwood. I wasn't in a cage or a cell, so I didn't need to destroy." One of the last meetings centered on a book that inadvertently had been dropped in a mud puddle. The consensus was that it was not the fault of the boy who dropped it and that all should share in the cost of the replacement of the book. (When the book finally was returned, no fine was levied.)

Item 3: Young people want to learn and become competent. Natural directions of growth became apparent when students were encouraged to choose activities that appealed to them and to learn in their own ways. Parents, however, were often quite unsure that their offspring could be learning anything important if allowed to make their own choices. At one parent meeting a father commented, "My son isn't learning anything."

The teachers encouraged him to talk and then asked, "What isn't he learning?"

"For one thing, math."

"Do you think he has a desire to learn this?"

Both father and mother said they were sure he did. The teachers reflected that they were glad this was the case. However, the parents' complaints continued.

"Six weeks have gone by and he doesn't have a math book. Why can't he have one if he wants one?"

"We are happy to know that he wants a book," Mr. Monroe replied. "It may be that the one he wants is not on the shelf with the other math books. But if he will tell us what he wants, we will get it for him right away. We drive to the library in Oregon City [twenty miles away] every Friday."

As the dialogue continued it became clear to everyone that only the parents, not the son, were interested in a mathematics book. The teachers gently explained that, as Montaigne made clear centuries ago, learning under compulsion has little hold on the mind. Fortunately this boy did find a need for mathematics soon—as he worked on plans to convert the woodshed into an industrial-arts center—and he raced through sections of several books in record time and with high comprehension and recall.

One of the areas where much growth was apparent at Fernwood was in the ability shown by boys and girls to present ideas orally. It became obvious, as days passed, that young people learn to talk by talking and they learn what they think and where they stand by making these thoughts and stances first conscious and then public. A free situation peels away the traditional school culture—leaving no protocol to hide behind, no excuse of "overdue homework" to prevent one from facing oneself or coming to terms with a situation. Reality is no longer disguised by daily routines.

Lacking cloaks and masks, the students had no recourse but to examine themselves and think about the basic issues and relationships. Who am I? What is the world all about? How can I live the kind of life I want to live and be the self I want to be in this world? (Some began to talk about the "openness" that places in Alaska still offered and to mourn the loss of the frontier.) Competence, in the most basic sense, is a matter of learning to live one's own life, joyfully and zestfully, and these feelings can only come when there is a prior feeling of independence and autonomy—of being in charge of one's own life.

As the boys and girls came to understand how they felt and thought, acceptance of their physical selves—their teen-age, out-of-hand awkwardness—grew. And gradually the young people began to accept one another, including even gauche, foot-in-mouth clumsiness, and to accept adults. Their verbal talents and poise advanced to such a level that by spring when the experimental group was asked to speak to a graduate seminar at Portland State College, almost all came eagerly, although this meant giving up free time after school. The level of self-confidence and the sure-footedness of these adolescents in talking to the college people were such that the professor spontaneously remarked that he wished his graduate students could do so well.

An area of competence important to school authorities was the fact that these students did not "lose ground" by being out of the regular school program for almost four months. All but two did better work and received higher grades upon return to school than they had done prior to the free experience.

Item 4: Young people want to help one another and to share. They easily invent and readily engage in altruistic and empathic projects where there is freedom and time to get to know one another and to discover what needs to be done. Not only did we observe many examples of helpful and responsible behavior at Fernwood, but parents also reported changes.

Parent meetings were a part of Fernwood from the beginning. A father or a mother or both of almost every family participated on a weekly or biweekly basis. Many of the adults felt they gained much in a personal sense from the group sharing. However, there were apprehensions about the program. Surely a program so much enjoyed by children could not involve real learning. At first some felt that if students chose what to learn they would only select the trivial and unimportant, and there was a feeling among parents that discovering friends was not a "matter of consequence." Gradually new perceptions emerged.

At one such meeting an arthritic father whose misanthropy had set him apart from his neighbors for years rose to confess: "I've told my children when to learn, when to work, and what to do all their lives. When they didn't jump, I used a belt. And now I realize that I've been wrong. If they have freedom and love, they choose what to do better than I can tell them."

Other parents attested to newly expressed helpfulness on the part of their children. Front yards lost their litter and rooms became neat. Squabbles with siblings diminished. Parents, some of whom had been school dropouts, began to see the point. At first the statements came in the guise of faint praise and were personal in nature. "Anything you'd do is bound to be better than what they did to us in school." Later applications were more universal. "The world is in such a mess that anything you can do to teach love is for the good."

Students learned to live together in such ways that hostilities and hurt feelings diminished, sharp elbows became round and smooth, and long toes were shortened. And upon return to the regular school, Fernwood youngsters often explained the inconsistencies of teacher behavior and the need for the young to be tolerant of their elders to students who had not experienced Fernwood.

Item 5: Young people have an intrinsic sense of beauty and appropriateness. This will emerge as esthetic judgment and taste if they are at liberty to make things and to express themselves. By such participation, they come to appreciate not only the products but also the efforts of others. And if given encouragement to express themselves they find a gift of language. One boy reflected on the beauty he had experienced the week before:

> I particularly enjoyed the feel of things, kicking the sand and letting it fan out and slide down, feeling the grass crinkle under my feet. And that day we were on the trip I looked at the river slowly going on its way, then rushing over the rocks, and smoothing off again into a pool. At night I watched the stars fall, burning up before they hit earth. And I listened as the trees whispered words into my ear.

Item 6: Young people are eager to become more aware of themselves and to find a philosophy to live by. This striving gradually merged into efforts by the Fernwood students to become their best possible selves, to find something important to live by and for, and to commit themselves to. As Louis Raths comments in his *Values and Teaching,* "When a self is recognized values can develop." This happened in the free program. As we have seen, the young people found words to express themselves and found they had thoughts worth expressing. Gradually they became free to wonder about the mystery that surrounded them—the secret of life itself. And they began to talk about this and many other things that were important to them. No one laughed at these concerns. Awe became natural and human nature could reveal itself.

Self-discovery and philosophical conjecturing were never forced, but the young people generally chose talking at length with each other and their teachers over more obvious delights such as taking trips. (Two Volkswagen buses and a school bus were available for this aspect of the program.) These choices might have been quite different if the teachers had been different people. Some teachers do not, by their very outlook on life, invite philosophical discussions. Some do not inspire. And some are so lacking in self-confidence and self-control that when they allow their students freedom, bedlam results. Nor can all teachers be effective as counselors. Here the personal equation is all-important. The counselor must enjoy being with people, be interested in them for their own sakes, and he must wish them well. Beyond this, he should know what he values and what he is willing to dedicate himself to.

The Fernwood teachers were mature in these ways and thus were able to help the boys and girls make some order out of this confused and confusing world. As for the young people, they had all the time they needed—hours, days, or weeks—to consider various alternatives, to speculate about the ethics of each situation, and to weigh the immediate and long-term consequences of choices. Most importantly, they were free to select the alternatives that truly appealed. (It is obvious that children who are punished or coerced by grades or group opinion are not free to choose.) Thus interests and feelings were tried out and acted upon and those that remained cherished after close examination came to take on the stature of values.

Item 7: Individual differences and unrealized potential dictated self-selection and individualized learning. The freedom in Fernwood was such that students could learn in their own ways about things they wanted to know. Most of the suggestions about things to do came from the children, although the teachers did encourage them to visit the Portland Art Museum, the airport, and the zoo. Books were always available and new ones could be obtained on the weekly trips to the library. Some became so addicted to reading that parents complained. The mother of one of the girls was a chronic complainer—a woman of easy virtue who welcomed a variety of men into her home but felt her daughter's love of books showed an inability to focus on important matters.

As the young people became practiced in decision making, they learned to center their interests—a boy learned much about history by studying the strategies of Napoleon and Caesar and re-enacting battles in a sand pile at home—and to widen their horizons—four girls decided to go to England and read the daily papers diligently searching for jobs for fourteen-year-olds. When they could not find work, they decided to become columnists and began writing a teen-age column which they sold to the local paper. Later a publisher of a Northwest teen-age paper "discovered" their talent and one was asked to become his editor.

Item 8: Individual differences and unrealized potential dictated that we expand the learning environment. This new educational setting incorporated a larger environment—reached out to home and community and beyond to the state and to the world. More of knowledge and more of life were admissible as curriculum. Since we held that students could learn from anything and from any of the worlds—natural, esthetic, technological, and human— they must be freed to do so. They could learn what they needed and when they needed to without waiting for a unit in curriculum or "to be taught."

The learning environment—what it was permissible to learn from and about—was virtually unlimited. Students learned to shingle roofs by assisting their fathers and neighbors; they learned about southern Oregon by planning and taking a five-day trip to historic Jacksonville and Crater Lake National Park; they learned about animals by assisting the Portland zoo veterinarian as he went about his daily tasks, and about flying and planes by spending whole days (not taking an hour's tour) at the airport. Thus they came to experience themselves and the world.

The end came suddenly and unexpectedly (we had planned originally for a year's program) when we received word the first week in December that the grant was canceled and our infant program was not to survive. The children were disconsolate and one of them wrote a letter which reflected how we all felt.

DEAR MR. PRESIDENT JOHNSON,
I am in a school class for 7, 8 and 9th graders. It is an experimental class where we have full freedom. We have our own government consisting of one chairman, one assistant chairman, one secretary, and one treasurer. This class works

on the idea that students will want to learn. We are very
concerned about our next funding period. It may be cut off
by the Northwest Regional Educational Research Laboratory. This may happen because their funds were cut in two.
Dr. Elizabeth Drews, who is responsible for our project, is in
Washington, D.C., looking for other sources of money and
talking to her friends about our class, hoping to influence
them. Would you please talk to someone too?

Sincerely,
A FERNWOOD STUDENT

19. THE NEW SCHOOL—
VANCOUVER

ANNE LONG

*An extraordinary memoir of a sensitive teacher's
attempt to let her students govern themselves, Anne
Long's moving personal letter to a friend portrays a*
Lord of the Flies *society and seeks its causes.*

*Anne Long shares the responsibility of the New
School—Vancouver with two other teachers.*

I began my teaching career in the public school system of
Vancouver. After my first chaotic year, I was asked to resign my
position, to be rehired and placed in a different school, which
was my inspector's way of accomplishing two ends: first, that I
would not become a member of the permanent staff of the school
board (by being rehired I would be on probation for a second
year); and second, that I would have a chance in a new setting to

establish for myself "the correct, authoritarian image" befitting a teacher. During my second year, I did conform more to the standards generally accepted by teachers, in terms of discipline, classroom management, etc., because I wanted to keep my teaching position. As a result, my second year was less chaotic, less strenuous, less fun, less meaningful. Then came the opportunity to teach in the New School, at which I jumped.

When I first began teaching in the New School, it was under the direction of a man who was academically oriented, and at best, it would have been classified as a progressive school. Children were allowed to talk, chew gum, eat their lunches pretty much when they chose, wear whatever they wanted to. But there were regularly scheduled classes, and attendance in the classes was, although not openly stated that way, compulsory. The students were expected to complete whatever work was presented to them, and if they didn't get it done in class time, they forfeited their recess or free activity period in order to do so. Generally, I would say that the type of work presented to the children during this year was more stimulating, more relevant to them, more flexible, and more fun for them than any public school program could ever be. But it was still a program very much determined by the adults, with specific skill and understanding goals in mind. During the beginning few months of that year, I was constantly feeling that the children were not "doing enough"; that they were not involved in "constructive" activities enough of the time; that they were not *producing* enough in terms of written material—evidence of their time consumed. But as the year wore on, this attitude of mine wore off; and by the end of that first year, I found I had done a complete about-face in terms of my expectations and notions about methods to be used in communicating values in the educational process. I felt then, as I do now, that if school experiences are to be meaningful, they must arise from and revolve around things in which children are genuinely interested. And that if children are to become deeply involved in their own education, they must be in a situation where they are able to make major decisions about how they are going to spend their own time in this process. My leanings toward "free-er" schooling at that time were influenced, and confirmed, by my having the opportunity, during the Easter recess, to spend a week in San Francisco, visiting such schools as Walden Center, Berkwood, the Peninsula School; speaking with their directors and teachers and speaking with Jim Herndon, author of *The Way It Spozed to Be,* who at that time was running a four-class free school within a public junior high school.

During the course of my first year in the New School, the director was constantly under the gun from the parent body (whose society owned and operated the school) for being overly authoritarian in his dealings with various students. Halfway through the year he announced his intention of resigning at the end of the school year; so the search was on for a new director. I halfheartedly announced my candidacy for the post, being somewhat leary of the potential destructiveness of parental intervention and control, having witnessed its effects on the director. I didn't really take my candidacy seriously, nor did anyone else. After advertising on a global level and screening a number of local people, the parent committee came up with a candidate whom they billed as the messiah of the New School. The other two teachers and I, who planned to stay with the school the following year had a brief opportunity to meet and talk with him. After he left, we spoke together and found we all had the same reservations about the way he planned to run the school. At the parent meeting which was to approve his appointment as director, we came forward with our reservations—that a totally unstructured school would not take into account the needs of all children. The result was a decision to bring him back for a weekend conference with us, postponing a final decision on the matter of his appointment until we had had a chance to discuss with him our reservations and see what the outcome of these discussions would be. The outcome was positive. We agreed that we would have a "structured" morning, with students remaining in their classrooms with their teachers for whatever type of classroom activities the teachers saw fit to provide, organize, or assist; and the afternoons would be unstructured, with students attending or not whichever class things might be offered, such as art, music, drama, etc., as they chose. He was duly appointed, and I would say that I, at least, began my second year at the New School with a real sense of great things to come.

However, after the first month or two of school, I began to feel some misgivings. With no compulsory classwork—or for that matter, no expectation of class work—an anti-academic attitude, if anything, pervaded the school; students were quick to reject anything that even half looked like a regular lesson, no matter how skillfully it was devised. They were quick, too, to test, to see just how far their "freedom" extended. Many were, I feel, surprised, even dismayed, to discover that freedom was, in the director's eyes, at least, limitless. They began, almost immediately, with smoking—cigarettes, if they could get them, but most made pipes out of acorns, corks, or clay and were smoking anything and everything—tea, grass (the common garden variety), sawdust, dandelion leaves—you name it, they tried it. It was a school-wide activity, right down to the five-year-olds, even my own—which was a real test of my belief. However, as the director predicted, it was a passing fancy, and in about a week or two it died out. Not, however, the availability and familiarity with matches. Next began an era of fire-lighting, three weeks short but a thousand long. They began in wastebaskets downstairs, mostly in the washrooms. These episodes jangled me out of my freedomite stupor, and the sheer stupidity of the irresponsibility of allowing these burnings, which had spread to little piles of paper on the basement floor, and finally to a three-foot crawl space under a wooden stage, appalled and terrified me into taking action against these dangerous activities. I began collecting the matches of those kids I knew to have them; sniffing around the basement five or six times a morning, flushing out those kids who persisted in lighting fires—or candles, which they had installed in the numerous wooden shantytown-type forts that had been built in just about every available space in the basement—confiscating their matches, and giving them the royal what-for about it. In the end, threatening to send them home from school if I caught them at it again. The director, throughout all of this, remained calm and soothing, stating that the children didn't really want to burn the school down, therefore, there was nothing to worry about. These inside burnings finally ended when he conceded to my anxiety about them (the only concession he made all year) and bought an incinerator, and the fires moved outside into the play yard. There all burnings were supposed to be supervised but were not, and they consumed numerous bottles of rubber cement, plastic hula-hoops, which were brandished about as torches, and anything else that was burnable. I wasn't terribly happy about this arrangement, but felt relieved that the building and children in it were no longer endangered and that those children who did not "need" to take part in fire-play did not have to be subjected to its hazards. Needless to say, all these incidents caused me to begin questioning the validity of the premises on which we were operating. And, unfortunately, they were not the last. During the first two months of school, more than twenty children were withdrawn.

After that initial shattering of the free-school image by fire, my faith was never quite the same. I kept looking to myself for the cause of the failures that everywhere glared at me. For five months I trained my critical eyes inward. I wanted so much to believe in the school, the freedom, the children, and their ability to assume responsibility. But throughout that time I constantly saw things that were wrong, that had nothing to do with me or my role with the children. I registered them with patience, understanding, sympathy, faith—but I registered them.

The Monkey Patrol was a name that soon became known throughout the school. It was a group of four boys: two ten-year-olds, one eleven-year-old, and one twelve-year-old. They made it their business to make life difficult for those who were not members of their group, particularly those at their own age level. They spent much of their time building forts, fighting over materials for the fort-building, wrecking forts built by other kids, disrupting the activities of kids involved in less boisterous pursuits, wrecking school equipment and furniture and the very school itself. Many of the plasterboard downstairs walls sustained enormous holes. This destructiveness was not their work alone, but they certainly did their fair share. Our director took it upon himself to try to help these kids work their way out of their problems. He won acceptance by the group by accepting any and all of their antisocial and destructive behavior without batting an eye. They soon learned that they could do no wrong in his eyes. Never would he correct, preach, or disapprove; he was their friend. They were an exclusive group, and he allowed them that luxury. He took them on outings on their own (leaving his entire class to fend for itself) and bought them any amount of candy and pop that they desired. One day he was taking a trip downtown to do some shopping and asked if anyone would like to go along. Naturally, the Monkey Patrol went. A short time after they had left, one youngster came moping through our room. When asked what was troubling him, he replied that he had wanted to go to town with the director, but the Monkey Patrol had not allowed him to do so. The director had not intervened. Later that day, the kids in the Monkey Patrol showed me the stuff they had "boosted" on their trip. I said I didn't think it was anything to be so proud about and asked what the director had said about the stuff. They told me he didn't know; he had left them in the toy department while he went off to do some school shopping. The following day I asked him about both issues. Well, he said, there had been no point in intervening on so-and-so's behalf; if he had insisted on his right to come, those other kids would have given him such an unmerciful bad time of it that he would have been more unhappy about going with them than he had been about staying behind. And the stealing? What would he have said to them about that? Oh, perhaps he'd have shown some interest in the things they had stolen—but no disapproval. They knew what they'd done was wrong; they didn't need him to tell them that. If he did, he'd only alienate himself from them; then he'd never have a chance to get to the real reasons for why they did such things, not that stealing itself is particularly abnormal behavior.

There were Cuisenaire rod fights, fort fights, paint fights, water fights. Student meetings, like A. S. Neill's at Summerhill, were screaming matches. Relations between students were a constant barrage of harassment upon harassment. Incident piled upon incident. I began feeling that I was living in the land of *Lord of the Flies.* No end to it was in sight. Student artwork was destroyed, pencils and rulers karate chopped, chairs broken up, desks smashed, sawed in half. The ditto machine became a juvenile pornography and hate-literature plant. "A report of the shithead of the New School. ⸺ ⸺ is a pig. Confirmed by ⸺ ⸺. So-and-so eats out ⸺ ⸺ in a drawn-out knockdown orgy. ⸺ ⸺ talks about fucking so much you get the idea she wants to be fucked. C'mon . . ." And another— "News of the School. Gess wut everybuddy, ⸺ ⸺ is a prostitute. ⸺ ⸺ the fish finally got a fuk out of her. in reterne he took her a bridel for her hoarse." Or "Every good boy should fuck his sister." Etc., etc. Staff relations became strained in the apparent and growing disagreement about how each of the various incidents should be handled.

Somewhere around mid-January I came to the conclusion that it was the director's approach that was wrong, not mine. At the January meeting, he proposed that the school be shut down altogether, since the staff didn't seem to have any hopes of agreeing about how the school should be run. The school was closed down for three days to allow us the opportunity to hash out our problems. *T*-grouping was suggested. That three days only confirmed for me my certainty that the director was not going to change his approach at all, and that if anyone was going to change anything, to bring the school operations onto a more tolerable plane, it would have to be those of us who found it intolerable—myself and two other teachers. He was apparently not only not going to do anything to help, but seemed to emit an unspoken "I dare you to try." Financial troubles besieged the school due to the large number of dropouts in the first two months. January, February, and March were heavy with troubled parent meetings, none of which solved anything. Finally, in mid-March, a large parent meeting passed a motion to split the school: the majority of students and teachers would remain in the building owned by the society, the minority would be free to withdraw without being responsible for fees for the remainder of the year. Myself and two other teachers were left with twenty-seven children. I believe around seventeen went with the director, and two or three took the opportunity to withdraw entirely, from both factions.

The weekend of the split, the remaining parents put on an enormous, two-day work party. Truckloads of rubbish were carted away, walls were repaired or in some instances replaced, and the entire upstairs of the school received its first washing and waxing in months. I had expected the final three months to be one long battle to bring the kids down, but to my pleasure and surprise, they responded with enthusiasm to the new order. Sure, we still had hassles—and certainly no one got very much "schoolwork" done—but it was now a pleasant, relaxed place to be in. The tension, which virtually hummed before, between staff-staff, staff-student, and student-student, was gone. It was a complete transformation. Myself and two teachers (one who stayed, and one who had left for the year) immediately petitioned the parent group to pass the school into our hands. This was accomplished, without much ado, at a meeting in May or June.

During the summer, I surprised myself when I came to write reports on the students who were moving on to public schools. The year which had stuck in my mind as a parade of horrors, was in fact laden with a number of positive, happy memories. Memories of things done with the kids, which will undoubtedly remain vivid in their minds too. We had made a film together. Screening time, three minutes. It took two days to make: one for rehearsing, setting up lights, figuring out camera angles; one for the actual shooting. It is rough, amateurish, but very funny. A number of children made their own three-minute films, using stop-action technique, painting, shooting, painting, shooting. One parent conducted a series of "urban-living" trips, and the students in my group got to see the inside of the police station, a downtown public school, Chinatown, the Chinese school, the Salvation Army. We visited junk yards and secondhand stores, went horseback riding several times, went swimming. We hiked up two mountains—one during the winter, through snow; the other in the late spring, dusty and sweltering hot. At the top we discovered masses of snow shrinking from the sun under the outstretched evergreens. We were taken on a tour of the water front, saw the warehouses, grain-loading facilities, had the concept of container shipping explained to us, saw the giant cranes that had been constructed to accommodate this type of operation, and went through a Greek freighter from bridge to galley, were served Greek coffee and Coca-Cola from bottles with the name in Greek. On another occasion we went through a Russian freighter, this time from the bridge to the bottommost engine room, were shown a film about the life of Lenin, with dubbed-in English, exchanged gifts with the seamen, then wound our way back to our cars between the towering grain elevators and flocks of pigeons. I read aloud to them *The Hobbit* and Lenny Bruce's *How to Talk Dirty and Influence People*. We talked a lot. We did a public-opinion survey, and the kids (eleven-to-thirteen-year-olds) canvassed people in three locations—downtown, and at both universities—in an attempt to find out where the most "liberal" attitudes were to be found. Throughout the year they did a lot of art work; before Christmas we had a two-week binge of batiking, but during the last three months it really flourished. One kid made a papier-mâché elephant, painted it blue with purple designs, and mounted it on casters. Several worked on a six-foot dragon. They made and collaged geometric shapes from cardboard. But best of all, for me—and I think for them—we had a five-day stay on one of the gulf islands between Vancouver and Vancouver Island. We stayed in a cabin that was part of a farm. The main house was an eighty-year-old structure with a large kitchen, heated by a grandiose wood-burning stove. We talked with the people we were staying with about guns, gun laws, laws, animals, slaughtering animals—to city kids unfamiliar, cruel—the Canadian election, politics, pets, the history of the island. We wandered in the woods, saw more deer than I can recall, found several animal skeletons, fought over who was going to sleep where, what we should have for supper, who should eat first, who should clean up, and generally went through the throes of the problems of living together. We walked in to another farm that is only accessible by foot, horse, or boat. To get to it from where we were staying, we had to hike to the top of an enormous bluff, then lace our way across the hazardous sheep trails that crossed the face of the bluff. The wind up there was cool, and we took our time, taking in the place as we went. Way, way down below us, we could see the farmer, riding his tractor, accompanied by his St. Bernard. He was so far down that he was smaller than a Dinky toy, and yet the dog could hear us, or see us. We heard him barking, and later, when we arrived at the farm, the farmer told us he had been barking at us. The farmer raised sheep and beef cattle, kept horses, cats, a tame goat called Woden, who liked to have his horns kicked, a tame deer that we never did see, and that huge St. Bernard. The dog was old and smelly. We walked through pasture after pasture, looking for horses, but found only cattle, thistles, and bones. The farmer served us tea, pop, and fig-filled cookies. His wife showed us how to spin, and some of the sweaters she had knit from the wool she had spun. We all tried to spin but couldn't, and our attempts were soon abandoned when the farmer said he had some old sheepskins the kids could have—not cleaned or dressed, but salvageable. His two daughters came home from school on their ponies and let our kids take turns riding. We finally pulled out of there laden down with dirty old sheepskins and two or three cow skulls that had been found in the pastures. Of course there's more, but you get the idea.

It was a memorable year.

I began this year, my third at the New School, with a determination that things would be different, better. My two colleagues and I all knew what had been wrong last year and understood and shared one another's goals, values. I figured the thing to do was to get the kids involved in activities, physically and emotionally involved. I have the senior class, kids nine through thirteen. Ten of them were new to the school, six left over from last year. I wanted them to see things, to feel things, to understand and question things. To transform these experiences into some comprehensible form through writing, artwork, drama, dance. My approach was that I would provide the materials, the stimulants, the atmosphere, and they would become involved.

Involved with things, ideas. What I hadn't reckoned on was their involvement with themselves, and the values that they brought with them—some from their homes, but mostly from their public school experiences. I did provide materials, stimulants, and atmosphere, as best I was able. But what was lacking for many of them was the "You have to do this, and you have to do it now." Without that, and without the incentives of report cards, exams, grades, the everyday school-type activities have no appeal. My stance was "This is what I expect . . ." and the return hand I was dealt was a game of "Do I have to?", or alternately, "Make me." The only rules I stated were that I would not allow destruction of property, either school or private, and that no child would be allowed to spend his time harassing any other. And what if they did, anyway? They would be asked to go home and stay home until they were prepared to spend their time in a more constructive manner. Several have been asked.

At first I had them writing every day, first thing in the morning. I provided several topics each day—imaginative, good-fun topics, I might say. Most everyone wrote, but only a few gave anything of themselves; and most of what I read, between their lines, said "I am expected to write something today and every day and I don't want to, but here it is anyway. I'll sure be glad when this page is filled 'cause then I can stop and get on with my own affairs." So I dropped the activity, figuring that if that was all they were doing, I was only prolonging their conviction that writing is a tiresome, meaningless task that had no relationship to their real life or experiences. So I posed for myself the question, How do I get to their real interests, concerns? After the child turns off, or has his real interests and concerns turned off by a public school system that refused to recognize the individual, that spends all of its time standardizing and regimenting children, there seems to be no route for him to those real, alive but buried needs, interests, and concerns but through the process of self-discovery. And how does a teacher program for self-discovery when each child has had different reactions to all the various experiences he has had and when each child has different needs that may have been thwarted in different ways? I soon came to the conclusion that I could not provide "a program" for this type of process. Unless I chose to ignore this whole facet of the developing child and held on to the security of an "academic program" and some sort of authoritarian means of having the children participate in that program, then I was faced with the task of redefining my role as a teacher. There really was no choice.

This redefinition has not been an easy job, and I am still stumbling around in the process of doing it. There are several elements which make it extremely taxing personally. The first, I suppose, is my own inability to cope with the knowledge that I am never sure that what I am doing is right. Without any specific guidelines or standards against which to gauge myself, self-doubt always hovers near. I was, along with just about all other teachers, brought up in an environment where right and wrong were clearly defined. It is not easy to live with and overcome uncertainty, especially when one is dealing with other people's lives. Add to this the problem of dealing with parents who are concerned about their children's lack of involvement in an academic program and you usually end up with a double dose of self-doubt. I was afflicted with this ailment (double-doubt) during the fall, when one of the parents of children in my class well-meaningly, rationally, went about attempting to help me to deal with the lack of involvement from which she felt her youngster was suffering. Her arguments were calmly and clearly articulated, and thus, very persuasive. She felt that her child, and the others in the group as well, would become involved in investigating various natural phenomena, mathematical principles, and other "ideas" if they were provided with more materials with which they could work, and thus discover. That one would not have to force or coerce the children in any way, but that the materials themselves would do the job. At that point I did quite a bit of wallowing around, wondering if I had what it took to be a good teacher, etc. I had tried out the idea of doing an over-all study of the city of Vancouver. I figured on spending a good amount of time out in the community with the children, letting them see and find out things for themselves, then coming back to the school and in some form or another recording and interpreting their observations. Once a week, I thought, we would take a field trip. I planned to begin the study by looking at the city from a cultural point of view. What different ethnic communities exist in the city? Where are they located? Why did they locate there? In what ways are they similar to and different from the community life the children know—and why? Our first field trip was to Chinatown. Before we left the school I asked the children to think about the various things they would see in the shops, about the materials used in the various articles, about the prices, the foods, etc. We went into the shops on both sides of the three-block length of Chinatown, food stores, knickknack shops, furniture and clothing stores. I talked to several storekeepers about China, Formosa, Russia, Communism, and the local Chinese community. We got to see the dragons' heads used in Chinese parades and celebrations, where they were stored, and what seemed like hundreds of uniforms worn by the men who go inside them. We had lunch in one of the less Western restaurants. Some kids refused to eat anything, making no quiet matter of their distaste for "that junk." Their behavior was less than mannerly; at one table they poured pop over one of the dishes and were generally rowdy. Most of them bought as many china or wood animals and figures as their money would allow. When we got back to school I tried to get them to write about the various things they had seen. The results were much like the written work I described earlier—containing no interest, no detail, no life. The next day I tried to have a discussion about the Chinese community, the prices of the various objects, the materials used in them, why those prices, those materials, etc.; they ho-hummed and talked about last night's TV episode of *Bewitched*, and generally let me know that they really couldn't care less. At that point I dropped that particular project.

I had been having an amount of difficulty at the end of each school day in getting the children to assist with the cleaning-up, putting-away process. Paints and brushes, inks, pens, clay and clay boards, scissors, etc., were forever being left out, and none of the children would willingly assume any responsibility for cleaning them up. I asked, nagged, pushed, and pleaded, but cooperation was nil. Finally I got tired of the whole business, since I was having to pay such a price in unpleasantness for every bit of work that I managed to get out of each kid; I dropped the whole issue, figuring that if I left the room exactly as they left it, and told our janitor to do the same, perhaps in a few days the state of the place would impair their activities and bother them into doing something about it. This, I thought, would lay the groundwork for a look at how we pollute our environment. My mind drifted off into fantasies of visiting the city dump, running tests on our city lakes and streams for pollution, investigating air pollution, etc. I felt it couldn't fail. It was based on the well-founded educational principle of beginning with the immediate, personal experience of the children in a real situation that affected them and leading from that into the larger world of their city community to see how the same problem was or wasn't dealt with there. My enthusiasm was short-lived. In two days the kids knew what was going on in terms of my position and the janitor's noninvolvement. I should have anticipated their first reaction; it might have made me more able to cope with it. They ranted and raved that if I and the janitor weren't going to do anything about it, they sure weren't either. On top of that they were generally impatient with me over the fact that I could no longer lay my fingers on a pair of scissors (etc.) when they wanted them. Instead of riding above all their clamor, as I had intended, I got angry and let them know what I thought about their general attitude, and ended up the day organizing a cleanup. Maybe it would have worked if I could have held out long enough—I'll never know.

Finally I had to make my peace with myself and acknowledge that I had come to the point in my thinking where I agreed with our ex-director's premise (as I understand it) about children in the educational process, at least those children who have had four or five years of public schooling to work out of their systems. Children just aren't going to get involved with ideas or other people's concerns or feelings until they have sorted out their own identities and egos well enough so that they can move into those other areas without fear of losing themselves. I have concluded from my experience, with these particular children anyway, that until they have reached that balance point, that certainty of their own identity, there are only two reasons that any one of them will become involved in any activity. The main one is ego-gratification. If an activity will give them status *within their group,* they will participate, even put a lot of time, energy, and thought into it. The second, which gives evidence of awareness of things beyond the self, is if the child decides he needs to master a certain skill, or body of information, in order to cope with public school. This occurs only to the older children in the group. There are two or three children in my group who are sure enough of their identity to involve themselves freely in whatever activities genuinely interest them. Because of their independence they are on the periphery of the group's social activities. They reject the battle over pecking order and therefore are generally rejected by those who are bound in that battle.

I'm very skeptical about those enthusiastic young student teachers who "believe" in free schools, and who come to us to discover our "secret." Maybe our secret is that we haven't found any secret yet and probably never will. Maybe our success is in precisely that area which gives us the most difficulty: the uncertainty, the vagueness. Perhaps our children grow into focus because the function of our school is so ill-defined and their role in it, too, is undefined. I begin to think that we should stop calling our school a school and call it something like The Institute for Self-Definition. People, even intelligent and educated ones, are all too often inclined to think of schools as places where their children are going to learn readin', writin', an' 'rithmetic. And when a school goes about trying to educate a child without necessarily having large, daily doses of those subjects, then people begin to question just what's going on. Whereas if we used that other title, then they couldn't ask so many questions, since they have no predetermined ideas about such an institution, having never attended one; and they would listen to descriptions of what's going on and what we're trying to do in an altogether new context. They'd stop defining us against their old school experiences. But so long as we are a school, we are, by tradition, and by inclination, tied to doing some things that regular schools do. We all feel that the skills taught by traditional schools are valuable tools, without which the process of self-definition could not be completed.

So what do I, as a teacher in this school, do in light of the premises in which I believe? I mean, what do I do with myself during those six hours every day when I'm there with those children? Reading is taught in our primary class, to the child who is ready to learn. Every day there is a reading "lesson." If the child is ready to learn, he participates, and through participation learns the skill. If not, he quietly goes on about his own business. He is not set against reading by being forced, but gradually, through exposure, becomes ready to tackle it himself. With my "seniors," nine-to-thirteen-year-olds, I have fallen into a pattern of "doing math" first thing every morning. This began because a boy who will be going into public junior high school next year got worried about how he was going to make out. Each day I worked with him, using Cuisenaire rods, attempting to build up some understanding about what fractions are all about. Other kids asked if I would give them some work and help with it. Now pretty well all of the children, except two or three die-hards, work daily on math. I remind one or two that their books are there, in the box, with some work in them—nothing more. If they do it, I mark it, help them with it, and lead them into the next concept. After that's over, usually between 10 and 10:15, another teacher comes in to work with them on science projects. He has just started with us and is kind of feeling his way around. The first couple of things he did, he had everyone involved; then interest lagged. Now, those who are really interested in doing a specific project with his assistance hound him; the rest, the novelty over, go about their morning work of drawing, bugging someone, fighting about something, playing a game—Monopoly, chess, cards—playing roughhouse downstairs, going to the store for candy, eating lunch, snooping around the primary room to see what's going on there, etc. During this time I work with one or two kids who are not doing science, and who want more individual attention than I could give earlier; or I set up the kiln, make some phone calls, or do any number of administrative jobs awaiting attention. The afternoons are established as an art time. Two or three weeks before Christmas we began work on batiks. I set up a waxing table, explained how the process works, and let the kids go at it. Most of them kept at it for a full two weeks, waxing, dyeing, rewaxing, dyeing the same piece, until they had achieved richly colored, subtly patterned designs. The batiks were then washed, ironed out, and sewed on burlap. Clay, papier-mâché, paint, ink, collage—we go through all media, a week or two at a time. Just about everyone becomes involved, then they lose interest and we go on to something else. Throughout all these afternoons, I help kids get materials they want, show them how to do something if asked, talk with them, settle arguments, break up fights, talk with them, listen to them, offer opinions, withhold opinions, tell jokes, tell stories, laugh, get angry, get excited, comfort, scold. A couple of times I have blown my lid, yelled indignantly, and sent some kids home. One group for continually harassing one kid who is their preferred target. Another kid for being a snotty little bitch about how much cleanup she should be doing. Everyone thought it was pretty funny, myself included, the time that I got mad, shot off my mouth, and sent two kids home—only to find my entire speech recorded by some kid who had been messing around with the tape recorder.

I suppose, to summarize my role, I could simply say that I am an adult whose job it is to help children with whatever tasks they have taken upon themselves. I treat them as I would treat any other person, with consideration and respect. I don't often get too much of it back from them, at least not at first. But it comes. For example, once after a prolonged discussion with one girl about how I didn't like it when she burped in my face in front of the public-health nurse, how I felt about it, how she wouldn't do that in front of her mother, and how there are other reasons for not doing it besides the threat of punishment, I told her that I felt I was generally considerate toward her, and that if she needed help I would give it to her as quickly and as well as I could, and that in return I would appreciate the same kind of consideration.

I explained how difficult it is for me to be pleasant with her if she burps in my face, and yet it seemed she had never thought about that at all. She was getting a bit "cute" with me by the end of our conversation, as comes through in her final comment, "Well, gee, when you've been brought up on punishments all your life, it's hard to think about not doing nasty things for any other reason." I felt she understood my point, so left it at that. So far, she hasn't burped in my face again.

One of my colleagues feels, and quite rightly too, I believe, that if we didn't take in children with public school background, but formed our senior group only from students who have had all their preschool and primary schooling in our school, then there would not be the need for the remedial work (in terms of attitudes) at the senior end of the school. However, ever since the school has been operating, 1962, I don't believe it has ever had a senior class without bringing in some students from the public system. After youngsters have had four, five, or six years in our school, they are often eager for a broader selection of friends than is possible in our small groups. Too, they often become interested in participating in team sports, which, again, our numbers do little to facilitate.

I myself feel, in spite of the strain and the bad times, that this remedial function is a valid one, and I would not like to see ourselves shun the outside community for fear it would disturb our blissful, self-contained one. We certainly could not begin to take on all the "problem children" that worried parents wish us to enroll; we have neither the training nor facilities for that sort of undertaking. But with children who are elsewhere classified as "normal," I feel we have a chance of succeeding, and therefore a reason to try.

Of the twenty in my senior group during the "Free School" year, two were enrolled in the school from an early age because of parental belief in the need for a human kind of education, and the remaining eighteen were enrolled because they, or another child in their family, were having *some difficulty* in coping with the regular school. Of the sixteen families of these children, twelve of the fathers worked in the professions—teachers, architects, social workers, engineers, etc.—three fathers were involved in business, one father was unknown to us (not living with the mother), and six of the mothers were involved with professional jobs or other full-time commitments outside their homes. Two families had remarried divorcees, and in all the rest but one, children lived with both their parents. All were economically within the middle-class income range, from lower-middle through upper-middle. Twelve of the twenty were of Anglo-Saxon Canadian or American extraction; the others were Jewish or German Canadian immigrants. Of the twenty children, about nine had real "problems," not merely "difficulties," serious enough in the public school system for their parents to look for alternate schooling. But most of the problems were not ones that the teachers of these youngsters considered to be terribly serious, and many, many children with worse problems remain in the system. Of the nine, I would say eight had emotional-attitude hang-ups; and of this eight, I would say that four had their hang-ups caused by their negative school experience, and the other four had their emotional hang-ups amplified by their schooling. Of the nine with problems, five had academic difficulties, and of these, in a public school, only one would be classified as "abnormal," in that she was a girl with a "subnormal" I.Q. Out of the entire twenty children, I would say that only one of these children would be, in any way, classified as abnormal in a public school; that one being the slow learner. Two, maybe three, of the rest may have come to the principal's attention for some reason or another at some time during the school year, but in my opinion none of them would have made the principal's "worry list."

Some information about Vancouver's public schools will probably bring the New School into sharper relief. I'll describe the average by describing the best. Individually, in schools throughout the city, teachers are testily dipping their toes into various experimental schemes. But these schemes, from what I can discover of them, are basically alterations in curriculum: a relaxation of previously held standards; a recognition of the fact that children of the same age don't all learn at the same rate (new, aren't they?!!); a realization that "bright" children can, and will, if pushed, do more, achieve more.

I know of one program where a university professor is working with two primary teachers in the system to attempt to put across a mathematics program whose emphasis is on the fun of playing with and learning about numbers. This man openly states to children that if they aren't enjoying what they are doing then there's no value in it. He has two young and enthusiastic teachers working with him; yet I know, from speaking with one of them, that she does not carry this philosophy over into her teaching of other subjects. In a discussion between the staff of our school and some liberal-minded public school teachers, she explained her method of achieving silence in her grade-one classroom—something to do with standing silently before them and looking stern. She found it difficult to understand how any teacher could have difficulty with such a simple task but later admitted that the children were undoubtedly responding to some authoritarian thing which she had established. Two of the four public school teachers who took part in this discussion had no qualms at all about the correctness of their being prescriptive about what children need to learn in order to get on in the world, and their responsibility to their classes to see that they "get it." Both felt what they were doing to be extremely free-wheeling and revolutionary; yet in no way does it affect the personal relationship that each had with his students. The other two seem to be questioning the over-all system more and are regarded as oddballs in their schools, getting a bad time from their students (in the way I had in my first year of teaching), other teachers, their principals, and, of course, their inspectors.

I know of two public schools in the Vancouver area that are attempting to effect change on a school-wide basis—one, a newly constructed, open-area elementary school and the other a high school with some lively administrators. I have visited neither. Of the open-area school, I am told that teachers are engaged in team teaching, that grade-seven students act as guides, showing visitors around, and that children in the school are quiet and engaged in activities. Of their curriculum, I have heard nothing, but feel strongly that it, rather than the "whole child," would be the main concern of the teachers in this school. The high school has abandoned bells, detentions, and presumably corporal punishment. However, I am told the lessons go on much as they always have, with the teacher telling, explaining, what the kids have to learn, and that disruptive behavior is curbed with threats of visits to the principal's office. The comment of an ex–New School student (who academically is achieving very well), on the difference between an up-tight high school he attended and this progressive one, pretty well sums up the extent of the progress: "At the other school they tortured you to death, here you just die."

So, from these few contacts I have had with what is going on in our public schools, I can only conclude that they haven't changed much since I was in them, and that they are, in fact, very repressive. Corporal punishment is maintained, being used to a greater and lesser extent, depending on the bent of the principal. Children are lined up and shut up. They are the raw material with which the teachers work. The teacher has the responsibility and power to shape the child to his mold. This wouldn't be so bad if it weren't for the fact that somewhere along the way many, many teachers have lost, or never had, their sensitivity, their creativity, their artfulness.

I can't but agree with Jim Herndon's *The Way It Spozed to Be,* which concludes that the system isn't going to make the radical changes it needs to fast enough to satisfy the needs of its consumers. The school system of Vancouver, along with those in the general metropolitan area, about one million in population, is like some mammoth giant from the past, trying to run with broken legs to catch the jets and missiles that pierce his heaven.

I should emphasize, I suppose, that despite my reservations about the "total freedom" disaster last year, I don't mean to challenge the notion that under freedom the child will be more productive and a better learner. Nor do I feel I've disproved the belief that without pressure to compete, children will become more sensitive and kinder to one another. My experiences are not general throughout the New School and can be attributed in part to the fact that my group was formed from students with public school backgrounds. I've described experiences because I feel that there are many pitfalls involved in free-progressive educa-

tion which those interested in free schools should be aware of.
It's a hard enough job to cope with the wear and tear of this type
of learning, even without the mistaken preconception that if
you're free with children, everything will be gro-o-ovy. The meaningful learning that children do in a "free" situation hardly ever
resembles the regular-school type of learning at all. Children,
people, learn sensitivity and kindness when they have unlimited
opportunity to relate with one another. The learning process is
painful and nasty to observe, and is often disappointing, discouraging, and disillusioning. When you're involved in the daily
fray, you're often unable to see and take reassurance from the
long-term growth of the child. People all too often make snap
judgments about things, and I am sure that anyone visiting our
school, who isn't already radically predisposed, must go away
convinced that we are all raving loonies, and that nothing constructive, in any terms, could come from such an environment. So
I feel people must be told what happens in a free school, or when
they try it and everything does not go smoothly, they will rush
back to the security of the old ways, with a genuine feeling that
they did try it and it doesn't work. Moreover, they are then in a
position to make pronouncements which only further hinder any
hopes of change. There was a perfect example of this type of
thing a few months ago in an article in a provincial teacher's
magazine entitled "Come As You Please: It Didn't Work for Us."
It was a report on a two-month experiment with the grade-ten
students in a high school. Briefly, no one was *made* to attend
classes. That was the only alteration on the behalf of the school.
Result? You guessed it—many, many kids skipped school, or particular classes. The conclusion? Kids are irresponsible, need
structure, supervision, etc., etc., *ad nauseam.* Was there any criticism of the course of studies being offered? Of course not! Very
few question the validity of it all.

I should like people to make the distinction between children
who have spent their entire school lives in a free-progressive
school and those children who have been admitted after four or
five years of public schooling. I feel secure in asserting that those
children enrolled in our pre-school and primary groups are, and

will continue to be, engaged in productive learning, with a minimum of acting out, so long as they stay within our school for four
to six years; and that the growth of these children closely paral-
lels the "free school" philosophy and ideology. Children who
have learned from their public school experience, on the other
hand, that learning is a drag; that adults are the bosses, and, as
such, are always right; that their fellow students are out-and-out
rivals for status, recognition, praise . . . all that is "worth while"
in that system of education—these are quite a different kettle of
fish. Those who are going to work with such kids should realize
this and be prepared for it.

I suppose that what I am really trying to say is that free-school
advocates, like their public school counterparts, are inclined to
focus on the positive, happy side of their experiences, without
also sharing their doubts, their unhappy experiences, their misgivings and their failures. Unless these aspects too, probably
larger than half our experiences, are shared with those who are
just turning our way, we will lose them.

I strongly believe that an Institute for Self-Definition should be
a full-time program, not a summer workshop or afternoon arrangement supporting a more formal program. I cannot say it
long or loud or clear enough: Until children have established
their identity, they cannot and will not become genuinely involved in the pursuit of any academic discipline. Therefore our
school-institution will conduct itself, on a full-time basis, with
this in mind. It cannot do otherwise, with our point of view. The
primary children, who have not been turned off themselves, will
learn the skills they need, which will undoubtedly include reading, writing, and arithmetic. The older children, the remedial
class, will probably do very little of an academic order. But their
learning will be very meaningful. They will learn that there are
adults who believe that fun and learning happen at the same
time. They will learn that adults-teachers are people; people who
have moods; who get happy, sad, angry, pleased, tired; people
who have likes and dislikes; who become excited about different
things; who have differing skills. Through free discussions they
will find out what their teacher thinks about the local political

scene, the war, hunting, the traffic or air-pollution problem, what feels better, wet or dry sand, mud squishing through the toes— any matter at all that comes to their attention or curiosity. They learn a great deal this way because the questions come from them, not the teacher. They are matters about which they are curious, and they are free to exercise their curiosity.

I suppose that I could say that this year's students are becoming kinder, more humane, and more creative in their work, play, and personal relations than were last year's on the whole; but I would hardly attribute this to my direction. The factor that contributes most heavily to this, I feel, is the plurality of leadership that is apparent in our school. The children are aware that the school is run by three of us, who have formed a co-op, and that no one person is in charge or has authority. Because of this, the teachers in our school jointly discuss problems and make group decisions. For the purpose of dealing with outside institutions, we have allocated titles to ourselves, mine being "Director"; I assume certain directoral roles when it comes to dealing with the outside, and yet my position in these dealings is determined by discussions and decisions made on a group basis. This mutuality of responsibility works within the school, too, and the children accept it and respond to it.

I am thoroughly convinced that 95 per cent of all the "academic learning" that goes on in public schools is meaningless blather to the children engaged in it. That the real lessons these children learn have to do with the unpleasantness of learning, the lack of joy in books, the grind of doing arithmetic, the drudgery of answering other people's questions instead of one's own, the vast distance between themselves and their teachers, between anything meaningful in their lives and their schooling. As one youngster expressed it to me: "Being in school is like being on a bus; you sit there and watch the world go by, and you can't get off until three-fifteen."

TEACHING "UNTEACHABLES": THE ACID TEST

20. THE BOARDMAN ELEMENTARY SCHOOL

Evans Clinchy

Even in the most hopeless-seeming urban school systems, like the one described by Jonathan Kozol in Part One, school reform is possible. The decentralized Boardman Elementary School, described by Evans Clinchy, offers an experimental, high-quality program within the Boston public school system where Kozol taught.

Evans Clinchy is a general consultant to the Educational Planning Center of the Boston Public Schools.

Larry is black, handsome, and angry, a strapping twelve-year-old lad who comes from a broken home in Roxbury, Boston's Negro ghetto. At first glance, Larry would seem to be a perfect candidate for destruction in an all-black ghetto school in a large American city such as Boston.

Indeed, his record during his early years in school indicated that he was headed in that direction, for it was a record of constant trouble, periodic expulsions, and repeated recommendations for psychological treatment. While school itself may have caused many of Larry's problems, not all of his difficulties originated there. He often appeared at the school door with large welts on his body, apparently caused by a belt buckle because his mother feels that force is her only means of controlling him. He cannot stand to be touched or shoved. When this happens, he is likely to lash out in a lethal fury, often causing severe injury to his unlucky or unwise antagonist.

Yet no one has ever tried to deny that Larry is bright as hell. His eyes and his whole face crackle with intelligence, but it is an intelligence that has rarely been directed at doing well in school.

For the past two years, however, Larry has not undergone destruction in the Boston public school he has been attending, the Boardman Elementary School—a small, ninety-three-year-old condemned building smack in the middle of a Roxbury urban renewal area. At about the time of Larry's arrival, Boardman had just become the first school in a new experiment within the Boston public school system, something that in Boston is called a "model demonstration subsystem." The idea is similar to the three "demonstration" school districts in New York City: IS 201, Two Bridges, and Ocean Hill–Brownsville. Unlike the decentralized districts in New York, the Boston subsystem does not have an independent governing board. It does, however, have a great deal of administrative autonomy and operates without many of the restrictions that bind other big-city school districts.

From the outside, the Boardman school looks like a typical ghetto school. Inside it is not at all typical. True, the lighting is not all it should be. Paint is peeling from the walls, and, in winter, the cold wind rushes in through the loose window frames. No one wants to put money into a building that will be torn down. But, as many visitors have said, the shock of the building wears off quickly. The bleak entrance hall is typical of the distinctive quality of the life of the school, for it serves as the auditorium and art studio, so that a visitor may have to pick his way past a papier-mâché snowman, a windmill, a play rehearsal, or a singing group. Even the stairway walls have been painted with crazy murals by the children.

Nor are the classrooms typical either. In many there are no desks for either students or teacher, just a few tables and some chairs. For the most part, the rooms are filled with materials and things for children to do—ranging from microscopes, balance beams, growing plants, gerbils, turtles, and tadpoles, to Cuisenaire rods, an easily worked printing press, a puppet theater, an electric typewriter, and a set of photographs taken in Roxbury and set up so that children can look at familiar places and write stories about them.

These materials are often, but not always, grouped in particular parts of the room according to subject matter. There may be a math corner, a science corner, or an animal section. There is almost always one corner, partly screened off and equipped with more comfortable chairs, filled with books on many different topics and at many different levels of difficulty. None of these are textbooks or graded readers, but rather storybooks, books of riddles or puzzles, or books about rockets, lost cities, or buried treasure.

Throughout most of the school day, the children can choose the materials they want to work with. They can read, work with another child on the balance beam, take care of the animals, work out problems on the Cuisenaire rods, or type out a story on the typewriter. The teacher moves about the room helping children do what they have themselves chosen to do. At times, because the teacher keeps track of what each child does, she will suggest a certain activity for a certain child or a group of children. If a few of the children have not chosen to do any math of late, she may pull several of them together into a small group and get them started on some math work. A teacher may also suggest a large and complicated project—a puppet show or a field trip into the surrounding neighborhood to see what's going on and to provide inspiration for stories and pictures. The children who wish to get involved in the project may do so. In most cases, if they do not wish to volunteer, they may continue with whatever else they are doing.

It is a strange way to run a school. And how does it work for a young man like Larry? When Larry first came to Boardman he was not at all sure he was going to like it any better than any of his other schools. Indeed, Boardman at that time was not much different from any other ghetto elementary school. But because it was part of the "model demonstration subsystem," Boardman was staffed with volunteer teachers from other Boston schools. It was also supported with additional federal money under Title I of the Elementary and Secondary Education Act, which made it possible to buy substantial quantities of extra materials and to add extra teachers, curriculum specialists, teacher aides drawn from parents and the larger Roxbury community, and extra administrative help.

But extra money, extra people, and extra materials, while necessary, were not sufficient to make Boardman radically different. The crucial element has been autonomy—with mandate of the subsystem to be experimental, to think about different and better ways of educating children and to try them out. It may sound delightful and easy, but it wasn't. The teachers, for the most part, were accustomed to following the "curriculum," the set of rules governing what should be taught, when, and how. These rules had become habitual for the teachers, and it was no easy task suddenly to cast them off and become free and "experimental," whatever that was supposed to mean.

Nor was it easy for Larry and the older children in the school to learn that instead of always doing what they were told to do, they were now supposed to exercise their own powers of choice. Even more disturbing, they were now supposed to be responsible for what they did. If they embarked upon a scientific experiment with their microscopes, they were now encouraged to keep at it until the question they had started with was answered, until they actually got the bulb to light or found out what that was they saw through the microscope. They were now supposed to figure out for themselves why the bulb lit up or why a human hair had all those different parts. They were not just supposed to find the answer in a book and remember it in order to give the right answer back on a test. In short, they were expected to ask themselves questions and find the answers on their own (with help from the teacher).

All of this started slowly at Boardman. Different teachers

began it in different ways and with differing degrees of success and enthusiasm. There is a name for the type of instruction at Boardman—the developmental classroom—but there is no pat formula. What it means essentially is that the teacher (or teacher and assistants) and the children must make the decisions about what goes on in the room, about the materials and what is done with them, about class activities, about individual projects, and themselves be responsible for whatever learning takes place or fails to take place.

Larry's first teacher took the message of freedom with great seriousness. The children were allowed almost free rein. In those early days, the staff still had not had much experience with "self-instructional" materials, that is, materials that children could work with on their own with minimal assistance or direction from a teacher. And none of the children had any experience with running their own educational lives. The result in Larry's room was close to chaos, a condition to which Larry was no small contributor.

For, like his teacher, Larry took the message quite seriously. Given the opportunity to make his own decisions, Larry made at least one clear decision—he was damn well going to do just exactly what he wanted to do, and if any other kid interfered, that kid was going to get it in the chops. But gradually, to everyone's surprise—and this may well have included Larry himself—he discovered that one thing he wanted very much to do was to find out what makes things grow. Although some of the other teachers and children thought they were pretty good at getting things to grow, they soon realized that they were in the presence of a genius. Larry could get almost anything to grow—grass, plants, fungi, almost anything at all. He could grow them in paper cups, in coffee cans, in mud, in sand. And that is what Larry did, almost exclusively. He not only grew things but read about them endlessly. He became, in short order, a savant in plant biology and began to teach his speciality to other children, especially children from the primary classes.

Unlike Larry, the primary children, for the most part, have not had any experience in other schools, so in many ways, theirs are the most interesting classes in the school. These younger children (the equivalent of first through third graders, although they are all mixed up in the same room) do not have ingrained routines to unlearn. So they take to the busy, hectic life of their classrooms with enormous gusto. All of the materials in the room are labeled—the rabbit, the fish, the electric typewriter, the door, the chalk. No one tells a child what something is. He has to learn to read it for himself. One of the crack teachers, Mrs. Jane Fitzgerald, has tried a form of "organic reading."

If a child wants a word, Mrs. Fitzgerald writes it on an index card and gives it back to the child. Each child thus begins a collection of his own words, and these then are turned into stories which the children collect into books and illustrate. The children type out many of their stories on the typewriter, which is slowly being recognized as one of the most useful inventions in the history of education.

Take Anthony, for instance, one of Mrs. Fitzgerald's prize pupils, who is the official typewriter teacher. Although it is often difficult for an adult to understand what Anthony is saying, the other children have no difficulty when Anthony takes over and gives one of his lectures on how to operate the electric typewriter. If you don't know how it works, go ask Anthony, but you'll have to wait your turn, for the typewriter is one of the most popular "self-instructional" materials in the room.

The Boardman classrooms are full of Anthonys, male and female. They drive the teachers quite mad with their questions, their unquenchable energy, their ideas and projects. In fact, every room at Boardman is now staffed with a full-time teacher assistant drawn from the community and often with a student-teacher as well. It takes that many adults just to keep track of what all the children are doing, just to answer all their questions and give them all the special attention and the constant approval they need.

Tough high school kids, as well as sweet young innocents, respond to this kind of freedom in the classroom. Last year, a small high school operation that was part of the demonstration subsystem was crammed into one end of a building that also housed the junior high that was part of the subsystem. The high school, consisting of two grades (nine and ten) and about 150 students, had been in full-fledged existence only since September 1967. Both the teachers and the students were wary and spent most of the year carefully feeling their way toward each other. By spring, the staff had made a good many departures from the traditional way of running a high school. For instance, the teachers began working in an interdisciplinary fashion—combining art, English, and social studies in a study of heroes. This involved an analysis of the Gary Cooper role in *High Noon,* the Sidney Poitier character in *Raisin in the Sun,* and a study of the Trojan War (this was quite a hit). The students are also making their own films with the help of an expert (and black) film-maker, studying Afro-American history, and hearing local (and militant) civil rights speakers.

Then came April 4, 1968. When the news struck that Martin Luther King had been assassinated, no one knew quite what to do or what might happen. Everyone on the staff appeared at school the next day expecting riots. Surprisingly, most of the students showed up, too. They, like the rest of Roxbury, were "up tight." Handbills were being distributed throughout the neighborhoods by local groups warning the black residents to "cool it," claiming that the white police were going to exterminate the black population of Roxbury.

In this atmosphere of tension, the teachers and the students confronted each other on the morning of April 5. It quickly became apparent to the staff that a small group of the "bandits," the really tough, turned-off cases, both male and female, were emerging as the student leadership (none of them having been elected to the formal student government). The first thing the students wanted was a moratorium on classes and the convening of an assembly, run by and for themselves alone, to decide what they were going to do. The proposal was presented to the two women who were running the school, Miss Grace Whittaker and Miss Theresa Hamrock, and they bought it.

When school resumed the following week, the "junta" and classroom representatives drew up a list of demands for changes in the operation of the school, including suggestions for new school rules, all typed and run off on the ditto machine by the students themselves. The list contained about fifteen items, falling roughly into two groups. One group revolved around a desire for all of the regular rituals that go with traditional high schools —a longer graduation for the ninth grade, a semiformal dance, a class day, a class picture, and "A SYMBOL TO IDENTY OUR SELVES AND WHAT WE STAND FOR."

The second group of demands aimed to establish the fact that they were autonomous human beings and had a right to exert some control over their own destiny in school. This was not exactly a preview of the violent scenes at Columbia University or in Paris, but the mood of the students in the colleges, the resistance to being treated as incompetent juveniles unable to take any responsibility for their own behavior—these had a familiar ring to the Roxbury high school students.

The list of demands called for some small adjustments in school rules and ended with this one: "BEFOR A STUDENT CAN BE SUSPENDED HE OR SHE MUST BE DESIDED BY THE BOARD. WHEN A STUDENT COMES BACK THEY MUST BE ACCOMPLIED BY A PARENTS. A BOARD MEMBER MUST BE PRESENT." One intent of this regulation was immediately clear—the students want a piece of the administrative action that galled them most, the ability of the staff to kick them out of the school at what appeared to be the administration's whim. But that was not all. Suspensions have led to heated confrontations between the school staff and angry parents who think their child has been unjustly treated. What the students wanted, they explained later, was, yes, some say over why people should or should not be suspended, but also a chance to make it clear to parents that a suspension was not an arbitrary, ruthless act on the part of the staff. The reason for having the board member present when the parents brought a student back was *to protect the staff*. It would be up to the board member to explain why both staff and students had decided that a suspension was necessary. The staff accepted the establishment of the board and the proposed new rules.

But what does all this experimentation—in the long run—

prove? One thing that has to be said immediately is that in the one or two years that these schools have been in operation, there has not been any large, across-the-board jump in the scores on standardized reading and achievement tests. The most we can say is that the subsystem students do not fall further behind each year on the tests.

Has the Boardman School been able to "rescue" Larry, to save him from destruction? In a sense, yes, but in many other real ways, no. Yes, he liked going to school there. It gave him a chance to develop in many ways that a traditional school would not have. But Boardman was not able to provide Larry with the kind of psychological help he needed in order to curb or cure the anger and violence inside him (his last assault required six stitches in the head of his victim). Residential care away from his mother plus a Boardman-type school might rescue Larry, but this, Boardman has not been able to provide. Larry may never be rescued. As for the general run of children at Boardman, we just don't know yet. No child has had a chance to start at the age of four at Boardman and graduate to a junior high or middle school.

But in many areas, and especially in ways that do not show up on tests, we think that considerable advances have been made. We feel that the attitudes of the children, especially the younger ones, have been almost magically transformed. Something must be happening at the upper levels, too, if students are devising rules to help protect teachers.

As for teachers, there is little doubt now in their minds that these black ghetto children can learn, that they have great intellectual energy if they are given a chance to use it. At the high school, while there is still considerable despair about reading levels and finding adequate materials, there is also, especially after the assassination drama, the beginnings of a tremendous respect for the "bandits," an admiration for their sense of independence and their self-reliance. Teachers are now beginning to worry about the more docile students.

Even the brief history of the subsystem says with some clarity that *decentralization can work* and is absolutely necessary to the establishment of viable schools. Individual teachers and administrators must have the autonomy to act as adult professionals, plus the additional money to make change possible. It is equally clear that there must be a great deal more involvement of parents and community people, perhaps not to the extent of total control, but at least to the point where they feel they have a real voice in what happens to their children—and thus some honest responsibility.

It is also quite clear that, as yet, the subsystem, which includes a total of only 700 of Boston's 93,000 public school children, has not had time to have a major impact on the roughly 23,000 other black children in the city or on the remaining 70,000 white children. We are only just beginning to wrestle with the problem of spreading what goes on in the subsystem to other schools—which will depend to some extent on whether anyone wants what goes on in the subsystem to be spread.

The most important thing of all, however, is the simple knowledge that it really is possible to operate first-rate schools in the middle of a black ghetto. We do not pretend to have all of the answers. But we do know that the children are perfectly educable. We know that, given sufficient freedom, money, and interest on the part of white America, the schools can be changed. There is hope for ghetto schools—if we really give a damn.

21. THE PENNSYLVANIA ADVANCEMENT SCHOOL
Farnum Gray

Sometimes it is necessary to break ghetto students out of their regular schools and give them an entirely different experience. The Pennsylvania Advancement

> *School concentrates on emotional rather than aca-*
> *demic growth, using group therapy, role-playing, and*
> *psychodrama.*
>
> *Farnum Gray is curriculum writer on the staff of the*
> *Pennsylvania Advancement School.*

"I'm in a glass cage!" he cried. "I can't talk to you, but you can talk to me. Communicate with me!"

The students circled the teacher, shouting insults.

"Look at that thing in the cage!"

"Ha, haaaa! He can't get out!"

The shouting seventh- and eighth-grade boys were in an improvisational drama class at the Pennsylvania Advancement School, which despite its name is not a school but a laboratory for developing new ways of learning and releasing creativity. Working with students selected from Philadelphia's eight school districts, the staff (a group of artists, dancers, writers, actors, researchers, teachers, and specialists in media technology and curriculum development) refines programs until they are conspicuously successful, at which time they are field-tested in the local public schools.

The students are boys whose work in regular schools is far below their capability—like Howard, one of the boys shouting the most obnoxious insults. Called Fat Albert by the other boys, Howard had the heft and waddle of Bill Cosby's comic character. A Black kid from the slums, he was likely to react to any difficult situation with "I'll beat the shit out of you!"

As the taunting boys circled the imagined cage, Chet, a gawky white boy, exclaimed: "Let's help him get out!"

The whole tone changed.

"We want to help you!"

"Let's break the glass and get him out."

Suddenly the teacher, George Mager, relaxed and smiled; the "cage" dissolved. Mager sat cross-legged on the floor and the boys gathered around him. His arms were around two boys, and all were enveloped in the warmth of his concern for them as they discussed what had happened. Eleven teachers who had come to observe at the experimental school sat at one side of the room. But for Mager and the boys, nothing existed outside their circle of light.

"What was it about?" Mager asked them. "What were you doing?" And the boys talked excitedly, trying to explain their actions.

Then Mager asked, "What *was* that glass cage?"

"It doesn't have to be a glass cage," Chet said intensely.

"What do you mean?"

"Well, you know, George, like lots of times when I'm with my friends, I feel like I'm in a glass cage."

Then Howard's gravelly voice said, "Whenever I'm at a party, I feel like I'm in a cage." He was more serious than the boys had heard him before. Howard revealed himself in that discussion. From that day, he started changing dramatically, gaining confidence in himself and winning the respect of the other boys. By the time he had finished his fourteen weeks at the Advancement School and was ready to return to his public school, Howard had become the acknowledged leader of the class. His case was no fluke. Of the eight boys in the class, seven made important gains in dealing with some of their most prominent personality difficulties. One made little improvement.

Howard's break-through followed considerable work with all of his teachers, who made a point of getting to know the boys and learning about their problems, both academic and personal.

The improvisational drama incident illustrates several qualities with which the Advancement School thinks schools should be strongly imbued. It was exciting. The students took an active part in determining the direction and content of the class. (For Howard, the content was his feelings about himself.) The sharpening of perceptions and the education of the emotions were important processes in the class. And it took place in a climate of friendly understanding, facilitated by a teacher who cared.

The school is on the third and fourth floors of what used to be a factory. Despite some handicaps—such as having a three-foot-

thick concrete pillar every five yards—the space has been made
into an inviting environment, though it doesn't look much like a
school. It has large areas of open space, with two L-shaped
rooms. Orange, blue-green, and red carpets run from wall to wall
throughout.

Stranger than the school's physical setting is its history. It
opened in November 1964 in Winston-Salem. Called the North
Carolina Advancement School, it worked for two and a half years
with underachieving boys from all over the state. It was controlled by the Learning Institute of North Carolina (LINC), a
nonprofit corporation set up outside the state's public school
bureaucracy to do educational experimentation. LINC's director
was Harold Howe II, who later went on to become the U.S.
Commissioner of Education.

The Carnegie Corporation, which had provided $500,000 to
help start the school, considered it "among the most far-reaching
and useful educational programs in America."

But the success was too conspicuous and so was the racial
integration. (It was the first integrated boarding school in the
South.) Since the school's founding the North Carolina Superintendent of Public Instruction had worked to get the school's
funds cut off.

On March 2, 1967, the State Board of Education and the
Superintendent of Schools changed course and recommended
that the school be put under their control. The state legislature
followed the recommendation.

Rather than try to work under the system's constraints, about
half the staff—headed by Peter L. Buttenwieser, who was the
school's director for its last year in North Carolina—accepted a
remarkable offer: Dr. Mark R. Shedd, the new Philadelphia
school superintendent, proposed to transplant the school to
Philadelphia to be an agent of change in his school system.

The entire professional staff left Winston-Salem, with a substantial number moving to the southern part of North Carolina to
establish another innovative school, The Charlotte Learning
Academy.

The Pennsylvania Advancement School opened its factory

doors in October 1967 with forty-three staff members—seventeen from the North Carolina predecessor. It serves from 150 to 220 students, depending on how many are needed for projects being carried on during a given semester, about 60 per cent Black, drawn from all sections of Philadelphia.

The school is a nonprofit corporation with a board of directors, working under contract to the School District of Philadelphia. Other than being a day school (classes meet from 9 A.M. to 2 P.M.), rather than residential, the setup is much as it was in North Carolina.

Challenged by Mark Shedd to make a constructive impact on Philadelphia's enormous, bogged-down school system, the school has begun by concentrating on two exceptionally receptive junior high schools, Sayre and Vaux. Three members of the staff who have teaching experience, and are specialists in English, social studies and math-science, work with teachers of the two schools on an individual basis.

In addition, visiting teachers from other schools get leaves of absence from their jobs to observe, get ideas, or carry out short curriculum development projects at the Advancement School.

The Advancement School's climate was described from a student's viewpoint by Jose Ortiz, a seventh-grader:

> This is a school that's different. You can ask me how and I'll tell you. In this school you're something. You're somebody to be known and cared about. Not pushed around, but treated with respect and dignity. In return, you treat the teachers with respect and dignity, and listen to what things they've got to say. When you have a problem you can go and talk to somebody about it, and they will try to help you with your problem.
>
> It's really different to be cared about. Usually in regular schools you and your teachers don't have a chance to know each other. You are two different people in the world.
>
> Not in this school. We talk a lot to the teachers. But not only that, we play games like ping-pong (Oh, the thrill of slamming on a teacher!), chess, checkers, Monopoly, and a

lot of cards. What we can discuss over a hand of blackjack or poker, you would be surprised on the subjects.

As Jose notes, one who assumes that the content of public education should be that which is between the covers of textbooks *would* "be surprised on the subjects" taken up at the Advancement School. They are the subjects inner-city boys normally talk about, and other subjects that they get into when they are encouraged to pursue their concerns through the familiar to the semifamiliar and then the unfamiliar.

They take up racial problems, the relationship between poverty and self-concept, and that staple of the mass media—violence.

With their own experiences providing much of the content, the students sharpen skills used in perceiving, analyzing, interpreting, and communicating. Students often start with the question "Who am I?" If they can learn to perceive and understand their own emotions and relate them to the emotions of other people, they sometimes gain in the ability to predict and control their own actions and empathize with the actions of others. This process may produce changed behavior, but if so, it is because the boy's perception of himself has changed, not because change was required or requested by the school. Improving human perception seems to be the best way of changing human behavior; advice, admonition, and punishment are of little use, if any.

Many Philadelphia junior high school students are far below grade level in reading and other basic skills, but trying to force them to catch up is ineffective unless the causes of their underachievement are dealt with. If a student begins to perceive himself as capable, and if he feels that his teachers and classmates value him as a person, he might become open to cognitive learning.

For Jeff, a stocky, Black twelve-year-old, the most relevant content was his own uncontrolled hostility. On his arrival at the Advancement School, he was an extrovert—very physical but without knowing how to express himself physically. To get attention, he hit, bumped, and grabbed people, or shouted.

For his teachers to force Jeff to suppress his feelings and study the conventional subject matter would have been absurd. He was not going to learn much if his energies were concentrated on trying to act passive while he seethed with aggressive feelings.

Jeff found that he did not have to be passive at the Advancement School. He was a nuisance, but he talked more and more honestly, particularly about his distrust of white people. In his improvisational drama class, he was getting better control of himself and his acting was starting to sparkle. In his fourth week at the school, Jeff watched one day as Ray, a former parochial school student, tried to convince a young woman not to become a nun. Sitting on a cushion in the semidark room, Jeff recalled that Ray had talked bitterly several times of how nuns had beaten him, preached at him, and otherwise abused him. The improvisation was especially interesting because the part of the young woman was played by Sister Fran, a nun who had come down from New York with a handful of the other black-clad teachers from the school where she worked. In introducing herself to the class, Sister Fran had said that she took an improvisational drama course for teachers at the Advancement School the past summer, and had brought other teachers from her school to learn about it and other Advancement School techniques.

As the improvisation started, Ray fidgeted in his checked sport coat and could not look Sister Fran in the eye. Finally he started to warm up, and his acting was believable as he said, "Nuns are crappy!"

"What do you mean by crappy?" Sister Fran asked.

"Well, they stink. Too holy!"

When the improvisation ended, Ray seemed livelier than usual as he sat next to Jeff.

Next, one "actor" was assigned to convince another that he should quit school to run numbers and push drugs. Jeff and his classmates liked it, and groaned when the teacher, George Mager, yelled "FREEZE" to end it. Then George stepped toward Jeff with a friendly smile and extended his hand. Jeff slipped his hand into the firm grasp, hopped up, and stepped into the spotlight.

George announced, "Jeff is a Black Power leader—Black militant. Okay?"

Then George gave a hand to Frank, a bright, sensitive white boy who was disheartened by the hostility Jeff and some of his Black friends were showing for whites. "You've got to convince Jeff not to be a Black militant," George instructed Frank. "Get your tension up," he told the boys. "Get your concentration. Okay? Here we go."

"I've heard a lot of rumors about you," Frank said.

Bouncing jauntily, Jeff snapped, "Like what?"

"You're going to get yourself in trouble. Going to make yourself a big man."

"That's right!" Jeff grinned and smacked his chewing gum. The boys' acting was real and electric.

"Well, what's the difference in Black and white? Can you tell me that?"

"Soul brothers," Jeff said haughtily.

"Soul?"

Jeff leaned forward and crooned, "So-o-o-o-oul."

"Well, I don't care what religion or anything anybody is," Frank said, pretending not to understand what kind of soul Jeff meant. "They're still just the same inside, and I think . . ."

"That's what you think!" Jeff knifed in.

"Look, did you ever see . . . uh . . . look in the news and see pictures of how the cops are beating the crap out of you guys cause you keep on bothering, running around, demonstrating, making trouble. Have you ever seen them? They go downtown. Break up and rob everything. You don't want to be like that, do you?"

Coolly, Jeff said, "Your soul do not like us. They want you."

Frank looked agitated. "Yeah. As I remember kidding you . . . going to church, you were pretty nice; but all of a sudden you've changed. You—"

"I still go to church."

"Yeah, but still you—"

"Once in a while," Jeff grinned arrogantly.

"Yeah! Once in a while! You're a hypocrite!"

"Ha, ha!" Jeff's laugh was half growl.

Frank said, "And look at the clothes you're wearing!"

"They're all right. Look at yours. Red socks," Jeff shouted

gleefully. He grabbed the neckband of Frank's long, red under-wear and jerked frenetically, crying, "Yeah, yeah, yeah!"

"FREEZE," George called out. Both boys stopped stock-still. Here was the point where the teacher had to enforce a structure that would protect the other boys. But he had to do it without forcing Jeff to be something he was not. To say, "You mustn't grab people, Jeff," might have caused a sullen withdrawal. But the time to stop the improvisation had not arrived. Frank prob-ably was aware of the implications of Jeff grabbing his longjohns, which the Black boy apparently regarded as typical garb for working-class white boys, and stopping now might leave Frank feeling overly frustrated.

The teacher said evenly, "All right, you're forgetting your tasks. What's your task? What do you have to accomplish up there? Get back to it. Move."

"I know I have longjohns on," Frank said. "It's cold outside. But what's this black socks; what's that for?"

"The leader!" Jeff said proudly.

"And you're walking around every day like this." Frank imi-tated Jeff's strut. "And you're always starting trouble in school—and mostly with white kids."

"Ahr-r-r-r. So what?"

"What is it with you? What do you want to be one of them for? All you want to do is start trouble and everything. There's no particular kid's color or anything."

"There ain't?" Jeff said with a marvelous sneer.

"There ain't, as you put it. Big deal. Wow! White trash, right? You don't really mean this stuff," Frank said, grasping Jeff's shoulder and shaking him.

"Yes I do!"

"I'm not messing with you any more. If you're smart, you knock it off." They circled each other suspiciously and Frank said, "You know something, you're going to get yourself in a lot of trouble. Just keep it up!"

"FREEZE."

George shook the boys' hands, and, with arms around their shoulders, guided them back to their seats. "Great acting," he said.

Jeff was not sure how much of what he had done was acting and how much was real. There was some of each in his performance, he felt, and he could think about it later. In the meantime, he basked in the appreciation of his classmates, who had been spellbound. Jeff had a good feeling about Frank, since the two of them had pulled off the success together.

And Jeff was now being aggressive in a new way. He was using his aggressiveness; it was not using him. It was not frustration taking him over; he was being aggressive because he wanted to.

To the adult visitors watching the class, it was obvious that the teacher had paired Jeff and Frank because he thought they had needs that could complement each other in the right kind of situation. Suppose the teacher had been wrong? The boys probably would have gotten something out of the exercise anyhow. As long as the teacher does not try to tell the students what makes them tick, and what changes they ought to make, there is no harm done if the teacher is wrong, although a teacher who usually guesses right can plan improvisations that will be more efficient in helping students develop. And it is not necessary for a teacher to decide whether a student is acting or expressing his own feelings; this ambiguity gives many students a sense of security which enables them to express feelings they might not admit even to themselves.

The class continued.

"New task," George told the group. "Think of something that you're afraid of. Now become specific in your head. Specifically. You must come up here and show us fear. Now concentrate specifically on what you could be afraid of.

"Now wait a minute; that's only half the job. Sometime, while one person's up here being afraid of something, I will go to somebody else and tap him on the shoulder. His job is to go up and help the person who is afraid—help him to not be afraid."

George guided Cathy into the spotlight. She was a tall, blond Antioch College student who worked at the school, and she and Jeff were good friends.

Cathy crouched on the floor, simulating great fear.

Then George's hand was stretched out to Jeff again.

Jeff swaggered up to the huddled girl and cracked, "Are you doing your yoger exercises?"

Jeff wanted very much to cheer Cathy up. But in his brusque efforts he jerked her to her feet and banged her against the wall. When she remained frightened, he pounded his fist against the wall and shouted gutturally, "What's the matter with you?"

After the "FREEZE," Jeff and Cathy sat on the floor in the spotlight and the boys talked about what had happened.

One said, "I think Jeff must have been feeling pretty frustrated, you know."

After they had talked awhile, George said, "Tell me this somebody: did you think he was helping Cathy? Yes or no?"

"No!" the boys chorused.

"He seemed to be scaring her more," Bob said. "When he got angry, she got even more scared."

George said, "Jeff, do you think there is an alternative way of doing this? Can you? Try it. Now this time—you may play it as you like—but this time you must try a different approach. Let's see if that's more successful."

Cathy started as before, but this time Jeff was gentle and concerned.

In discussing it afterward, the class remarked on the difference. "He helped her this time," a boy said.

"This sure was better," Cathy said. "When he got angry at me, the first time, it made me more scared. When he didn't seem to get upset because I was scared, it was much easier."

Then Sister Fran was the scared one and Ray, who minutes before had tried to convince her not to be a nun, was supposed to help her. In the discussion that followed, Jeff had some very definite opinions on how one helps somebody.

The class built to an exciting finish, and Jeff trotted off for a quick game of ping-pong before lunch.

Late that afternoon, Jeff happily ran up to George, and while talking to him, he punched him and pulled on his arm. George said, "Jeff, do I like you?"

"Yeah."

"Are you sure that I like you?"

"Yeah."

"Then you don't have to hit me any more."

Jeff got that look kids get when they've just seen the light. Said he'd learned a lot that day—a different way to act in class.

"Drama isn't limited to the classroom," George said. "You can be different outside the class, too."

Jeff got that look again. Maybe he didn't have to be rough, gruff Jeff any more.

In the days that followed, both adults and students praised Jeff for his striking improvement in consideration for other people.

Eventually, Jeff was everybody's buddy. In the drama class's chain-reaction exercises, Jeff took many of his turns to drape an arm around someone's neck and call him friend. It became unreal. In trying to find who he was through trial and error, Jeff went to the opposite extreme. His aggressiveness was now other-directed.

The praise lessened.

Jeff gradually realized that being supernice was not what he wanted.

One day there was an improvisation in which a teacher named Herb, who was visiting the class, timidly asked his boss for a raise, saying he had not had one in years and he really needed the money. George's instructions had been that anyone who wanted to help Herb could step into the improvisation. Jeff and several others went to Herb's rescue. The others wanted to help Herb become more assertive in talking with his boss, but Jeff—acting overbearingly friendly—wanted to steal some money and give it to Herb. In the discussion, some of the boys were critical of Jeff's superficial approach. They thought he was not helping Herb, only encouraging him to delay dealing with his real problem—his timidity. Herb thought so, too. Jeff was puzzled, and he thought about it.

One day when Jeff was looking to the teacher for praise, George said, "Do it for you, not for us."

After several of these experiences, Jeff quieted down and took to analyzing situations. He observed and listened to people keenly. He still had a strong need for affection, but he was going after it in more mature ways. By this time he was convinced that his teachers and classmates liked him and cared about him. He became more concerned about whether he was proud of himself than whether others were impressed. What do I want to be? he thought.

Once, in discussing an improvisation done by some other boys, Jeff said, "These kids are trying to please you, George. Everytime they get on the stage they start looking at you." His comment showed improvement both in understanding people's actions and in honestly saying what he thought.

Sometimes at the start of a class George would announce, "I'm not here today." Then he would go to the back of the room and sit down, and one or two of the boys would structure the class. One day when the boys had acclaimed Jeff as their leader for part of a class, he set up an improvisation that was a bitter argument between the most powerfully antiwhite boy in the class and another Black boy who tended to butter up whites. Was Jeff using the situation to externalize his own internal conflict?

Jeff was actively involved in a process of perceptual growth which was changing him from a person who was aggressive in very destructive ways to one who could assert himself constructively. If he can continue this learning process throughout his life, it will have been more important to him than anything he could have learned from a seventh-grade textbook.

Throughout Jeff's Advancement School term, George never told him he could not do something. Jeff stopped abusing people through his own decision, which he made by gaining new perceptions. Had George simply told him to stop hitting people, shut up, and be still, he might have perceived the instructions as a threat. If so, it could be expected that he would have clung to the perceptions he already had and his behavior would have rigidified.

When George gave Jeff his instructions for the second improvisation with Cathy, the requirement that he "must try a different approach" was perceived by Jeff as a challenge rather than a threat. Rather than narrowing his vision, as he might have if he had felt threatened, he rose to meet the challenge by creating a new, more successful mode of behavior for himself.

This description tends to look at a part of Jeff's development at the Advancement School through the stencil of phenomenological psychology. There are quite a few psychological stencils, replete with verbal labels, and teachers can benefit from knowing some of them. (Knowing only one is often worse than knowing none.) But for growing children, the verbal labels seem unnecessary. They benefit most from what they discover themselves.

At the end of Jeff's semester, one of his classmates said it had been meaningful. Asked what he meant by "meaningful," he talked about the changes other boys had made. His descriptions seemed accurate.

"But what about you?" he was asked.

"Oh, yeah—me," the muscular Black boy said. "Well, I've learned an awful lot."

"Can you tell me what you've learned?"

"No, man, no. It's all inside."

Teachers in most of the school's courses emphasize helping kids to seek and clarify their own values, choosing freely from alternatives and considering the consequences. Dr. Sidney B. Simon, Associate Professor of Education at Temple University, taught the Advancement School staff value-seeking techniques that are now used successfully by many of the teachers.

In some of the beginning activities, boys might be asked to rank Dick Gregory, Marlon Brando, and Claude Brown—each in a book they are reading or a movie they have seen—on a "manhood" scale. They might be asked to state before the class whether they feel lonely often, sometimes, or never—or whether they have ever told a friend that he has bad breath.

Ultimately, they learn the satisfaction of taking action, whether by writing a letter to the editor or taking part in community projects.

When the Pennsylvania school opened in October 1967, Shively Willingham, a former college football star, set out to help a group of tough young gang hangers-on to learn some science. Asked what they'd like to learn in science, they talked about snakes. So Willingham and the boys brought in reptiles, and later mice, cats, and gerbils, and the boys did things with them. Boys who were completely down on people showed remarkable concern for animals, and an animal laboratory with a wealth of learning possibilities evolved.

In keeping with the students' interest in subjects directly related to their own lives, the animal program has become at least as much social science as biology. The animal lab enables students to study ecology and psychology through experimental manipulation. The boys found that mice can learn to walk a tightrope better when rewarded than when punished. Some concluded that their iguana's health had been damaged by loneliness.

The students' "laboratory" extends outside the school building. Boys have made films contrasting different neighborhoods in the city, from the poorest to the richest. They have conducted door-to-door surveys in which they boldly asked residents their annual income, then colored a map of Philadelphia to show different income levels and other data they had gathered. They interview people such as policemen on the beat and disc jockeys. Some boys have spent time with men on their jobs, getting the feel of adult life in various kinds of workaday worlds, and perhaps to some extent bridging the generation gap.

Boys often prepare for teaching or other jobs outside the school with role-playing or other exercises that build feelings of personal effectiveness.

Success has been striking in using the junior high boys as teachers in elementary schools. For the most part they teach small groups of children with an elementary school teacher supervising. Some alumni of the program got jobs—with Advancement School sponsorship—as teacher's aides in the summer Get-Set program. Having the children look up to them builds the boys' self-esteem, and they develop empathy for their own beleaguered teachers.

Joe Cruz, a seventh-grader who taught third-graders, wrote:

> There was a boy in my room that the teacher told me to talk to because he didn't know English, so I talk to him in Spanish and when I left he wanted to come with me. In the morning he worked very hard, so when I came in the after-

noon he showed me what he had done. Every time I come I take him to the corner and talk to him, and he does better work than he used to.

After their teaching experience, one group of boys, accompanied by teachers, spoke before a district meeting of school administrators and answered questions about education.

Although poor reading is a common handicap for kids from ghetto backgrounds, Marvin Shapiro, the school's top reading specialist, thinks that bending kids over books and trying to force them to make sense of the printed words holds little promise. He says the major reading hump for deprived kids is at the level between the fifth and sixth grades, where more complex sentences and longer words are needed. At this level, the material the child is being asked to read is more complex than the language he and his family and friends use in talking. Therefore, a major need of these boys as they attempt to raise their reading levels is improvement in conversation. When a student becomes involved enough in a topic to accept a teacher's gentle nudging and strives to express his thoughts more accurately, he is preparing the way for reading improvement.

Students are given exercises in taste, hearing, sight, and smell to heighten their sensibilities, and even the toughest kids dance when it's introduced through athletic movement and acting out gang fights.

According to Marvin Shapiro, the school's many exciting, talk-stimulating activities "teach" reading.

Our research shows that students who do especially well in improvisation class also make impressive gains in reading proficiency.

"I never thought I would hear culturally deprived junior high school kids talking so articulately and animatedly," commented one visiting educator. "Their vocabularies are amazing."

Perhaps the most compelling impact the school is making is on the boys themselves, and those who learn from them what school can really be like. "He never talked about his other school," reports one parent. "He doesn't shut his mouth about this one."

22. THE CAM ACADEMY

*When youngsters drop or are pushed out of school,
education's failure is obvious, tragic, and complete.
The CAM Academy in Chicago, a private school in
the ghetto, was set up specifically to find ways which
public schools could use to reach these kids with a
radically different program.*

*The following profile of the program was written by
a group of visiting educators; the description of the
research design is the work of Jon Wagner, coordi-
nator of curriculum and research.*

The streets are wide and the traffic never stops moving, perhaps
because the drivers don't want to look at this area of West
Madison Street in Chicago. It's not that it's such a bad ghetto, as
ghettos go. There are stores like Goldblatt's and smaller, cheaper
neighborhood stores, for this is an old-line shopping district. It's
just that the remains of the riots following Martin Luther King's
death are all around, some of the store windows are still boarded
up and slogans cover the walls. The slogans are reminders that
the wounds are open, that, despite all the talk about civil rights
and welfare, the old problems are unsolved. An overwhelming
grayness, a perpetual smog on the mind, has settled in here and
it's not pretty to look at. So people drive through, their windows
up, their car doors securely locked, and their eyes fixed straight
ahead.

But if some driver ever did look, he'd see a surprising thing at
3932 West Madison. In the midst of a gray strip of small, non-

descript buildings, next door to a boarded-up store with "Black Power" and "Don't Vote" slogans crudely painted on the wood, is a two-story, modern red-brick building. The rest of the street is almost empty, but here people busily come and go.

The building is the headquarters of the Christian Action Ministry, a service organization begun by several West Side churches that saw the hopelessness of preaching the word of God to unemployed, uneducated, underfed, underhoused, and spiritually drained people. These churches decided to practice their teachings instead. CAM headquarters houses an employment agency; legal services; facilities for preschool, tutoring, and adult classes; a teen program; and a summer program.

But the most important part of CAM's program is its Academy. Its students are kids who were kicked out, pushed out, or dropped out of the Chicago public schools. The churches estimate that in the immediate vicinity of CAM headquarters alone 40 to 50 per cent of the kids fit into this category. Their future resembles that of their neighborhood. They are the potentially hard-core unemployed.

Despite being labeled failures because they don't fit the public school's mold, some of these kids still want an education. CAM Academy offers them a unique chance to get it. Aiming at the student who wants to continue his education after he leaves CAM, the school's flyer bills it as a "second-chance, nongraded high school with qualified teachers" and "Afro-American emphasis" in a modern and lively building. The school was set up as a model for the Chicago public schools. According to the flyer, CAM uses only "the most recent teaching methods."

CAM's unique approach to education enables its students to complete four to six years of public schooling in one to two years. Writing Workshop Director Paul Pekin claims that CAM graduates have a higher reading level than graduates of Chicago public high schools.

Pekin is the first to admit that CAM Academy's impact is not great numerically. Last year the enrollment was seventy-two; this year it is 170.

CAM's success with this enrollment, however, is nothing short of fantastic. After its first full year in operation, CAM graduated thirty-five students in June 1968 with its own certificate, which guarantees a tenth-grade reading level. Many students take and pass the public school system's GED examination, offered as the equivalent of a high school diploma. Twenty-two students were sent to college, and are still there, according to Principal Mike Cook.

Performance records are even better this year than last. Seven students had completed Math I and ten had finished English I by November 1, 1968; none had completed them at that time last year. Thirty-five graduated in June 1968; this year, thirty to thirty-five will have their certificates by Christmas.

CAM plays the longest shots available to perform this miracle. It is, in Pekin's words, a "for-real school with for-real teachers and for-real students and a for-real principal." But these for-real students have for-real problems that the school must work with.

Although the males have spent an average of 10.2 years in a Chicago public school and the females 8.8 years, their entering tests place them at the seventh-grade level. In exact figures, they average 7.75 in reading, 7.29 in math, and 7.40 in language. They have wasted from one to four years in a system that has failed them. Many have only one-half high school credit.

Sixty per cent have dropped out, been kicked out, or pushed out of one of the five public high schools in the area—Marshall, Crane, Flower, Farragut, or Austin. Before coming to CAM, students spent an average of a year and a half out of school; but the range is from immediate transfer to eleven years out of school. In day school, the average age is eighteen; in night school, it is 20.5.

CAM's courses are divided into three levels and students are placed according to the results of the California Test Bureau's Test of Adult Basic Education, Level D. In Level One, the student must complete Basic Math; English I, II, or Reading; Writing Workshop; and Observation and Inquiry. To complete Level Two, he must take Introduction to Science, Introduction to Culture, Humanities, Advanced Writing, Art, Drama, and Current Events. Sewing, Cooking, and Child Care are optional.

Level Three consists of individual research projects in Advanced Science, Humanities, and Culture under a teacher's supervision.

This whole program is based upon the concept of individual attention so that students move entirely at their own pace. All attendance is voluntary, said Pekin. The only discipline is self-discipline.

Physically, the building isn't just "lively" and "modern"—it's alive and it's "now." Whole worlds separate it from the dark, dingy halls and barren, cell-like classrooms of Chicago public schools. A man-size modern metal sculpture by Elmer Peterson stands in the foyer. Students themselves painted the Academy's walls in warm whites, bright oranges, reds, and yellows. Psychedelic posters, pop art posters, and student work hang in classrooms and offices alike. Although the Academy has its own library, paperback bookracks are found in almost all the rooms. Everything is brightly lighted—there are no dark corners.

The classrooms are friendly, informal, and almost loungelike in their setup. Every classroom revolves around a table-and-chairs concept; there aren't any back rows to be lost in or to hide in. The chairs are brightly colored molded plastic, the kind that are functional and still comfortable. You can always find a coffeepot and cups somewhere in the room.

Classroom doors are always open and students wander in and out freely. They know a particular teacher will always be there at the appointed time; but, more importantly, they know he is usually there all the rest of the time just talking, listening, working on student projects. None of the teachers have state educational certificates. They teach because they want to, Pekin contends. Students drift into Pekin's room with freshly written stories, ideas for stories or poems, or just to talk.

Take Calvin, for example. Calvin wandered in while I was talking to Pekin about his Writing Workshop. He was wearing mod-ish blue pants and a black shirt. I asked him how he'd heard about the school and he said that kids had told him about it one afternoon when he was out in the back yard "just messin'."

"There were a lot of sisters and brothers down here," he said. "I saw people I knew so I decided to look around."

Calvin talked constantly about everything—the new Beatles' album, a safari story he'd just written, and why he wrote safari stories. When he left, Pekin explained that when Calvin had come to the Workshop last year he wouldn't speak at all.

Pekin's Writing Workshop answers that riddle and exemplifies the progress possible in this school. The class is required of everyone because it raises the student's ability to handle English faster than any other course.

Pekin describes the class setup as a "place where something can happen." No teacher's desk dominates the room—Pekin calls himself a "director" rather than a "teacher." On one of the two tables a coffeepot and multicolored plastic cup holders are scattered around. Nearby there is a low round table surrounded by chairs where class is held. All work is kept in an open cabinet against the wall.

The Writing Workshop approach is used everywhere in the school: "We emphasize skills and concepts. We don't teach facts and figures because they always change. We teach them how to use those facts and figures and how to deal with them."

Pekin's Workshop is based on the "story workshop" method developed by his former teacher John Schultz. It involves, says Pekin, "disciplining the student to a certain sight, to really come to things instead of copping out." The class is small—average attendance is eight or nine; the round-table–coffee atmosphere is informal, but the method is disciplined.

The two-hour, once-weekly class combines reading, word study, and writing. The make-up varies everytime, but Pekin tries to "get writing out of people, one way or another." In the first class, Pekin usually reads the first chapter of Richard Wright's *Black Boy* as part of his plan to use Black authors and the classics as reading material. Readings are of five-to-six-page duration so they won't exhaust the students' attention span, he explains. After the reading, students must "recall" the "sharpest thing in their mind."

"CAM isn't hipped on adjectives and adverbs," says Pekin, referring to his total emphasis on the noun and verb in writing. "Too many adjectives indicate a weak noun and adverbs point out faulty verbs."

Pekin's language study method is unique. At first everyone sits in a semicircle and he asks each one for a word. Usually he gets words like "idealism" and "future" the first two or three times around. Then he asks for a word they can see. After each student has given two or three such words, he eliminates all words that can be seen in the room, like "coffeepot" and "cup." The object is to make the students "see" a word as they say it.

Next Pekin starts the class on noun-and-verb pictures so that they can associate one noun or verb with another. For example, a person picks a place, but instead of giving its name, he gives details, like "soda straw." The next person must give a verb that goes with "soda straw," like "sucks," until the whole image is formed.

"The verb is the thing" in Pekin's method, so after a few classes the group moves on to concrete verb images. Student Josh Fleming illustrated it this way: "Old man playing football in the park in the fall." Noun images are also used, like Josh's "Wine bottle in a garbage can with an open window and curtains blowing out."

This image making leads into story writing. Pekin gives his students fifteen minutes at the end of the class to write at top speed, without worrying about punctuation or grammar. "Just get it down," he says. He usually asks them to write about something they've talked about in class, but he will accept anything. Calvin writes short safari or space stories. Everyone in the class has his own notebook to write longer pieces at home. These are the pieces that Pekin put into this year's book, *Look What's Happening, Baby!*, sponsored by the Community Arts Foundation of Chicago.

The only problem in the Writing Workshop and in other classes is attendance. Pekin shakes his head. "You lose people and just when you think they're gone forever, they show up again."

Attendance is completely voluntary, but students discover they can do better if they come regularly. Eventually sixty per cent come two days or more a week.

The word "voluntary" is the key to the whole school. Students are self-disciplined and self-educated. The school exists to guide and encourage.

Students are attracted by this revolutionary approach, by this willingness to try something new. All classes are designed to fulfill the quote which opens the Curriculum Report:

"Give a man a fish and he will eat today.

Teach a man to fish and he will eat forever."

As a model school, CAM has decidedly proved its point to the Chicago public schools. But how do you measure the human impact? There's Josh Fleming, who never wrote or drew before he came to CAM in September 1967; he'll go to the Art Institute in January if he can get the money. And Calvin, who talks now. And twenty-two kids who actually went to college in spite of everything against them. All because of a different kind of school.

RESEARCH DESIGN

Tests administered to our present students during their years in public school have led us to appreciate the inadequacies of conventional testing devices for measuring intelligence, achievement, motivation, and creativity. The work that has been done by these students while at CAM Academy has shown their individual dossiers of standard test results to be irrelevant to their performance as a student.

We have found that achievement tests in math and English do give some indication of the level at which a student can perform in these areas. All students coming to the Academy are given the California Test Bureau test of general educational development before they begin their classes. This is a diagnostic test (we exclude no one on the basis of his performance on the test) and gives us some indication of the student's ability in arithmetic, reading, and language (grammar).

When students complete our math course or our English course, they take the corresponding sections of this test again. This serves as a post-test.

However, everything we believe about education is outraged by the narrowness of this approach. We are not running a trade school, nor do we look at education as training. We do feel that there is more going on here for our students than just learning a little math and English. If we did not feel that, we would not be here.

The problem is: How do we describe the "goals" of a "humanistic" curriculum? How do we describe what "else" is going on in this school? How do we evaluate it? And more importantly, how do we communicate what we are about to others?

We have tentatively adopted a model for our methodology: microecology. We will be studying the school as a living system, almost as if it were a living organism. We will be looking at the inputs to the school; the outputs from the school; the relationships among students, among the faculty, between students and faculty; the relationship between the school and the community, etc. In order to do this, we will be looking at attendance, the weather, visitors, field trips, the mood of classes, the mood of teachers, the informal and formal organization of the students and of the teachers, and we will attempt to be particularly sensitive to any changes in these variables over the year.

In order to make this study, we have instituted the following procedures. Students fill out our "Blue Sheet" as part of their registration. We ask them for general background information, such as age, sex, marital status, last high school attended, last date attended, etc. In addition to these questions, we also ask students what they want to do in life, and whether or not they are interested in college.

Each instructor takes attendance in his class (no small feat in a nongraded, noncompulsory, free-swinging school). In addition, he fills out a short form which asks about the mood of the class, visitors, and anything unusual which happened during the class. There is plenty of space for additional comments.

To the present date, our emphasis has been on cross-tabulating several of these variables, finding averages, medians, and ranges, and making a few tables. However, we are currently revising this design to include more instruments measuring attitudinal change. We are open to suggestion. We want to develop something different than the conventional dehumanizing statistics, but what? We would be very interested in knowing what testing or survey techniques have been developed to measure attitudinal change and development in other independent schools.

We are presently changing one component of our research design that has proved to be unsatisfactory: the involvement of students. We feel that the students should be involved in every aspect of the school, including curriculum development and research, and we have not made proper provisions for this to take place in the area of research. We have undertaken the following program to remedy this situation.

A course is being offered entitled "Educational Psychology." Students who want to take this course will be required to complete at least one course in the Academy before taking this one. The course will consist of a weekly seminar and discussion, and weekly readings. These discussions will focus on psychology of learning and memory, classroom techniques, and research design. The students involved in the course will then spend one period a day throughout the rest of the week working as assistant teachers in a class, actually teaching their own class, or working as a research assistant. In this manner we hope to involve the students in the actual research being done about their school and to share with them our notions of what we are doing. We will look to them for new ideas and new perspectives about our research, and we hope to teach them some statistics, some notions of what learning is all about, and give them classroom experience. Somehow, we feel it has to be their school.

23. A HARLEM CLASS WRITES
HERBERT KOHL

The creative energies of Black children, stifled by the conventional school program, were tapped by Herbert Kohl, who reported their extraordinary writing achievements in his book 36 Children.

SHOP WITH MOM

I love to shop with mom
And talk to the friendly grocer
And help her make the list
Seems to make us closer.
                    —*Nellie, age 11*

THE JUNKIES

When they are
in the street
they pass it
along to each
other but when
they see the
police they would
run some would
just stand still
and be beat
so pity ful
that they want
to cry
                    —*Mary, age 11*

Nellie's poem received high praise. Her teacher liked the rhyme "closer" and "grocer," and thought she said a great deal in four lines. Most of all the teacher was pleased that Nellie expressed such a pleasant and healthy thought. Nellie was pleased too, her poem was published in the school paper. I was moved and excited by Mary's poem and made the mistake of showing it to the teacher who edited the school newspaper. She was horrified. First of all, she informed me, Mary couldn't possibly know what junkies were, and, moreover, the other children wouldn't be interested in such a poem. There weren't any rhymes or clearly discernible meter. The word "pity ful" was split up incorrectly, "be beat" wasn't proper English and, finally, it wasn't really poetry but just the ramblings of a disturbed girl.

My initial reaction was outrage—what did she know about poetry, or about Mary? But it is too easy to be cruel about the ignorance that is so characteristic of the schools today. That teacher did believe that she knew what poetry was, and that there was a Correct Language in which it was expressed. Her attitude towards the correctness of language and the form of poetry was in a way identical to her attitude towards what sentiments good children's poems ought to express. Yet language is not static, nor is it possible *a priori* to establish rules governing what can or cannot be written any more than it is possible to establish rules governing what can or cannot be felt.

Not long ago when I was teaching a class of remote, resistant children in a Harlem school, as an experiment I asked these children to write. I had no great expectations. I had been told that the children were from one to three years behind in reading, that they came from "deprived" and "disadvantaged" homes and were ignorant of the language of the schools. I had also been told that their vocabulary was limited, that they couldn't make abstractions, were not introspective, oriented to physical rather than mental activity. Other teachers in the school called the children "them" and spoke of teaching as a thankless military task. I couldn't accept this mythology: I wanted my pupils to tell me about themselves. For reasons that were hardly literary I set out to explore the possibilities of teaching language, literature, and writing in ways that would enable children to speak about what they felt they were not allowed to acknowledge publicly. Much to my surprise the children wrote a great deal; and they invented their own language to do so. Only a very small number of the children had what can be called "talent," and many of them had only a single story to write and rewrite; yet almost all of them responded, and seemed to become more alive through their writing. The results of some of this exploration are given here.

I have subsequently discovered other teachers who have explored language and literature with their pupils in this way, with results no less dramatic. The children we have taught ranged from the pre-school years to high school, from lower-class ghetto children to upper-class suburban ones. There are few teaching techniques that we share in common, and no philosophy of education that binds us. Some of these teachers have tight, carefully controlled classrooms; others care less for order and more for invention. There are Deweyites, traditionalists, classicists—a large range of educational philosophies and teaching styles. If there is anything common to our work it is the concern to listen to what the children have to say and the ability to respond to it as honestly as possible, no matter how painful it may be to our teacherly prides and preconceptions. We have allowed ourselves to learn from our pupils and to expect the unexpected.

Children will not write if they are afraid to talk. Initially they suspect teachers and are reluctant to be honest with them. They have had too many school experiences where the loyalty of the staff and the institutional obligations of teachers have taken precedence over honesty. They have seen too much effort to maintain face, and too little respect for justifiable defiance in their school lives. I think children believe that there is a conscious collusion between all of the adults in a school to maintain the impression that the authority is *always* right, and that life is *always* pleasant and orderly. Unfortunately, the collusion is unconscious or at least unspoken. This is dramatically true in slum schools where the pressures of teaching are increased by understaffing and a vague uneasiness about race which is always in the air.

I was assigned to a school in East Harlem in September 1962 and was not sufficiently prepared for the faculty's polite lies about their success in the classroom or the resistance and defiance of the children. My sixth-grade class had thirty-six pupils, all Negro. For two months I taught in virtual isolation from my pupils. Every attempt I made to develop rapport was coldly rejected. The theme of work scheduled by the school's lesson plan for that semester was "How We Became Modern America," and my first lesson was characteristic of the dull response everything received.

It seemed natural to start by comparing a pioneer home with the modern life the children knew—or, more accurately, I thought they knew. I asked the class to think of America in the 1850's and received blank stares, although that presumably was what they had studied the previous year. I pursued the matter.

—Can anyone tell me what was happening around 1850, just before the Civil War? I mean, what do you think you'd see if you walked down Madison Avenue then?

—Cars.

—Do you think there were cars in 1850? That was over a hundred years ago. Think of what you learned last year and try again, do you think there were cars then?

—Yes . . . no . . . I don't know.

Someone else tried.

—Grass and trees?

The class broke out laughing. I tried to contain my anger and frustration.

—I don't know what you're laughing about, it's the right answer. In those days Harlem was farmland with fields and trees and a few farmhouses. There weren't any roads or houses like the ones outside, or street lights or electricity.

The class was outraged and refused to think. Bright faces took on the dull glaze that is characteristic of the Negro child who finds it less painful to be thought stupid than to be defiant. There was an uneasy drumming on desk tops. The possibility of there being a time when Harlem didn't exist had never, could never have occurred to the children. Nor did it occur to me that their experience of modern America was not what I had come to teach about. After two months, in despair, I asked the kids to write about their block.

WHAT A BLOCK!

My block is the most terrible block I've ever seen. There are at lease 25 or 30 narcartic people in my block. The cops come around there and tries to act bad but I bet inside of them they are as scared as can be. They even had in the papers that this block is the worst block, not in Manhattan but in New York City. In the summer they don't do nothing except shooting, shabing, and fighting. They hang all over the stoops and when you say excuse me to them they hear you but they just don't feel like moving. Some times they make me so mad that I feel like slaping them and stuffing and bag of garbage down their throats. Theres only one policeman who can handle these people and we all call him "Sunny." When he come around in his cop car the people run around the corners, and he wont let anyone sit on the stoops. If you don't believe this story come around some time and you'll find out.

—Grace, age 11

My block is the worse block you ever saw people getting killed or stabbed men and women in buildin's taking dope . . .

—Mary, age 11

The next day I threw out my notes and my lesson plans and talked to the children. What I had been assigned to teach seemed, in any case, an unreal myth about a country that never has existed. I didn't believe the tale of "progress" the curriculum had prescribed, yet had been afraid to discard it and had been willing to lie to the children. After all I didn't want to burden them or cause them pain, and I had to teach something. I couldn't "waste their time." How scared I must have been when I started teaching in Harlem to accept those hollow rationalizations and use the "curriculum" to protect me from the children. I accepted the myth that the teacher and the book know all; that complex human questions had "right" and "wrong" answers. It was much easier than facing the world the children perceived and attempting to cope with it. I could lean on the teachers' manuals and feel justified in presenting an unambiguously "good" historical event or short story. It protected my authority as a teacher which I didn't quite believe in. It was difficult for me; pontificating during the day and knowing that I was doing so at night. Yet could I cause the class much more pain or impose greater burdens with my lies than they already had? How much time could I have "wasted" even if I let the children dance and play all day while I sought for a new approach. They had already wasted five years in school by the time they arrived in my class.

So we spoke. At first the children were suspicious and ashamed of what they'd written. But as I listened and allowed them to talk they became bolder and angrier, then finally quieter and relieved.

I asked them to write down what they would do to change things, and they responded immediately.

> If I could change my block I would stand on Madison Ave and throw nothing but Teargas in it. I would have all the people I liked to get out of the block and then I would become very tall and have big hands and with my big hands I would take all of the narcartic people and pick them up with my hand and throw them in the nearest river and oceans. I would go to some of those old smart alic cops and throw them in the Ocians and Rivers too. I would let the people I like move into the projects so they could tell their friends that they live in a decent block. If I could do this you would never see 117 st again.
>
>   —*Grace, age 11*

For several weeks after that the children wrote and wrote— what their homes were like, whom they liked, where they came from. I discovered that everything I'd been told about the children's language was irrelevant. Yes, they were hip when they spoke, inarticulate and concrete. But their writing was something else, when they felt that no white man was judging their words, threatening their confidence and pride. They faced a blank page and wrote directly and honestly. Recently I have mentioned this to teachers who have accepted the current analyses of "the language" of the "disadvantaged." They asked their children to write and have been as surprised as I was, and shocked by the obvious fact that "disadvantaged" children will not speak in class because they cannot trust their audience.

Nothing the school offered was relevant, so I read the class novels, stories, poems, brought my library to class and let them know that many people have suffered throughout history and that some were articulate enough to create literature from their lives. They didn't believe me, but they were hungry to know what had been written about and what could be written about.

It was easier for the class to forget their essays than it was for me. They were eager to go beyond their block, to move out into the broader world and into themselves. We talked of families, of brothers and sisters, of uncles, and of Kenny's favorite subject, the Tyranny of Teachers and Moms.

We spoke and read about love and madness, families, war, the birth and death of individuals and societies; and then they asked me permission to write themselves. Permission!

Sharon came into class angry one day and wrote about a fight.

ONE DAY THERE WAS A BIG FIGHT

One day in school a girl started getting smart with a boy. So the boy said to the girl why don't you come outside? The girl said alright I'll be there. The girl said you just wait. And he said don't wait me back. And so the fight was on. One had a swollen nose the other a black eye. And a teacher stoped the fight. His name was Mr. Mollow. I was saying to myself I wish they would mind their own business. It made me bad. I had wanted to see a fight that day. So I call Mr. Mollow up. I called him all kinds of names. I said you ugly skinney bony man. I was red hot. And when I saw him I rolled my eyes as if I wanted to hit him. All that afternoon I was bad at Mr. Mollow.

I tried to talk to her about her paper, tell her that "it make me bad" didn't make any sense. And she explained to me that "being bad" was a way of acting and that down South a "bad nigger" was one who was defiant of the white man's demands. She concluded by saying that being bad was good in a way and bad in a way. I asked the class and they agreed. In the midst of the discussion Louis asked one of his characteristically exasperating questions: "But where do words come from anyway?"

I stumbled over an answer as the uproar became general.

—What use are words anyway?

—Why do people have to talk?

—Why are there good words and bad words?

—Why aren't you supposed to use some words in class?

—Why can't you change words as you like?

I felt that I was being "put on," and was tempted to pass over the questions glibly; there were no simple answers to the children's questions, and the simplest thing to do when children ask difficult questions is to pretend that they're not serious or they're stupid. But the children were serious.

More and more they asked about language and would not be put off by evasive references to the past, linguistic convention and tradition. Children look away from adults as soon as adults say that things are the way they are because they have always been that way. When a child accepts such an answer it is a good indication that he has given up and decided to be what adults would make him rather than himself.

It was in April, after their move to the new school, that I talked to the class about my limitations within the educational system. Before that, however, I found myself telling them about the demands that the system made upon them. There were compulsory achievement and, at that time, IQ, tests given halfway through the year, and it was on the results of those tests that the children's placement in junior high school would be based. Nothing else really counted; classes were formed on the basis of reading grades and my pupils *had* to do well. It was a matter of their whole future since in junior high school all but those few students put in the "top" classes (three out of fourteen on each grade) were considered "not college material" and treated with the scorn that they merited in their teachers' eyes.

The easiest way to bring this up in class was to tell the children exactly where they stood. I braced myself, and defying all precedent as well as my own misgivings, I performed the unforgivable act of showing the children what their reading and IQ scores were according to the record cards. I also taught a lesson on the definition of IQ and of achievement scores. The children were angry and shocked; no one had ever come right out and told them they were failing. It was always put so nicely and evasively that the children never knew where they stood. After seeing the IQ scores—only two of which were above 100, the majority being in the 80 to 90 range—and the reading scores, which with few exceptions were below grade level, the children were furious. I asked them what they wanted to do about it, and sadly they threw back at me:

"Mr. Kohl, what can we do about it?"

And I told them. Only I didn't say read more, or take remedial lessons, or spend another year in school, and you will be better off. I told them what middle-class teachers usually tell their pupils, what I heard myself while in public school in New York City, and what teachers in Harlem are usually too honest and scrupulous to tell their pupils. I said if you listen I will teach you how to take tests and how to get around them.

This scrupulosity of Harlem teachers and administrators with respect to tests is a curious psychological phenomenon, completely at variance with the irresponsibility they display in all other educational and disciplinary matters. Yet I think it is all too easily explicable. They feel their own failures with the children are vindicated if an objective test, objectively administered, shows the child to be a failure.

There were no sample tests available, to prepare the children beforehand. The assistant principal told me that if old tests were made available the children would have an unfair advantage over other children. I reminded him that keeping files of old tests was frequently standard procedure at middle-class schools, and that P.S. 6, a predominantly white school located less than a mile down Madison Avenue, even gave after-school voluntary classes in test preparation. He shrugged and told me that a rule was a rule. So I went to friends who taught in white schools and got copies of the old tests and sample questions that they used and went ahead with my plans. No one checked on what I was doing, and no one really cared as long as my class wasn't disruptive.

The first thing I had to do was familiarize the children with test instructions. I spent several weeks on practicing following directions as they are worded on the standard tests. The class asked me why such practice was necessary, and I explained that with all the fine writing they could produce, with all the words of praise and recommendation I could write, they would go no-where in junior high school unless those grades on paper were up to the standards the Board of Education set. The kids didn't like that idea, I don't like it; but we had to get tough and face the fact that like it or not they *had* to do well. When I put it that way they were willing to try.

After going through the reading of directions, I broke down the types of questions that were asked on the various reading tests and tried to explain something of the psychology of the people who created the test. I frequently found that some of the children were deliberately choosing wrong answers because they had clever explanations for their choices. They had to be convinced that the people who created objective tests believed as an article of faith that all the questions they made up had one and only one correct answer. Over and over, it is striking how rigid teachers tend to be and how difficult it is for children who haven't been clued in on this rigidity to figure out what the teacher expects in the way of suppression of original and clever responses. The children agreed to be dull for the sake of their future.

After these exercises we simulated testing situations, and the children gradually learned to cease dreading and avoiding the testing situation. Their anxiety decreased to a manageable level, and therefore they were able to apply things they had discovered in their own thinking, reading, and writing to situations that arose in the test.

Unfortunately I had no say in determining when the tests were given. Both the reading and IQ tests had to be given before February for administrative reasons, and so the full benefit of the year's work did not show in those tests. The IQ test was close to a disaster. True, there were about ten children who came up over 100 and one—Grace—who scored 135, but the children were not yet able to cope with the test and didn't show themselves as well as they could. With the reading test it was different. The children were almost ready and in a few short months performed the seemingly impossible task of jumping from one to three years in reading. There were a few children on fifth-grade level, about twelve on sixth-grade level, another twelve on seventh-grade level, and eight who ranged from the eighth to the twelfth grades. I couldn't believe it myself. When I told the results to the

children, they for once showed their pride in themselves unashamedly.

The children learned that they could do unpleasant but necessary work; they also knew that the test preparation was not all
there was to education, that the substance of their work, the
novels and stories, the poems and projects they created, were the
essential thing no matter how the external world chose to judge
them. They were proud of their work and themselves. I felt
thrilled and privileged to teach them and witness them create. I
offered what I could to them; they offered much in return. I am
grateful that over the course of the year I could cease to be afraid
and therefore respond to what the children had to teach me of
myself, of themselves and the world they lived in and which we
shared as human beings.

Not all of the children made it through the year; two moved,
and one, John, was too much for me to control. He was tough
and shook my confidence. It would take me another year before I
could reach children like him. We never fought, he didn't disrupt
the class; he just disappeared into the halls and then the streets. I
have to admit that I made a very feeble and false effort to stop
him; the rest of the class occupied me. The next year I had a class
of Johns, and seeing how easily they responded to adult confidence and trust, I have always regretted my lack of effort with
John. Yet I have to admit that I did not have the necessary
confidence as a teacher and as a human being the year I taught
the thirty-six children. It took the thirty-six children to give me
that.

The year did not come to a conclusion. It ended as all school
years must. Michael was beginning his third novel, Sam was
starting his first. It was the end of June; commencement came
with its absurd pomp, and then a farewell party. The children
had to move across the street to junior high school and to a new,
more chaotic and difficult world.

The following September meant meeting new children, concentrating my energy and feelings on them and letting go of my
preoccupation with the thirty-six children. It was sad yet exciting,
beginning again with an empty classroom. I waited nervously for

the children, refusing to think of my first words. At nine o'clock they came in quietly and hesitantly, looking me over. They were nervous too. I looked at my new class and told them how strange it felt to be in school again, starting another year, meeting new people. They agreed. One boy said he almost stayed home. A girl, Alice, said she came because she knew that she'd be having a man teacher. At that I introduced myself and asked the class to sit in any seats they liked. Everyone looked at me, puzzled. Then a big boy, Willie, said:

"You mean I don't have to sit in the back?"

"No."

"And you're not going to keep me at your desk to watch me?"

"Why, should I watch you?"

"Didn't they tell you?"

"Nobody told me anything about the class, I didn't ask. This is a new year, everyone starts from the beginning."

Our first day of school was not like my first day with 6-1. I felt free to encounter the children without preconceptions and explore with them what was meaningful to learn. The children didn't frighten me; there was no question of control since I knew I was in control of myself. Time and chaos weren't my enemies—a bit of disorder, time to explore and play were all expected to be part of our year together. I had no trouble talking to the class. In a sense we started together and therefore could plunge into things more quickly than was possible with 6-1.

Other teachers had warned me of my new class—it was 6-7, "the bottom." I was told that the children were illiterate, indifferent, dangerous. Someone claimed that most of them wouldn't even show up after the first week. In June some colleagues, as the children suspected, offered to point out "the ones" who would cause me the most trouble. I declined just as I had declined to look at the children's record cards in September.

The children looked older than the ones in 6-1, taller and more self-assured. They spoke about themselves freely and with great perception. They knew that they were rejects in the school, and they also knew that the school as a whole was a reject. Any adult pretense of the opposite would have closed them up altogether.

As soon as everyone was settled I began as directly as possible and asked the class what books they wanted to read. Naturally they asked for sixth grade readers. I told them I felt the books were too hard and they groaned.

"We're not so dumb, Mr. Kohl."

"I won't do that baby stuff again."

"Mr. Kohl, we can read anything."

I asked the children how well they thought they read and they became confused; no one had ever told them. They only knew that every year they got the same second- and third-grade books, which they knew by heart. My first lesson became clear. I took out the class record cards and dumped them on my desk. Then I explained to the class what grade reading scores meant, and what the significance of IQ was.

"If you are reading up to your grade level, that means in the sixth grade, you're supposed to have a score in the sixes; six point zero, six point one, and so forth. If you have average intelligence your IQ should be at least one hundred. Let's see what these cards say."

There was suspense in the room as I listed the scores: 3.1, 3.4, 2.0, 4.2, 3.1 . . . IQ's of 70, 75, 81, 78 . . . then anger.

"Mr. Kohl we're not that dumb."

"It's phoney."

"No one taught us that stuff, no one ever told us."

But they knew now. After a heated debate I threw my first question back at the class.

"Tell me what books you want to read."

The class chose fifth-grade books, ones they knew would be difficult for them in preference to ones that were on their supposed "level." They were ready to fight to read and learn, met my challenge, and kept on challenging themselves and me for the rest of the year.

One day during the first week Alice coyly proposed a bet.

"Mr. Kohl, I bet I can read anything on your desk no matter what those cards of yours say."

Her reading score was 3.4. I accepted and she went through all the books on my desk including a page of the novel I was reading on the way to school. I was perplexed and delighted.

"How can you do that and still have a three point four reading score?"

"I wouldn't read for those teachers. Listen——"

Alice picked up a book and stumbled through several paragraphs. She paused, stuttered, committed omissions and reversals, *i.e.*, read on a low third-grade level. Then she looked at my astonished face and burst out laughing.

Alice was tough and angry and brilliant. She was hypersensitive and incapable of tolerating insult or prejudice. In her previous years in school she had been alternately defiant and withdrawn. She was considered a "troublemaker" by some teachers, "disturbed" by others. Yet when offered something substantial, a serious novel, for example, or the opportunity to write honestly, she blossomed. During the year she became hungry to learn and less hostile. It was sometimes hard to find material to keep up with her voracious appetite.

Juan sat next to Alice in the front of the room, quiet and quixotic. When there was a good deed to be done Juan would be certain to volunteer and mess things up. He was shy, and according to the records I showed him had an IQ of 70 and was illiterate.

He listened intensely in class when I taught reading; otherwise he seemed to be somewhere else. He never spoke in class; yet after the Christmas holiday he came to me and told me that I had taught him how to read. It seemed that the idea that words were divided into syllables excited him, and so over the Christmas vacation he divided all the names under *A* in the phone book into syllables and learned how to read. I was astonished at his excitement over a fact of grammar that seemed dull and matter-of-fact to me. I encouraged Juan to write, and for all his struggle with the English language a beautiful, sad world emerged.

One cold rainy day I was going to school and I had to go 1,000 miles to get there and there wasn't no cars and no buses and train so I had to walk. I got soke a wet. I still had 500 more miles to go at last I almost got there and went I got there the school was close and I thought for a minute and then I remember it was a haliday and then I droped deid.

Many of the teachers laughed at the children, believed they didn't care about school, or anything, for that matter. Yet these teachers couldn't see the sad fact that no matter how poorly their students, most of whom were over sixteen, the dropout age, did in school, still they came—with what magical hope that one day they would find themselves reading, graduating, in college . . . still they came and were laughed at for it. The guidance counselors, blind to the beauty and pathos of youngsters of eighteen and nineteen still trying where they have failed so often, usually recommended leaving school.

Confronted by the human challenge of the classroom I reached into myself, uncovered a constant core which enabled me to live with my mistakes and hypocrisies, my weaknesses and pettiness; to accept as myself all the many contrary and contradictory things I was. I fought to be more human and I feel I succeeded. And because of all this I had to ask: What about the children? Of what worth is all this to the children? At one time I thought I knew, but not any longer. Certain uncomfortable questions became more and more insistent: Was it possible to function usefully within the existing school system? Must one get out and agitate to change the system? Or can one stay enclosed in a "successful" classroom ignoring everything that happens subsequently to one's pupils?

The thirty-six children are suffering from the diseases of our society. They are no special cases; there are too many hundreds of thousands like them, lost in indifferent, inferior schools, put on the streets or in prep schools with condescension or cynicism. When I think of my work as a teacher, one of the children's favorite myths, that of Sisyphus, continually comes to mind: the man condemned to roll a rock up a mountain only to see it fall back to the bottom, to return to the bottom himself and take up his unending task.

Books on
Radical School Reform
by the Contributors

ASHTON-WARNER, SYLVIA, *Teacher*. New York, Simon and Schuster, 1963.

CLARK, KENNETH, *Dark Ghetto*. New York, Harper & Row, 1965.

DENNISON, GEORGE, *The Lives of Children*. New York, Random House, 1969.

FANTINI, MARIO, and WEINSTEIN, GERALD, *The Disadvantaged: Challenge to Education*. New York, Harper & Row, 1968.

FRIEDENBERG, EDGAR, *Coming of Age in America*. New York, Random House, 1963.

———, *The Vanishing Adolescent*. Boston, Beacon, 1959; paperback, New York, Dell, 1962.

GOODMAN, PAUL, *Compulsory Mis-education*. New York, Horizon Press, 1964.

———, *Growing Up Absurd*. New York, Random House, 1960.

HERNDON, JAMES, *The Way It Spozed to Be*. New York, Simon and Schuster, 1968.

HOLT, JOHN, *How Children Learn*. New York, Pitman, 1967; also paperback.

———, *How Children Fail*. New York, Pitman, 1964; paperback, New York, Dell, 1967.

———, *The Underachieving School*. New York, Pitman, 1969.

KOHL, HERBERT, *36 Children*. New York, New American Library, 1967.

KOZOL, JONATHAN, *Death at an Early Age*. Boston, Houghton Mifflin, 1967.

347

LEONARD, GEORGE, *Education and Ecstasy.* New York, Delacorte, 1968.
MCLUHAN, MARSHALL, *The Medium Is the Massage.* New York, Random House, 1967.
POSTMAN, NEIL, and WEINGARTNER, CHARLES, *Teaching as a Subversive Activity.* New York, Delacorte, 1969.

About the Editors

Ronald Gross *is one of the nation's leading education writers and editors. His articles and essays have appeared chiefly in* The New York Times Magazine, Harper's, *and* Saturday Review; *in 1963 he won a Philip M. Stern Fund grant for such writing. Among his books are* The Arts and the Poor, Learning by Television, *and two previous anthologies,* The Revolution in the Schools *and* The Teacher and the Taught: Education in Theory and Practice from Plato to Conant.

Mr. Gross is vice-president and editor-in-chief of the Academy for Educational Development, a nonprofit consulting organization. Previously, he was associated with the Ford Foundation's Education Program and with the Fund for the Advancement of Education. He has served as a consultant to the U.S. Office of Education, the Aspen Institute for Humanistic Studies, the U.S. National Commission for UNESCO, the National Foundation, and other public and private agencies. During 1968–69, he was associate staff director for the Commission on Instructional Technology, which recommended an unprecedented national commitment to experimentation in education.

Mr. Gross is also widely known for his work in experimental poetry and intermedia arts. In 1967 he published a volume of found verse, Pop Poems, *and in 1968 a portfolio of visual, kinetic, and typescript poems,* A Handful of Concrete. *His essays on* Found Poetry *and* Concrete Poetry *in* The New York Times Book Review *were the first to introduce these international movements to the general American reading public. He has lectured widely on poetry, popular culture, and the language environment and taught contemporary literature at New York University and the New School for Social Research. At the National Book Awards in 1957 he conducted a symposium on "Poetry Now," with Allen Ginsberg, Robert Creeley, John Ashbery, Dick Higgins, and Walter Lowenfels. Mr. Gross has been active in most of the current innovations in poetic theory and practice—including use of computers, chance methods, other arts and technologies, and rock lyrics—and was the first to use the term "Expanded Poetry" to describe them.*

BEATRICE GROSS is an experienced elementary-school teacher with a master's degree from the Bank Street College of Education. She has also served widely as a reporter, interpreter, and consultant on educational innovations. Her articles and book reviews have appeared in *The New York Times Magazine* and the *World-Journal-Tribune,* and she has been a consultant to Aspira, Science Research Associates, Bobbs-Merrill Company, Milton Bradley Company, and the National Planning Project for Higher Education.